What Your Colleagues Are Saying . . .

"Fisher and Frey set the record straight about text-dependent questions. They demonstrate that text-dependent questions can ad literal understanding but also understandings about doesn't say, how the text works, what the text means reader, how the text might be read in a specific discipl With specific prompts and concrete examples, Fisher an how to use questioning as a central tool to address the State Standards."

NELL K. DUKE, EdD
University of Michigan

"Fisher and Frey have a knack for making complex topics accessible. They write in a jargon-free style that teachers appreciate, and their use of examples and analogies helps bring ideas to life. These are qualities their readers have come to expect, and this book does not disappoint. . . . Teachers will find here an abundance of fresh, practical ideas that are easy to implement. This book deserves a 'close read,' and I heartily recommend it."

MICHAEL MCKENNA
University of Virginia

"Doug Fisher and Nancy Frey are experts at linking research to educational practice. Their latest book, *Text-Dependent Questions,* provides teachers with the information they need to scaffold their students' deep comprehension through four levels of questioning. I am excited to share this book with teachers and colleagues!"

LINDA DORN, PhD
University of Arkansas at Little Rock

"*Text-Dependent Questions* solidifies Fisher and Frey's well-earned reputation as literacy experts who offer sane and nuanced interpretations of the Common Core State Standards. They remind us that close reading at its best is a social process, one involving teacher-learner interaction as well as student-to-student talk. While the recommended texts and sample questions are useful, the extended classroom examples are the true heart of the book, demonstrating how skilled practitioners flexibly devise and deploy high-quality questions to serve varied instructional purposes."

KELLY CHANDLER-OLCOTT
Syracuse University

"Fisher and Frey deliver another indispensable resource for teachers of adolescents across the curriculum as they strive to meet today's more rigorous standards. Mentoring students to grow from dependence on questions provided by others to developing the capacity to 'interrogate a text' themselves is fundamental to proficient reading of complex disciplinary texts. *Text-Dependent Questions* provides teachers with a carefully reasoned pathway for questioning a text as a requisite for close reading."

DOUG BUEHL
Author of *Classroom Strategies for Interactive Learning*

"Everything about this book is genuine. From the authors' candid appraisal of the myths surrounding close reading to their forthright recommendations for teaching, it is refreshing. Fisher and Frey have been there, lived the pedagogy, and generated much of the scholarship that makes *Text-Dependent Questions* both compelling and unpretentious. Readers who have heard this dynamic pair speak at conferences and other professional gatherings are in for a treat; Fisher and frey are indisputably on the frontline when it comes to engaging others in close reading."

DONNA E. ALVERMANN
The Omer Clyde & Elizabeth Parr Aderhold Professor in Education
Distinguished Research Professor of Language and Literacy Education

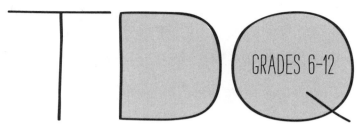

GRADES 6–12

TEXT-
DEPENDENT
QUESTIONS

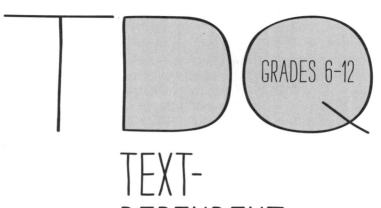

TDQ

GRADES 6-12

TEXT-DEPENDENT QUESTIONS

PATHWAYS TO CLOSE AND CRITICAL READING

DOUGLAS FISHER & NANCY FREY

WITH HEATHER ANDERSON & MARISOL THAYRE

Professional Learning Guide and PowerPoint slides by Laura Hancock available at www.corwin.com/textdependentquestions

CORWIN
LITERACY

FOR INFORMATION:

Corwin

A SAGE Company

2455 Teller Road

Thousand Oaks, California 91320

(800) 233-9936

www.corwin.com

SAGE Publications Ltd.

1 Oliver's Yard

55 City Road

London EC1Y 1SP

United Kingdom

SAGE Publications India Pvt. Ltd.

B 1/I 1 Mohan Cooperative Industrial Area

Mathura Road, New Delhi 110 044

India

SAGE Publications Asia-Pacific Pte. Ltd.

3 Church Street

#10-04 Samsung Hub

Singapore 049483

Publisher: Lisa Luedeke

Editorial Development Manager: Julie Nemer

Editorial Assistants: Francesca Dutra Africano
    and Emeli Warren

Production Editor: Melanie Birdsall

Copy Editor: Cate Huisman

Typesetter: C&M Digitals (P) Ltd.

Proofreader: Sue Irwin

Indexer: Sheila Bodell

Cover Designer: Gail Buschman

Marketing Manager: Maura Sullivan

Common Core State Standards (CCSS) cited throughout the book are copyright © 2010 National Governors Association Center for Best Practices and Council of Chief State School Officers. All rights reserved.

Photographs by John A. Graham.

Printed in the United States of America.

A catalog record of this book is available from the Library of Congress.

ISBN: 978-1-4833-3137-9

This book is printed on acid-free paper.

14 15 16 17 18 10 9 8 7 6 5 4 3 2 1

CONTENTS

Chapter 4. What Does the Text *Mean*?   97

Chapter 5. What Does the Text *Inspire You to Do?*   137

Texts and Questions for . . .

NOTE FROM THE PUBLISHER

The authors have provided links to video and web content throughout the book that is available to you through QR codes. To read a QR code, you must have a smartphone or tablet with a camera. We recommend that you download a QR code reader app that is made specifically for your phone or tablet brand.

QR codes may provide access to videos and/or websites that are not maintained, sponsored, endorsed, or controlled by Corwin. Your use of these third-party websites will be subject to the terms and conditions posted on such websites. Corwin takes no responsibility and assumes no liability for your use of any third-party website. Corwin does not approve, sponsor, endorse, verify, or certify information available at any third-party video or website.

Visit the companion website at
www.corwin.com/textdependentquestions
for the Professional Learning Guide and PowerPoint slides by Laura Hancock and access to the video clips and other resources.

ACKNOWLEDGMENTS

Corwin gratefully acknowledges the contributions of the following reviewers:

Barry Gilmore
Author
Memphis, TN

Kym Sheehan
Teacher and Curriculum Specialist
Charlotte County Public Schools
Port Charlotte, FL

Marsha Voigt
Educational Consultant and Literacy Coach
Barrington, IL

Jennifer Wheat Townsend
Literacy Specialist
MSD Pike Township
Indianapolis, IN

1

THE BUILDING BLOCKS OF *EFFECTIVE* CLOSE AND CRITICAL READING LESSONS

The students in Angie Holbrook's chemistry class have read a lot about the carbon cycle, as well as carbon pollution, and are faced with the task of making an informed recommendation to an elected official. More specifically, they have to write a coherent argument about carbon and its impact on the environment using evidence from the texts they studied in class as well as research they have conducted independently. They must make claims and supply evidence for those claims. They must connect evidence to the claims with warrants as well as recognize counterarguments and address them. Ms. Holbrook's students are not overwhelmed with the assignment. Instead, they are prepared. This preparation rests on the close reading of complex texts that her students completed as part of their schooling experience.

Close Reading Defined

Close reading is an instructional routine in which students are guided in their understanding of complex texts. The Aspen Institute, an educational and policy studies group with significant influence on practice, defines close reading in the following way (Brown & Kappes, 2012):

> Close Reading of text involves an investigation of a short piece of text, with multiple readings done over multiple instructional lessons. Through text-based questions and discussion, students are guided to deeply analyze and appreciate various aspects of the text, such as key vocabulary and how its meaning is shaped by context; attention to form, tone, imagery and/or rhetorical devices; the significance of word choice and syntax; and the discovery of different levels of meaning as passages are read multiple times. (p. 2)

There are a number of interrelated practices that combine to create a close reading experience. Importantly, not all texts deserve a close reading. Some texts are read for pleasure; others to find a specific bit of information. In these situations, close reading is not necessary. Close reading is also not necessary when the text is fairly accessible. In other words, close reading is typically used with complex texts—texts that do not give up their meaning easily or quickly.

The following salient features are necessary for students to learn to read closely (e.g., Boyles, 2013; Fisher & Frey, 2012):

- **Short, Complex Passages.** Texts selected for close reading typically range from a few paragraphs to a few pages. These texts are sufficiently complex to withstand multiple readings and challenge readers' thinking and understanding.

- **Repeated Reading.** Students reread the text, or parts of the text, for different purposes, to answer different questions, to find evidence for their inferences and conclusions, or as part of their collaborative conversations. Importantly, rereading is one of the primary scaffolds that are used during close reading. Inviting students to reread a text, looking for evidence or digging deeper into the meaning, can improve fluency and comprehension (e.g., Therrien, 2004). However, we were sensitive to the comments of Nichols, Rupley, and Rasinski (2009), who suggested that "continual reliance on repeated readings without appropriate guidance and support can lead to diminished student engagement and may not help students recognize that increased fluency provides for more focus on meaning" (p. 5).

- **Annotation.** Students write directly on the texts as they read, identifying central ideas, circling confusing words or phrases, and writing margin notes such as questions, reactions, and examples. Annotations can be used in narrative and informational texts, in both print and digital environments (Castek & Beach, 2013; Zywica & Gomez, 2008). Importantly, annotations serve as a scaffold as students must slow down their reading to annotate and continue to annotate as they discuss the text with others. Common annotations include the following:

1. *Underlining* for major points.

2. *Vertical lines in the margin* to denote longer statements that are too long to be underlined.

3. *Star, asterisk, or other doodad in the margin* to be used sparingly to emphasize the ten or dozen most important statements. You may want to fold a corner of each page where you make such a mark or place a slip of paper between the pages.

4. *Numbers in the margin* to indicate a sequence of points made by the author in development of an argument.

5. *Numbers of other pages in the margin* to indicate where else in the book the author makes the same points.

6. *Circling of key words or phrases* to serve much the same function as underlining.

7. *Writing in the margin, or at the top or bottom of the page,* to record questions (and perhaps answers) a passage raises in your mind (Adler & Van Doren, 1972, pp. 49–50).

See Figure 1.1 for a classroom poster for annotation and Figure 1.2 for a sample of a student's annotation.

Figure 1.1   Common Annotation Marks

- **Collaborative Conversations About the Text, Including Argumentation.** Students should interact with their peers and their teachers using academic language and argumentation skills as they discuss the text. These collaborative conversations are an important scaffold, as they provide students with peer-mediated instruction that is "based on principals of behaviorism and social theory" (Sperry, Neitzel, & Engelhardt-Wells, 2010, p. 256). In other words, when students read hard texts individually and independently and then answer questions, we do not define this as close reading. Students have to be interacting with others in such a way as to facilitate one another's understanding of the text.

Figure 1.2   Student Annotation Sample

Speech to the Troops at Tilbury.

Queen Elizabeth I – Speaker
1598

My loving people,

We have been persuaded by some that are careful of our safety, to take heed how we commit our selves to armed multitudes, for fear of treachery; but I assure you I do not desire to live to distrust my faithful and loving people. Let tyrants fear, I have always so behaved myself that, under God, I have placed my chiefest strength and safeguard in the loyal hearts and good-will of my subjects; and therefore I am come amongst you, as you see, at this time, not for my recreation and disport, but being resolved, in the midst and heat of the battle, to live and die amongst you all; to lay down for my God, and for my kingdom, and my people, my honour and my blood, even in the dust. I know I have the body but of a weak and feeble woman; but I have the heart and stomach of a king, and of a king of England too, and think foul scorn that Parma or Spain, or any prince of Europe, should dare to invade the borders of my realm; to which rather than any dishonour shall grow by me, I myself will take up arms, I myself will be your general, judge, and rewarder of every one of your virtues in the field. I know already, for your forwardness you have deserved rewards and crowns; and We do assure you in the word of a prince, they shall be duly paid you. In the mean time, my lieutenant general shall be in my stead, than whom never prince commanded a more noble or worthy subject; not doubting but by your obedience to my general, by your concord in the camp, and your valour in the field, we shall shortly have a famous victory over those enemies of my God, of my kingdom, and of my people.

Sheridan Shenk

My parents have to persuade me to go to the doctor's every time. They tell me its for my best interest, which does not make me any more willing. Sometimes I'm very stubborn. They have to resort to bribery. My dad tells me that if I go, he will take me out to lunch. My mom tells me that if I go calmly, she'll buy me something.

Queen Elizabeth is speaking to her troops with the intention to inspire them to go into battle.

I believe Elizabeth's speech was very successful. She walked the line between an equal and the person with the power. She put herself in the shoes of the soldiers by saying, "I am come amongst you." Although she went down to the lower class, she still kept her power as queen and the speaker. England was "her kingdom", the audience was "her people". Luckily she used her position of power to promise the listeners rewards if they act out of their valor. That fine line is where the true genius of this speech is held.

- **Text-Dependent Questions.** The majority of questions that are discussed during close reading require that students provide evidence from the text as part of their responses. The questions are not limited to recall but rather focus on various aspects of the text, including its structure, what it means, and what logical inferences can be drawn from it. As with many other aspects of close reading, the text-dependent questions serve as a scaffold for students. Teachers can ask questions strategically to focus student attention on specific aspects of the text that are challenging or confusing.

These salient features of close reading provide the scaffolds students need to understand the text. In addition, the way in which the lesson unfolds provides a scaffold for students. Close reading is not one-and-done reading. Rather, it is purposeful, careful, and thoughtful. As we have noted before, complex texts do not often give up their meaning quickly or easily. Instead, readers learn to look for different things as they interact with a given text during a series of successive interactions.

> When students read hard texts individually and independently and then answer questions, we do not define this as close reading. Students have to be interacting with others.

The Phases of Close Reading

Close reading leads student on a cognitive path that begins with establishing the literal meaning of a text and ends with an exploration into its deeper meaning and a plan for what should occur as a result of the reading. These phases, which may roll out over several lessons, encourage students to move from surface-level comprehension to deep comprehension:

- What does the text say?

- How does the text work?

- What does the text mean?

- What does the text inspire you to do?

These phases draw on the work of other researchers, notably Adler and Van Doren (1972) and Kurland (1995) and are the focus of the remainder of this book. As you can see in the table of contents, we devote an entire chapter to each of these questions. In considering close reading in the age of the core standards, we have linked specific question types to each of these phases. We refer to them as *phases* because they may be spread across one or more lessons, depending on how much time and discussion is needed to move students from surface-level comprehension to deep meaning. These should not be interpreted too narrowly as a recipe for a close reading lesson; rather, they should be used as a tool for organizing the journey through a piece of text. This approach to deep comprehension instruction should also not be viewed narrowly within the language of the Common Core. As we have noted, the research on close and critical reading extends back decades. Collectively, these guiding questions provide a means for addressing close and critical reading, whether you live in a region that has adopted Common Core standards or not. In addition, they are a method for addressing all the reading standards, as well as significant portions of the language, speaking and listening, and writing domain standards outlined in the Common Core State Standards documents (CCSSI, 2010a, 2010b). Over time, and with practice, students will ask themselves and their peers these questions as they engage with complex texts.

What Does the Text Say? The first phase concerns the literal meaning of the text, especially as it applies to explicitly stated information, as well as the central ideas or themes. Students aren't always able to determine these central themes during the first or second reading. Often, this understanding emerges more fully as the discussion progresses. The ongoing conversation in the classroom about a piece of text gives students ample opportunities to formulate and comprehend the use of language conventions and functions, especially as students in this initial phase seek to explain and give supporting evidence. These interactions with one another allow them to use talk in a variety of contexts through the communicative tasks associated with collaborative peer conversations. See Figure 1.3 for a table of intersecting anchor standards, which will be more fully explored by grade level in Chapter 2.

How Does the Text Work? A second cognitive path involves the mechanics of the piece, especially as it applies to vocabulary, the structure of the text, and the author's craft. The College and Career Readiness (CCR) reading **standards 4, 5,** and **6** capture the importance of zooming in at the sentence and paragraph levels. The language standards, especially CCR.L.4 and CCR.L.5, describe the essential nature of understanding figurative language, connotative meaning, and word solving. Although vocabulary is conventionally addressed early on in a reading lesson, we prefer to allow it to gestate for a bit before examining words and phrases closely. Our experience has shown us that taking time in the lesson to discuss vocabulary in the context of the reading pays off, as the overall structure of the text builds an important bridge between literal (what the text *says*) and inferential levels

Figure 1.3   Intersection of ELA Standards: *What Does the Text Say?*

Anchor Standards for Reading	
1	Read closely to determine what the text says explicitly and to make logical inferences from it; cite specific textual evidence when writing or speaking to support conclusions drawn from the text.
2	Determine central ideas or themes of a text and analyze their development; summarize the key supporting details and ideas.
3	Analyze how and why individuals, events, and ideas develop and interact over the course of a text.
10	Read and comprehend complex literary and informational texts independently and proficiently.
Anchor Standards for Language	
1	Demonstrate command of the conventions of standard English grammar and usage when writing or speaking.
3	Apply knowledge of language to understand how language functions in different contexts, to make effective choices for meaning or style, and to comprehend more fully when reading or listening.
6	Acquire and use accurately a range of general academic and domain-specific words and phrases sufficient for reading, writing, speaking, and listening at the college and career readiness level; demonstrate independence in gathering vocabulary knowledge when considering a word or phrase important to comprehension or expression.
Anchor Standards for Speaking and Listening	
1	Prepare for and participate effectively in a range of conversations and collaborations with diverse partners, building on others' ideas and expressing their own clearly and persuasively.
4	Present information, findings, and supporting evidence such that listeners can follow the line of reasoning and the organization, development, and style are appropriate to task, purpose, and audience.
6	Adapt speech to a variety of contexts and communicative tasks, demonstrating command of formal English when indicated or appropriate.

(what the text *means*). Figure 1.4 features a table of intersecting anchor standards for this phase; these standards will be discussed in more detail by grade level in Chapter 3.

What Does the Text Mean? As the students' understanding of the text expands, the next cognitive path involves integrating knowledge and ideas in order to locate deeper, at times hidden, meanings and to make logical inferences based on what the text says. This speaks to some of the qualitative elements that make a text more complex, especially those that involve layers of meaning. As students discuss texts, especially those that present arguments, they are encouraged to examine them closely in order to evaluate whether or not the arguments support

Figure 1.4   Intersection of Standards: *How Does the Text Work?*

Anchor Standards for Reading	
4	Interpret words and phrases as they are used in a text, including determining technical, connotative, and figurative meanings, and analyze how specific word choices shape meaning or tone.
5	Analyze the structure of texts, including how specific sentences, paragraphs, and larger portions of the text (e.g., a section, chapter, scene, or stanza) relate to each other and the whole.
6	Assess how point of view or purpose shapes the content and style of a text.
10	Read and comprehend complex literary and informational texts independently and proficiently.

Anchor Standards for Language	
3	Apply knowledge of language to understand how language functions in different contexts, to make effective choices for meaning or style, and to comprehend more fully when reading or listening.
4	Determine or clarify the meaning of unknown and multiple-meaning words and phrases by using context clues, analyzing meaningful word parts, and consulting general and specialized reference materials, as appropriate.
5	Demonstrate understanding of figurative language, word relationships, and nuances in word meanings.
6	Acquire and use accurately a range of general academic and domain-specific words and phrases sufficient for reading, writing, speaking, and listening at the college and career readiness level; demonstrate independence in gathering vocabulary knowledge when considering a word or phrase important to comprehension or expression.

Anchor Standards for Speaking and Listening	
1	Prepare for and participate effectively in a range of conversations and collaborations with diverse partners, building on others' ideas and expressing their own clearly and persuasively.
4	Present information, findings, and supporting evidence such that listeners can follow the line of reasoning and the organization, development, and style are appropriate to task, purpose, and audience.
6	Adapt speech to a variety of contexts and communicative tasks, demonstrating command of formal English when indicated or appropriate.

the claim. Because deep meanings of texts are often subjective and speculative, debate and disagreement are more likely to occur. Properly channeled and celebrated, these alternative points of view give students the chance to evaluate other speakers' points of view and their use of rhetorical devices. In investigating what the text means, students focus on the author's purpose and the inferences they can make based on their understanding of the text. Students also come to understand what a text means when they analyze multiple texts on the same theme or topic. Figure 1.5 has a table of intersecting anchor standards aligned with the question of text meaning. These concepts will be revisited by grade level in Chapter 4.

Figure 1.5   Intersection of Standards: *What Does the Text Mean?*

Anchor Standards for Reading	
7	Integrate and evaluate content presented in diverse formats and media, including visually and quantitatively, as well as in words.
8	Delineate and evaluate the argument and specific claims in a text, including the validity of the reasoning as well as the relevance and sufficiency of the evidence.
9	Analyze how two or more texts address similar themes or topics in order to build knowledge or to compare the approaches the authors take.
10	Read and comprehend complex literary and informational texts independently and proficiently.
Anchor Standards for Language	
1	Demonstrate command of the conventions of standard English grammar and usage when writing or speaking.
3	Apply knowledge of language to understand how language functions in different contexts, to make effective choices for meaning or style, and to comprehend more fully when reading or listening.
6	Acquire and use accurately a range of general academic and domain-specific words and phrases sufficient for reading, writing, speaking, and listening at the college and career readiness level; demonstrate independence in gathering vocabulary knowledge when considering a word or phrase important to comprehension or expression.
Anchor Standards for Speaking and Listening	
1	Prepare for and participate effectively in a range of conversations and collaborations with diverse partners, building on others' ideas and expressing their own clearly and persuasively.
2	Integrate and evaluate information presented in diverse media and formats, including visually, quantitatively, and orally.
3	Evaluate a speaker's point of view, reasoning, and use of evidence and rhetoric.
4	Present information, findings, and supporting evidence such that listeners can follow the line of reasoning and the organization, development, and style are appropriate to task, purpose, and audience.
6	Adapt speech to a variety of contexts and communicative tasks, demonstrating command of formal English when indicated or appropriate

What Does the Text Inspire You to Do? This final phase of close reading, which becomes more of a critical reading, is the one we find teachers are often best at, as they deeply understand the texts they are using. In fact, many of these texts are ones that have inspired them in some way. In this case, the *you* in the question refers to the student, who takes what has been learned from the text to create a new product. These questions are better described as tasks, in that they are expressed through formal debate, Socratic seminar, presentations, investigations and research, tests or other assessments, and writing from sources. These tasks may involve reconsidering a previously discussed text in light of the newer one, or may play a role in research or investigation. Therefore, the table in Figure 1.6 includes writing anchor standards, as many of the

Figure 1.6 Intersection of Standards: *What Does the Text Inspire You to Do?*

Anchor Standards for Reading	
7	Integrate and evaluate content presented in diverse formats and media, including visually and quantitatively, as well as in words.
8	Delineate and evaluate the argument and specific claims in a text, including the validity of the reasoning as well as the relevance and sufficiency of the evidence.
9	Analyze how two or more texts address similar themes or topics in order to build knowledge or to compare the approaches the authors take.
10	Read and comprehend complex literary and informational texts independently and proficiently.

Anchor Standards for Language	
1	Demonstrate command of the conventions of standard English grammar and usage when writing or speaking.
2	Demonstrate command of the conventions of standard English capitalization, punctuation, and spelling when writing.
3	Apply knowledge of language to understand how language functions in different contexts, to make effective choices for meaning or style, and to comprehend more fully when reading or listening.
6	Acquire and use accurately a range of general academic and domain-specific words and phrases sufficient for reading, writing, speaking, and listening at the college and career readiness level; demonstrate independence in gathering vocabulary knowledge when considering a word or phrase important to comprehension or expression.

Anchor Standards for Speaking and Listening	
1	Prepare for and participate effectively in a range of conversations and collaborations with diverse partners, building on others' ideas and expressing their own clearly and persuasively.
2	Integrate and evaluate information presented in diverse media and formats, including visually, quantitatively, and orally.
3	Evaluate a speaker's point of view, reasoning, and use of evidence and rhetoric.
4	Present information, findings, and supporting evidence such that listeners can follow the line of reasoning and the organization, development, and style are appropriate to task, purpose, and audience.
6	Adapt speech to a variety of contexts and communicative tasks, demonstrating command of formal English when indicated or appropriate.

Anchor Standards for Writing	
1	Write arguments to support claims in an analysis of substantive topics or texts, using valid reasoning and relevant and sufficient evidence.
2	Write informative/explanatory texts to examine and convey complex ideas and information clearly and accurately through the effective selection, organization, and analysis of content.

3	Write narratives to develop real or imagined experiences or events using effective technique, well-chosen details, and well-structured event sequences.
7	Conduct short as well as more sustained research projects based on focused questions, demonstrating understanding of the subject under investigation.
8	Gather relevant information from multiple print and digital sources, assess the credibility and accuracy of each source, and integrate the information while avoiding plagiarism.
9	Draw evidence from literary or informational texts to support analysis, reflection, and research.

tasks involve informal and formal writing. These will be explored more completely by grade level in Chapter 5. The best close readings are those that leave students with a lot of questions that they still want to answer. Often, the results of close reading are independent research, as students are inspired to find the answers to their own questions.

How Much Frontloading Is Too Much (or Not Enough)?

The Bard never said, "To frontload or not to frontload, that is the question," but we, like Hamlet, are faced with a dilemma, and ours is causing all of us to re-examine this instructional practice. And that's a good thing, by the way. Educators must be willing to question longstanding assumptions about our practices in light of new information. Isn't that what critical literacy (which we actively encourage in our students) is all about?

Of growing concern is that the general approach of dismantling any and all obstacles that are in a reader's way diminishes the opportunity to resolve problems. In other words, we need to thoughtfully and intentionally allow for problems to emerge, so students can attempt to work them out. This can pose a challenge for well-meaning teachers who have used a preteaching approach that frontloads the main points of the text in advance of the reading. There's logic in doing so: The less time devoted to discussion of the text, the more likely it is that students will require some frontloading. In other words, if it's a "once-and-done" text, then more frontloading is going to be required.

In addition, the characteristics of the learner at times necessitate frontloading. For example, a student who is new to the language of instruction is likely to require more frontloading. Others may have limited background knowledge that is going to significantly impact their ability to integrate new knowledge. But to remove *all* struggle from a reader's path also removes the need to deploy the strategies we've been teaching them. Imagine a medical student's education that included an exhaustive

Resolving problems builds stamina, persistence, and confidence. But we also don't want students to quit in frustration or avoid more challenging pieces in favor of the comfort zone.

list of diseases and their treatments, but no experience at applying this knowledge with real patients in real time. In a similar way, students learn about what to do when comprehension breaks down. But if readers have little classroom experience in regaining understanding of a text, they are not going to do so on their own when reading independently. This in turn can stall their growth in accessing increasingly complex text. When they are doing close reading, students can practice and apply their problem-solving skills. And resolving problems builds stamina, persistence, and confidence. But we also don't want students to quit in frustration, or avoid more challenging pieces in favor of the comfort zone. We have no problem with students selecting texts that are in their comfort zone, especially for independent reading, but that zone should expand over the course of the year.

The characteristics of a close reading discussed earlier are important precisely because they are *distributed* scaffolds, rather than frontloaded ones.

It is important to recognize that scaffolded instruction doesn't happen only in advance of the reading. It also occurs *during* the reading and rereading of a text. The characteristics of a close reading discussed earlier are important precisely because they are *distributed* scaffolds, rather than frontloaded ones. Rereading, with guidance, provides students with the time to soak in information. Collaborative conversations with peers provide a means for students to clarify and consolidate. The habit of annotation ("reading with a pencil") slows down the reading process so that students can understand the text more deeply. Newkirk (2012) writes,

> To read slowly is to maintain an intimate relationship with a writer. If we are to respond to a writer, we must be *responsible*. We commit ourselves to follow a train of thought, to mentally construct characters, to follow the unfolding of an idea, to hear a text, to attend to language, to question, to visualize scenes. It means paying attention to the decisions a writer makes. (p. 2)

In addition to the three aforementioned distributed scaffolds (multiple readings, collaborative conversations, annotations), there is a fourth: thoughtfully planned text-dependent questions. These questions move students from literal to inferential and critical levels of meaning, both within a single book or article and across multiple texts.

> ### The Distributed Scaffolds of Close Reading
> 1. Multiple Readings
> 2. Collaborative Conversations
> 3. Annotations
> 4. Thoughtfully Planned Text-Dependent Questions

Text-Dependent Questions
Drive Close Reading

This last point is the focus of this book. The questions teachers and students ask about a text serve not only as a scaffold for student learning but also as a main driver of close reading itself. These questions frame the extended discussion of a text and invite students to coconstruct knowledge in the company of their teacher. These questions advance students through a process of more deeply understanding a text.

Phase 1: What Does the Text *Say?*

General understanding questions cause students to attend to the major points in the text, such as the sequence of events, the story arc or important plot points, or the main claim and the evidence furnished. These are paired with *key detail questions* that drill down further, especially in exploring the relationship between the main ideas and the supporting details. These are often phrased as *who, what, when, where, why, how much,* or *how many* kinds of questions. The purpose of these key detail questions is not to quiz students on minutia, but rather to link the major idea of the piece to the details the author has furnished that directly support it.

Angie Holbrook's chemistry students are examining the transcript from a portion of a speech delivered by President Barack Obama at Georgetown University in June 2013. They have been studying the carbon cycle and carbon pollution in their class and have a solid working knowledge of both. In addition, they have read articles from *Scientific American* as well as their textbook. But they have not yet synthesized the information such that they can apply it critically by using their scientific literacy to understand the intersection of science, technology, and society. As described in the Next Generation Science Standards for high school, "Though the magnitudes of human impact are greater than they have ever been, so too are humans' ability to model, predict, and manage current and future impacts [HS-ESS3–5]" (NGSS Lead States, 2013). By using a close reading approach of a speech delivered by a world leader on the topic of climate change, Ms. Holbrook hopes to have students consolidate their knowledge about the carbon cycle and carbon pollution with an argumentative text type. Therefore, her initial general understanding and key detail questions invite students to identify the main message:

- *What are the three parts to President Obama's plan to reduce carbon emissions, and how will it be carried out?*

- *What are the next steps for the government to take to put Mr. Obama's plan into action? Where in the text can you find steps?*

- *What does he believe are the next steps for the people?*

Phase 2: How Does the Text *Work*?

The next category of text-dependent questions involves the mechanics of the text. Questions about *vocabulary words and phrases* are essential, because they provide students with opportunities to resolve the unknown. Such questions may be directed to the denotative meaning by prompting students to use their structural and contextual analysis skills. Importantly, they can also include questions about the connotations of the word or phrase, including mood, tone, and the use of analogies. Going deeper still, *text structure questions* ask students to locate the ways in which cause and effect, problem–solution, compare–contrast, temporal order, or extended description are used by the writer to maintain a logical flow in an expository piece. Within a narrative text type, devices such as flashback, foreshadowing, time lapses, cliffhangers, and surprise endings are worthy of query. Vocabulary plays an important role here as well, especially in connecting signal and transitional words and phrases to the structures utilized. Text structure questions do not only zoom in on a few sentences. Text structures also unfold across paragraphs and passages, especially as they forward a plot, an explanation, or an argument. Therefore, questions that cause students to apply literary analysis (e.g., characterization, narration, and point of view) give students a chance to see text structures at play over a longer piece of text.

> Within a narrative text type, devices such as flashback, foreshadowing, time lapses, cliffhangers, and surprise endings are worthy of query.

Finally, *author's craft questions* cause students to notice the writer's deliberate use of word choice, syntax, dialogue, and epilogues, and choice of genre to shape the message. These may include the ways in which the author uses text features such as illustrations, diagrams, captions, and footnotes to convey information. Ms. Holbrook returns her students to the mechanisms used in the speech:

- *What are key words and phrases that the president uses to link his plan to carbon pollution?*

- *What are the key words and phrases that the president uses to link his plan to green energy approaches?*

- *In what instances does the president link this plan to other agencies and branches of government? Why is that important?*

Phase 3: What Does the Text *Mean*?

Are you tracing the trajectory of the questions? We began with discussion of the literal-level meaning of the text (general understanding and key detail questions), and then moved to examining the mechanics of the piece (vocabulary, text structure, and author's craft). This forms a solid foundation for the next category of questions, which involve the deep meaning of a text. *Author's purpose questions* probe the stated and hidden or subversive intentions of the author (but not all authors have such intentions) and the relationship the writer has to the topic, especially in questioning credibility and expertise. Students in grades 6–12 explore rhetorical structures in argumentative writing used by the author to lay out a formal line of reasoning, especially in examining the use of *ethos* (the writer's credibility), *pathos* (the emotional appeal), and *logos* (formal logic and reasoning) to back claims. Questions that invite *intertextual connections* foster the habit of thinking across texts to compare, contrast, and consider how different writers address similar themes and subjects.

These questions invite *opinion with evidence or argument* and result in some task.

Ms. Holbrook's questions now move toward examining audience and purpose and toward locating examples that build a case for the president's plan:

- *Who is the audience for this speech? How do you know? What in the speech helped you to determine who the audience is?*

- *How does the president use the Clean Air Act of 1970 as an argument to support his plan?*

- *What makes Obama's speech credible? What evidence does the president present?*

Phase 4: What Does the Text *Inspire You to Do*?

A final category of questions is reserved for encouraging students to move beyond the text at hand by taking action. These questions invite *opinion with evidence or argument* and result in some task. They invite students to take a critical stance by examining power structures, considering alternate perspectives, and posing problems themselves that lead to action (McLaughlin & DeVoogd, 2004). Such questions lead to research or investigation, and are expressed through debate, presentations, or writing. In other words, students use the text as a platform for what will occur next. In Ms. Holbrook's chemistry class, students compose letters to a policy maker or legislator commenting of the president's plan. They cite evidence from the text of the speech, and evidence from their own study of the carbon cycle and carbon pollution is to be used to support their own claims about the proposed plan.

The progression of text-dependent questions used by Ms. Holbrook and others featured throughout this book provide an added benefit, in that teachers are able to check for understanding, make formative assessment decisions, and ensure that students engage in critical thinking. The Depth of Knowledge (DOK) framework (Webb, 2002) is a widely used method for gauging the rigor of thinking necessary to successfully perform a task. The four cognitive levels described in the framework are as follows:

Level 1: Recall and Recognition tasks

Level 2: Skills and Concepts tasks

Level 3: Strategic Thinking and Reasoning Tasks

Level 4: Extended Thinking tasks

The DOK is used, for instance, to determine whether assessment questions address the full range of critical thinking. In addition, it is used to align instructional practices and curricular materials. The range of text-dependent questions described throughout this book have been developed to aid teachers in moving students systematically across of continuum of increasing complexity. Figure 1.7 further describes the relationship between DOK and text-dependent questions.

Figure 1.7   Relationship Between Depth of Knowledge and Types of Text-Dependent Questions

	Level 1 (Recall)	Level 2 (Skill/Concept)	Level 3 (Strategic Thinking)	Level 4 (Extended Thinking)
General Understanding *What does the text say?*	Identify sequence of events, major plot points, story arc, or main claim and evidence furnished.			
Key Details *What does the text say?*	Answer questions about information provided directly in the text (i.e., who, what, when, where, why, how much, or how many).	Determine importance of ideas, link main idea to supporting details.		
Vocabulary *How does the text work?*		Identify denotation: Use structural and contextual analysis to resolve meaning.	Identify connotation and shades of meaning, figurative language and analogies; interpret mood and tone.	

	Level 1 (Recall)	Level 2 (Skill/Concept)	Level 3 (Strategic Thinking)	Level 4 (Extended Thinking)
Structure *How does the text work?*		Locate text structures (cause and effect, problem and solution, description, chronological order).	Link major concepts or ideas across paragraphs and passages; interpret elements of text using literary analysis (e.g., characterization, point of view, narration).	
Author's Craft *How does the text work?*			Identify the ways a writer's decisions about word choice and text structures serve to convey experiences, information, or arguments.	
Author's Purpose *What does the text mean?*		Locate stated purpose of the text, if applicable; analyze author's relationship to the content of the piece.	Determine hidden or subversive intentions and hypothesize possible motivations or interests.	Critique author's purpose using rhetorical structures and formal reasoning; link these to historical, sociological, or psychological phenomena.
Intertextual Connections *What does the text mean?*				Compare and contrast information or viewpoints across multiple texts.
Opinion With Evidence or Argument *What does the text inspire you to do?*			Identify missing or incomplete information that merits further investigation.	Construct formal original arguments using textual evidence; reflect on the role of one's own biases in interpreting the text; formulate a plan of action or next steps for investigation or research.

Source: Adapted from Norman Webb's Depth of Knowledge Chart © 2002 and Types of Text Dependent Questions Chart, Fisher & Frey © IRA 2012.

The point of a close reading is to foster extended discussions about a piece of text, so that the group can coconstruct the meaning.

Use Text-Dependent Questions Judiciously

Text-dependent questions are the product of the teacher's close reading of the text. This in itself is a habit to build, as many of us are more accustomed to examining the content (that is, the literal level of the text) without going much further. That means that we have to allow ourselves a bit more time to sit with a piece of text we've selected for a close reading in order to locate the structural and inferential levels of meaning. If you're having trouble in doing so, even after time spent reading closely, then perhaps it isn't a good choice for a close reading, as it may not be "juicy" enough to warrant that level of attention.

Resist the urge to turn close reading into an independent activity. The point of a close reading is to foster extended discussions about a piece of text, so that the group can coconstruct the meaning. Close reading is social learning at its best. That means that it is critical for the teacher to listen attentively to what is being discussed. After the initial literal meaning of the text has been established, many text-dependent questions raise insights and observations by students that will surprise you. Be prepared for that. Watch the line of thinking develop across the group, and allow them the time to process their ideas. Text-dependent questions are not about waiting for one student to utter the correct reply, and then moving on. It's about dialogic teaching, where "teachers and students act as co-inquirers, collaboratively engaging in a generation and evaluation of new interpretations of texts" (Reznitskaya, 2012, p. 446). Students are encouraged to elaborate on answers, teachers monitor their conversational moves to keep the discussion moving forward, and all group members (not just the teacher) monitor and maintain the flow of the conversation (Reznitskaya, 2012). During close reading lessons in our classrooms, we discourage students from raising their hands and waiting to be called on, as it makes us feel like traffic cops. We encourage them to speak directly to one another, not solely to us. And we encourage them to ask their own questions about the text and what it means to them.

Listening attentively means that some of the text-dependent questions you carefully prepared might not get used. In many cases, the thinking you hoped to provoke in your students through a question is addressed in the discussion of another. That's what often happens. The purpose of these questions is to build the habit of thinking critically, and because of this, the cognitive path students set out on isn't always predictable. We develop these text-dependent questions to keep in our back pocket, so to speak. We'd rather have them available, but never used, than fail to unearth an important point that is essential to students' deeper understanding.

Be prepared for the close reading lessons you've crafted to take a different period of time than you have expected. Some are shorter, in that students move more quickly through a discussion of a text than you had expected. More often, they will stall at a point you had not anticipated. "I taught them this already. They should know this," you'll think. When they hesitate and struggle, view it properly as an indication that you are provoking deeper thinking. That's exactly what you want to achieve in a close reading lesson. You are building the habit of reading closely and interrogating the text. Don't expect that all these text-dependent questions will be addressed in one lesson. We teach at the high school level, and our close reading lessons are typically 45 minutes or an hour long. Often, close reading lessons extend over two or three periods. In other words, we return to the same piece of text but with a different intent. Sometimes we work with other teachers to use an interdisciplinary approach, such as examining a speech in English class for its rhetorical structures and in history class for its political context and implications.

QUESTION • YOURSELF

Close reading of complex texts builds a habit for students, a habit that will serve them well throughout their lives. Like all habits, good and bad, an investment of time is required. When a group of researchers examined the time it took for people to develop fairly simple habits (self-selected ones such as drinking more water each day or doing sit-ups before breakfast), they found that the average number of repetitions required was 66 before the person reached a plateau (Lally, van Jaarsveld, Potts, & Wardle, 2010). Interestingly, some people developed a habit in 18 days, whereas others took 254 days. These researchers noted that

- Missing a single day did not reduce the chance of forming a habit

- A subgroup took much longer than the others to form their habits, perhaps suggesting some people are habit resistant

- Other types of more complex habits may well take much longer

What does that mean for us? For one thing, students aren't likely to develop the habit of reading closely very quickly. It will take time and practice. For another, there may be some students who develop this habit quickly and others who need more time and support to do so. Unlike learning to eat a piece of fruit each day or walking for 15 minutes, which were some of the habits people in the study decided to develop, reading closely is a complex cognitive process and not a relatively simple behavior. To complicate this further, we intentionally raise the complexity of the text with which students are trying to develop this habit. We say this to provide some reassurance that the effort does pay off, eventually. At first, it will require a lot of guidance and support. Over time, students assume increased responsibility for their discussions about complex texts. We know that they have developed this habit when they assume responsibility, asking each other the type of questions outlined in this book. And it's pretty rewarding when a group of students meets to talk about a complex piece of text, slowly and intentionally uncovering the big ideas and comparing those ideas to their own, expanding their understanding of the world around them.

Videos

To read a QR code, you must have a smartphone or tablet with a camera. We recommend that you download a QR code reader app that is made specifically for your phone or tablet brand.

Videos can also be accessed at
www.corwin.com/textdependentquestions

Video 1.1 Doug Fisher and Nancy Frey reveal how repeated reading and collaborative conversation can give students the opportunity to acquire new knowledge.

Video 1.2 Several teachers discuss the importance of collaborating with other instructors to provide a range of texts that can help students acquire different skills.

Video 1.3 Teachers give insight into bringing excitement back into the classroom—both for the students and the instructors.

Video 1.4 A successful classroom is full of students who are willing and able to engage, but they need a teacher to lead them in their learning.

2

WHAT DOES
THE TEXT **SAY**?

The habit of reading closely begins with inspection. Inspections of facilities, products, and services all rely on formal processes. As citizens, we count on inspectors to keep our food chain safe and our transportation systems running smoothly. These inspectors are trained experts who are knowledgeable about what they are inspecting, and they begin by taking a measure of the characteristics of the item. What they select to measure is not the product of convenience; inspectors know what they are looking for and seek specific information in order to gauge quality and estimate the nature of what they are inspecting.

Close reading helps students become, in part, text inspectors. Developing the skill of inspection requires expertise: knowing what to look for. Middle and high school readers are not yet experts, although they are developing the ability to take the measure of a text in order to understand its characteristics. However, as the texts become more complex in terms of content and style, they need guidance in how to do so. Unfortunately, sometimes students are simply told what is important and are not given a chance to develop the skills to inspect a text on their own. This leaves them sorely lacking in the ability to inspect a text when not in the company of the teacher. But how can we help our students build these skills?

The text-dependent questions point students to the elements of a complex text so that students can gather useful information. Targeted questioning is crucial, because it serves to focus students' attention on important parts of the text without telling them what the text says. Like good inspectors-in-training, students build the habit of detecting clues—as well as spotting and resolving problems—when they have frequent practice and when they receive feedback about their efforts. But the key to a good inspection is in knowing where to look and what to look for. The text-dependent questions designed for use during early readings of a text provide students with a model of inspection they internalize over time. In this chapter, we focus on the first phase of inquiry, understanding what the text says.

An Invitation to Read Closely: *Literal*-Level Questions

Although frequently maligned, questions about the ideas and concepts directly stated in the text set the stage for deeper understanding. To be sure, it is a problem when the questions posed to readers fail to progress beyond explicit meaning. But understanding the literal level of a text is the gateway to analysis and conceptual thinking. Adler and Van Doren (1972) noted that the first two of the four questions readers pose to themselves focus on determining the gist and identifying the details. In their words,

> Although frequently maligned, questions about the ideas and concepts directly stated in the text set the stage for deeper understanding.

"What is the book about as a whole?"

"What is being said in detail, and how?"

"Is it true, as a whole or in part?"

"What of it?" (pp. 46–47)

But they caution that readers' ability to address the last two questions is predicated on having satisfactorily answered the first two, noting that "you have to know what is being said before you can decide whether it is true or not" (p. 47). Adler and Van Doren were concerned with the questions readers ask themselves. In this book, we focus on questions that teachers and students ask related to complex text such that collaborative conversations and deeper meaning result.

Why Students Need This Type of Questioning

The complexity of thinking required of adolescents accelerates between grades 6 and 12. These increased expectations present a challenge for students entering middle school and exiting high school. Many ninth graders struggle with the increased demand as they move from middle school to high school; twelfth graders face the expectations they will soon confront as college and career applicants. Some of these students have performed below grade level expectations for most of their school careers. It should be obvious why struggling readers benefit from text-dependent questions that shift their attention to the points that help them identify the general content of the piece—it slows down initial instruction. Too often a teacher might breeze by these questions, allowing the high-achieving students to reply to them. When this happens, we've seen the looks of confusion and then disengagement on the faces of struggling readers who can't seem to get an initial toehold on the meaning of the text. Discussion of these points furnishes an important scaffold for those who initially struggle with a text and reduces the likelihood that they will simply push it away and mutter, "This is stupid." And this is what struggling readers really believe: that they are stupid. By posing questions that invite students to locate a sequence of events, the major plot points, or the arc of a story, we can assist these students in gaining a general understanding of a text. Over time, this habit translates into a bit more persistence with difficult pieces of text—and hopefully into a stronger belief in themselves as capable learners.

> Discussion of these points furnishes an important scaffold for those who initially struggle with a text and reduces the likelihood that they will simply push it away and mutter, "This is stupid."

Questions about the explicit meaning of the text are beneficial for struggling readers. The probing question that follows the initial question makes all the difference. Those probes invite students to furnish evidence to support their answers. Consider the learning effects on two different questioning cycles:

> **Mr. Ramirez:** *According to this article, what evidence supports Wegener's 1912 proposal of continental drift?*
>
> **Evan:** There's fossils and rock layers on different continents that are really similar to each other.
>
> **Mr. Ramirez:** Exactly. *What later findings in the 1960s confirmed his proposal?*

The students in the earth science class who read and understood the content of the text are able to follow this line of questioning. But those that have a shakier grasp of the reading are already trying to figure out how their classmates knew the answer. A follow-up probe asking for evidence untangles some confusion for these readers:

> **Mr. Ramirez:** *According to this article, what evidence supports Wegener's 1912 proposal of continental drift?*
>
> **Evan:** There are fossils and rock layers on different continents that are really similar to each other.

Mr. Ramirez: *Can you tell us where you found that information? I'd like everyone else to look as well.*

Evan: (after searching for a few moments) It's in the second paragraph. There are two sentences that say, "Scientists of the time had known that similar fossils of ancient creatures had been found on different continents. In addition, the edges of land masses thousands of miles apart appeared to have strangely similar rock layers."

Mr. Ramirez: *Does everyone see that? I'd like you to underline that point and make a note in the margin about it. But now I have another question. How does this tie to continental drift?*

Olivia (a struggling reader): Keep going, 'cause it's in the next sentence. Right here it says: "Alfred Wegener proposed in 1912 that continental drift, or the movement of Earth's tectonic plates, explained these two phenomena."

The follow-up probe in the second example slowed down the instruction enough to allow others to catch up. The added voice of another student expands the conversation from a single exchange with an individual to one involving another learner. As well, the direction to the entire class to look in the text and annotate it invites fuller participation and transforms the learning environment from a passive experience to an active one.

But what about those students who can already locate this information? Doesn't dwelling on literal level questions bore them? We argue no, because the probe is asking them to do what many of them are not accustomed to doing, which is citing textual evidence. In the language of the Common Core State Standards (CCSS) students at the secondary level are expected to "cite specific evidence when offering an oral or written interpretation of a text . . . to use relevant evidence when supporting their own points in writing and speaking, making their reasoning clear to the reader or listener" (CCSSI, 2010a, p. 7). Whether you are in a state or territory that is directly tied to the CCSS or not, citing and using supporting evidence to support your points is a critical skill. Students are required to do so in the research papers and literary essays they write, and in debates and Socratic seminars they participate in. Even in conversation, and certainly in debate, a speaker is required to provide evidence. The ability to do so is a skill and a habit. By requesting that students supply such evidence in discussion, we build both.

In our experiences, students catch on quickly to this procedure. Students who are consistently asked to provide evidence begin furnishing evidence on their own without prompting. They point out an important phrase or sentence in a passage as they reply to a query—"At the top

> Whether you are in a state or territory that is directly tied to the CCSS or not, citing and using supporting evidence to support your points is a critical skill.

of page 36, in the second sentence, it says. . . ." In turn, their annotation skills improve as they start anticipating what will be asked of them. They mark up the text and enumerate examples and arguments. And in the meantime, students who struggle get better at locating and attending to key details, because they hear the explanations of others concerning the location of this information and make efforts to explain it themselves.

But students who read at and above grade level benefit as well from the development of this habit. We've encountered many adolescents who are reaching the outer limits of their ability to glean facts from a text and are now confronting unfamiliar challenges as they read more complex ones. Some of the more basic comprehension approaches that were sufficient in the earlier grades are now beginning to fail them. Even among those who are still going strong, few are adept at utilizing evidence from texts in their writing. In particular, they lack the ability to select the phrases and sentences that best support their claims. Routinely requiring students to supply evidence about the text builds this skill. Over time, skill becomes habit.

Why Classroom Discussion Is Crucial

The positive effects to be gained by attention to the general meaning of the text and the key details of the text are muted, if not entirely undone, if we ask students to do this work in silence, as an independent activity. Turn to the back of any school textbook, and you'll find questions derived directly from the text. Yet telling students to read the chapter and then answer the questions at the end of it doesn't result in much learning. At best it is a recognition and recall task. What's missing? In a word, discussion.

Telling students to read the chapter and then answer the questions at the end of it doesn't result in much learning. At best it is a recognition and recall task.

Classroom discussions allow for the coconstruction of knowledge. Discussion elevates the act of reading deeply from a private one to a public one. But dialogic teaching, that is, teaching through discussion, is not an endless round of Q and A. It is also not telling students what the text is about as a frontload, before they've ever read the text. As we noted in Chapter 1, simply telling students what they should think and know is insufficient and ineffective. In fact, it breeds dependency, as students come to rely on the teacher, and not themselves, as the interpreter of text. In their study of nearly 2,000 eighth and ninth graders in more than 100 classrooms, Nystrand and Gamoran (1991) demonstrated that robust classroom discussion resulted in higher levels of reading comprehension. Importantly, they described three necessary features of discussion, distinguishing it from other facets of classroom talk:

- Sustained dialogue, not just short questioning cycles

- Uptake, such that the teacher poses new questions derived from the comments of students

- Authentic questions that do not always have a single correct answer

Wilkerson and Son (2011) reviewed studies focused on dialogic teaching, including such well-known approaches as Question the Author (Beck, McKeown, Hamilton, & Kucan, 1997), Paideia seminars (Billings & Fitzgerald, 2002), and Grand Conversations (Eeds & Wells, 1989). Although each differs in terms of its philosophical roots—QtA owes a debt of gratitude to Vygotsky, Grand Conversations are grounded in the work of Louise Rosenblatt, and Paideia is based on Socratic talk—all were effective at deepening conversation. However, Wilkerson and Son caution "that the success of discussion hinges not on increasing the amount of student talk per se, but in enhancing the quality of the talk" (p. 371).

> Simply telling students what they should think and know is insufficient and ineffective. In fact, it breeds dependency.

Questions focused on the literal level of meaning of a text will not accomplish the kind of critical thinking we seek from our students. But they are the start of the journey. To put it plainly, students must have a solid foundation of understanding about what the text says before they can get to what the text means. We do not view this as a bottom-up approach to comprehension. While we discuss the development of text-dependent questions in a linear fashion, in practice we often find ourselves deploying them in a more iterative fashion. For example, a discussion focused on deeper meaning, say on an author's hidden purpose for writing a piece, may loop back to a re-examination of the definition of an overlooked term. An exploration of the logical inferences that can be made from a text may require further analysis of the details from the text. Having said that, we recognize that conversations about complex text begin with text-dependent questions designed to clarify the general understanding of a text and the key details we'll need to determine what exactly the text says.

Students discuss the author's purpose for writing the selection they have read.

How Examining *What the Text Says* Addresses the STANDARDS

The heart of the CCSS resides in learning from, talking about, and composing texts. Text-based discussions teach students about how to approach, analyze, and evaluate texts. In addition, regular exposure to and discussion of complex texts provides students with extensive experience looking at what authors do to convey experience, inform and explain, and formulate reasoned arguments. While this book is not about writing, it should be noted that adolescent writers are, in part, apprenticed into composition through discussions of mentor texts. As is noted on the webpage for Gallagher (2011), "If you want to learn how to shoot a basketball, you begin by carefully observing someone who knows how to shoot a basketball. If you want to be a writer, you begin by carefully observing the work of accomplished writers" (http://www.stenhouse.com/html/write-like-this.htm). As students read and discuss complex texts, they begin to approximate this type of writing and thinking into their own creations.

Discussions framed by text-dependent questions allow teachers to address standards in reading and language as well as speaking and listening. These domains don't exist in isolation from one another. As we read, we marshal what we know about language. As we discuss a text, we enact our speaking and listening skills to understand and be understood. The concise nature of the standards is a signal to us that a given lesson is likely to teach toward standards that traverse the domains. In focusing first on what the text says, students acquire skills and habits in reading, language, speaking, and listening.

Reading Standards

The first cognitive path, to determine what the text says, is described in **reading standards 1, 2, 3,** and **10. Standards 1** ("read closely") and **10** ("complex texts") bookend the comprehension standards listed in between. As discussed previously, the prompts used as a follow-up to text-dependent questions build the habit over time of citing textual evidence, which in turn makes it more likely that students will provide evidence in their writing, not just in their discussions. Text-dependent questions that focus on the general understanding of a text help students locate the theme or central idea, and key detail questions cause them to examine the ways in which these items relate to the overall meaning (**standard 2**). This is a complex interaction that goes far beyond simply identifying the main idea. The subtle clues that foreshadow a major event, the assumptions that are laid out at the opening of an argument, the background information that is referenced in an essay—all of these are key details that have been carefully constructed by the author. Taken together, these details not only provide the foundation for drawing inferences; they are also critical for constructing an accurate summary. Figure 2.1 provides an overview of the standards that focus on what the text says.

Figure 2.1   Reading Standards That Focus on *What the Text Says*

Standard (Grade)	Literary	Informational
1 (6)	Cite textual evidence to support analysis of what the text says explicitly as well as inferences drawn from the text.	
1 (7)	Cite several pieces of textual evidence to support analysis of what the text says explicitly as well as inferences drawn from the text.	
1 (8)	Cite the textual evidence that most strongly supports an analysis of what the text says explicitly as well as inferences drawn from the text.	
1 (9–10)	Cite strong and thorough textual evidence to support analysis of what the text says explicitly as well as inferences drawn from the text.	
1 (11–12)	Cite strong and thorough textual evidence to support analysis of what the text says explicitly as well as inferences drawn from the text, including determining where the text leaves matters uncertain.	
2 (6)	Determine a theme or central idea of a text and how it is conveyed through particular details; provide a summary of the text distinct from personal opinions or judgments.	
2 (7)	Determine a theme or central idea of a text and analyze its development over the course of the text; provide an objective summary of the text.	
2 (8)	Determine a theme or central idea of a text and analyze its development over the course of the text, including its relationship to the characters, setting, and plot; provide an objective summary of the text.	
2 (9–10)	Determine a theme or central idea of a text and analyze in detail its development over the course of the text, including how it emerges and is shaped and refined by specific details; provide an objective summary of the text.	
2 (11–12)	Determine two or more themes or central ideas of a text and analyze their development over the course of the text, including how they interact and build on one another to produce a complex account; provide an objective summary of the text.	
3 (6)	Describe how a particular story's or drama's plot unfolds in a series of episodes as well as how the characters respond or change as the plot moves toward a resolution.	Analyze in detail how a key individual, event, or idea is introduced, illustrated, and elaborated in a text (e.g., through examples or anecdotes).
3 (7)	Analyze how particular elements of a story or drama interact (e.g., how setting shapes the characters or plot).	Analyze the interactions between individuals, events, and ideas in a text (e.g., how ideas influence individuals or events, or how individuals influence ideas or events).
3 (8)	Analyze how particular lines of dialogue or incidents in a story or drama propel the action, reveal aspects of a character, or provoke a decision.	Analyze how a text makes connections among and distinctions between individuals, ideas, or events (e.g., through comparisons, analogies, or categories).

(Continued)

Figure 2.1 (Continued)

Standard (Grade)	Literary	Informational
3 (9–10)	Analyze how complex characters (e.g., those with multiple or conflicting motivations) develop over the course of a text, interact with other characters, and advance the plot or develop the theme.	Analyze how the author unfolds an analysis or series of ideas or events, including the order in which the points are made, how they are introduced and developed, and the connections that are drawn between them.
3 (11–12)	Analyze the impact of the author's choices regarding how to develop and relate elements of a story or drama (e.g., where a story is set, how the action is ordered, how the characters are introduced and developed.)	Analyze a complex set of ideas or sequence of events and explain how specific individuals, ideas, or events interact and develop over the course of the text.
10 (6)	By the end of the year, read and comprehend literature, including stories, dramas, and poems, in the grades 6–8 text complexity band proficiently, with scaffolding as needed at the high end of the range.	By the end of the year, read and comprehend literary nonfiction in the grades 6–8 text complexity band proficiently, with scaffolding as needed at the high end of the range.
10 (7)	By the end of the year, read and comprehend literature, including stories, dramas, and poems, in the grades 6–8 text complexity band proficiently, with scaffolding as needed at the high end of the range.	By the end of the year, read and comprehend literary nonfiction in the grades 6–8 text complexity band proficiently, with scaffolding as needed at the high end of the range.
10 (8)	By the end of the year, read and comprehend literature, including stories, dramas, and poems, at the high end of grades 6–8 text complexity band independently and proficiently.	By the end of the year, read and comprehend literary nonfiction at the high end of the grades 6–8 text complexity band independently and proficiently.
10 (9–10)	By the end of grade 9, read and comprehend literature, including stories, dramas, and poems, in the grades 9–10 text complexity band proficiently, with scaffolding as needed at the high end of the range. By the end of grade 10, read and comprehend literature, including stories, dramas, and poems, at the high end of the grades 9–10 text complexity band independently and proficiently.	By the end of grade 9, read and comprehend literary nonfiction in the grades 9–10 text complexity band proficiently, with scaffolding as needed at the high end of the range. By the end of grade 10, read and comprehend literary nonfiction at the high end of the grades 9–10 text complexity band independently and proficiently.
10 (11–12)	By the end of grade 11, read and comprehend literature, including stories, dramas, and poems, in the grades 11–CCR text complexity band proficiently, with scaffolding as needed at the high end of the range. By the end of grade 12, read and comprehend literature, including stories, dramas, and poems, at the high end of the grades 11–CCR text complexity band independently and proficiently.	By the end of grade 11, read and comprehend literary nonfiction in the grades 11–CCR text complexity band proficiently, with scaffolding as needed at the high end of the range. By the end of grade 12, read and comprehend literary nonfiction at the high end of the grades 11–CCR text complexity band independently and proficiently.

Another facet important to understanding what the text says requires that students be able to trace the arc of a character's development over the course of a literary text, or accurately follow the chain of ideas and events that occur in an informational one (**standard 3**). Doing so requires the reader to consolidate a number of sources of information, including words and phrases that signal a chronology or progression, and to accurately visualize the events as they transpire. All of this can tax working memory, especially in dense informational text. For example, a passage in a biology textbook on how neurons in the brain communicate with other cells at the synapse is going to provide a detailed description of the sequence. Consider this paragraph in a text used in a psychology class:

> The process of signaling has several stages. Neurons first receive a signal that is either in a chemical form (a neurotransmitter, or a chemical in the environment for sensations such as smell) or a physical form (such as a touch in somasensory receptors in the skin, or light in photoreceptors in the eye, or electrical signals at electrical synapses). Those signals initiate changes in the membrane of the postsynaptic neuron, changes that make the electrical currents flow in and around the neuron. The electrical current acts as a signal within the neuron, potentially affecting the neuronal membrane at sites remote from the input synapse. (Gazzaniga, Ivry, & Mangun, 2009, p. 27)

The text-dependent questions posed by the psychology teacher are intended to slow the reader down in order to correctly sequence this phenomenon. Her questions about the order of the events and the two types of signals (chemical and physical) encourage students to parse dense texts into manageable parts in order to understand them. For example, she might ask these questions:

- *Let's start by tracing the sequence of events in the signaling process. How does it begin?*

- *When the signal is transmitted, what occurs in the membrane? If you're having trouble locating that information, move down several sentences.*

- *Keep going to trace the sequence. The membrane changes to accommodate an electrical signal. What is the result?*

- *Now go back into that paragraph again, because there's some key information about the possible sources of the signal. Where do these signals come from?*

- *What are examples of the two types of signals? The authors are using those examples to help us understand the similarities and differences between the two.*

These literal-level questions, coupled with her prompts that assist students in locating information, or reminding them to cite and name the evidence, build foundational knowledge about the information contained in the passage. The few extra minutes spent attending to the details of this pivotal paragraph set up the next portion of the passage, which is devoted to a discussion of ionic currents and a scientific illustration of the process. Later in the chapter, we will focus on questions about what the text says and how these questions can be used with complex texts in middle and high school English and social studies as well as science classrooms. A table containing the corresponding literacy standards for history/social studies, science, and the technical subjects can be found in Figure 2.2.

Language Standards

Language encompasses both speaking and writing, and the discussions that result from text-dependent questions have the power to build the language skills of students across both domains.

Language **standard 1** focuses on students' command of standard English. In grades 6–8, students are expected to use the appropriate pronouns, understand different sentence structures, form and use appropriate verbs, and recognize inappropriate shifts in voice and mood, among other things. This expectation is further delineated in grades 9–10 in terms of complex grammatical structures. In grades 11–12, knowledge of these structures is framed in terms of their changing forms across time. Conventions are reinforced through consistent use of prompts that encourage students to cite textual evidence, as they incorporate appropriate conventions into their speech. In terms of language registers, classroom discourse is usually *consultative*, meaning that discussion is at an academic or professional level and is about concepts and phenomena that remain in the abstract. Events from the past are discussed in history, while physical, chemical, and biological phenomena are central in the sciences, and universal themes

Figure 2.2 Reading Standards in History, Science, and the Technical Subjects That Focus on *What the Text Says*

Standard (Grade band)	History/Social Studies	Sciences and Technical Subjects
1 (6–8)	Cite specific textual evidence to support analysis of primary and secondary sources.	Cite specific textual evidence to support analysis of science and technical texts.
1 (9–10)	Cite specific textual evidence to support analysis of primary and secondary sources, attending to such features as the date and origin of the information.	Cite specific textual evidence to support analysis of science and technical texts, attending to the precise details of explanations or descriptions.
1 (11–12)	Cite specific textual evidence to support analysis of primary and secondary sources, connecting insights gained from specific details to an understanding of the text as a whole.	Cite specific textual evidence to support analysis of science and technical texts, attending to important distinctions the author makes and to any gaps or inconsistencies in the account.

Standard (Grade band)	History/Social Studies	Sciences and Technical Subjects
2 (6–8)	Determine the central ideas or information of a primary or secondary source; provide an accurate summary of the source distinct from prior knowledge or opinions.	Determine the central ideas or conclusions of a text; provide an accurate summary of the text distinct from prior knowledge or opinions.
2 (9–10)	Determine the central ideas or information of a primary or secondary source; provide an accurate summary of how key events or ideas develop over the course of the text.	Determine the central ideas or conclusions of a text; trace the text's explanation or depiction of a complex process, phenomenon, or concept; provide an accurate summary of the text.
2 (11–12)	Determine the central ideas or information of a primary or secondary source; provide an accurate summary that makes clear the relationships among the key details and ideas.	Determine the central ideas or conclusions of a text; summarize complex concepts, processes, or information presented in a text by paraphrasing them in simpler but still accurate terms.
3 (6–8)	Identify key steps in a text's description of a process related to history/social studies (e.g., how a bill becomes law, how interest rates are raised or lowered).	Follow precisely a multistep procedure when carrying out experiments, taking measurements, or performing technical tasks.
3 (9–10)	Analyze in detail a series of events described in a text; determine whether earlier events caused later ones or simply preceded them.	Follow precisely a complex multistep procedure when carrying out experiments, taking measurements, or performing technical tasks, attending to special cases or exceptions defined in the text.
3 (11–12)	Evaluate various explanations for actions or events and determine which explanation best accords with textual evidence, acknowledging where the text leaves matters uncertain.	Follow precisely a complex multistep procedure when carrying out experiments, taking measurements, or performing technical tasks; analyze the specific results based on explanations in the text.
10 (6–8)	By the end of grade 8, read and comprehend history/social studies texts in the grades 6–8 text complexity band independently and proficiently.	By the end of grade 8, read and comprehend science/technical texts in the grades 6–8 text complexity band independently and proficiently.
10 (9–10)	By the end of grade 10, read and comprehend history/social studies texts in the grades 9–10 text complexity band independently and proficiently.	By the end of grade 10, read and comprehend science/technical texts in the grades 9–10 text complexity band independently and proficiently.
10 (11–12)	By the end of grade 12, read and comprehend history/social studies texts in the grades 11–CCR text complexity band independently and proficiently.	By the end of grade 12, read and comprehend science/technical texts in the grades 11–CCR text complexity band independently and proficiently.

permeate literature. Experience discussing abstract concepts and ideas is vital for adolescents, who will utilize the consultative register throughout their professional lives.

Language **standard 3** focuses on how different language is used in different contexts. The language structure itself is important in many texts. For example, a discussion of *Canterbury Tales* by Geoffrey Chaucer would include his use of Middle English, which bears little resemblance to the English spoken today. While Chaucer's contribution to literature was in writing in the vernacular of time rather than in Latin or French (which was the convention at the time), 19th century poet Paul Laurence Dunbar wrote some of his works in the African American vernacular English that predated the Civil War, while other pieces were written in conventional English. A study of these works begins with making meaning of conventional and dialectical uses of the language. As well, discussion of nearly any text written in standard English provides students with the opportunity to replicate the syntax used by the author. As writing researcher James Britton remarked, "Writing floats on a sea of talk" (1983, p. 11). The text-based discussions lead to the use of similar language structures in their written work. The language standards that focus on what the text says are shown in Figure 2.3.

Speaking and Listening Standards

Without question, text-based discussions are at the core of the speaking and listening standards. **Standard 1** is all about participation in small- and large-group discussions. Importantly, text-dependent questions can be posed to the entire class, but explored more fully in small groups, before returning once again to whole class debriefing. In fact, this is an excellent way to ensure that more students have an opportunity to participate. Students are required to

- refer to evidence from texts (1a)

- pose and respond to questions (1c)

- consider multiple perspectives of speakers (1d)

Standard 4 addresses the presentation of information and evidence. This is not exclusively about formal presentation; it includes the extemporaneous speech of discussion. As students participate in discussion driven by text-dependent questions, they hone their ability to present ideas such that they are understood by others. These extend beyond simply identifying a sentence or short passage so that others can locate it. The real skill is in linking that evidence to a line of logic—in other words, providing the reasoning about why the evidence is relevant to the query. Figure 2.4 contains a list of the speaking and listening standards that relate to what the text says.

Text-based discussions provide an initial starting point for exploring a reading in depth. Questions about the general understanding of the text, and the key details that frame it, invite students into the reading and allow those who are less sure to gain a firmer footing.

Figure 2.3 Language Standards That Focus on *What the Text Says*

	Grade 6	Grade 7	Grade 8	Grades 9–10	Grades 11–12
1	Demonstrate command of the conventions of standard English grammar and usage when writing or speaking. a. Ensure that pronouns are in the proper case (subjective, objective, possessive). b. Use intensive pronouns (e.g., myself, ourselves). c. Recognize and correct inappropriate shifts in pronoun number and person. d. Recognize and correct vague pronouns (i.e., ones with unclear or ambiguous antecedents). e. Recognize variations from standard English in their own and others' writing and speaking, and identify and use strategies to improve expression in conventional language.	Demonstrate command of the conventions of standard English grammar and usage when writing or speaking. a. Explain the function of phrases and clauses in general and their function in specific sentences. b. Choose among simple, compound, complex, and compound-complex sentences to signal differing relationships among ideas. c. Place phrases and clauses within a sentence, recognizing and correcting misplaced and dangling modifiers.	Demonstrate command of the conventions of standard English grammar and usage when writing or speaking. a. Explain the function of verbals (gerunds, participles, infinitives) in general and their function in particular sentences. b. Form and use verbs in the active and passive voice. c. Form and use verbs in the indicative, imperative, interrogative, conditional, and subjunctive mood. d. Recognize and correct inappropriate shifts in verb voice and mood.	Demonstrate command of the conventions of standard English grammar and usage when writing or speaking. a. Use parallel structure. b. Use various types of phrases (noun, verb, adjectival, adverbial, participial, prepositional, absolute) and clauses (independent, dependent; noun, relative, adverbial) to convey specific meanings and add variety and interest to writing or presentations.	Demonstrate command of the conventions of standard English grammar and usage when writing or speaking. a. Apply the understanding that usage is a matter of convention, can change over time, and is sometimes contested. b. Resolve issues of complex or contested usage, consulting references (e.g., *Merriam-Webster's Dictionary of English Usage, Garner's Modern American Usage*) as needed.

(Continued)

Figure 2.3 (Continued)

	Grade 6	Grade 7	Grade 8	Grades 9–10	Grades 11–12
3	Use knowledge of language and its conventions when writing, speaking, reading, or listening. a. Vary sentence patterns for meaning, reader/listener interest, and style. b. Maintain consistency in style and tone.	Use knowledge of language and its conventions when writing, speaking, reading, or listening. a. Choose language that expresses ideas precisely and concisely, recognizing and eliminating wordiness and redundancy.	Use knowledge of language and its conventions when writing, speaking, reading, or listening. a. Use verbs in the active and passive voice and in the conditional and subjunctive mood to achieve particular effects (e.g., emphasizing the actor or the action; expressing uncertainty or describing a state contrary to fact).	Apply knowledge of language to understand how language functions in different contexts, to make effective choices for meaning or style, and to comprehend more fully when reading or listening.	Apply knowledge of language to understand how language functions in different contexts, to make effective choices for meaning or style, and to comprehend more fully when reading or listening.
6	Acquire and use accurately grade-appropriate general academic and domain-specific words and phrases; gather vocabulary knowledge when considering a word or phrase important to comprehension or expression.		Acquire and use accurately general academic and domain-specific words and phrases, sufficient for reading, writing, speaking, and listening at the college and career readiness level; demonstrate independence in gathering vocabulary knowledge when considering a word or phrase important to comprehension or expression.		

Figure 2.4 Speaking and Listening Standards That Focus on *What the Text Says*

	Grade 6	Grade 7	Grade 8	Grades 9–10	Grades 11–12
1	Engage effectively in a range of collaborative discussions (one-on-one, in groups, and teacher-led) with diverse partners on grade 6 topics, texts, and issues, building on others' ideas and expressing their own clearly.	Engage effectively in a range of collaborative discussions (one-on-one, in groups, and teacher-led) with diverse partners on grade 7 topics, texts, and issues, building on others' ideas and expressing their own clearly.	Engage effectively in a range of collaborative discussions (one-on-one, in groups, and teacher-led) with diverse partners on grade 8 topics, texts, and issues, building on others' ideas and expressing their own clearly.	Initiate and participate effectively in a range of collaborative discussions (one-on-one, in groups, and teacher-led) with diverse partners on grades 9–10 topics, texts, and issues, building on others' ideas and expressing their own clearly and persuasively.	Initiate and participate effectively in a range of collaborative discussions (one-on-one, in groups, and teacher-led) with diverse partners on grades 11–12 topics, texts, and issues, building on others' ideas and expressing their own clearly and persuasively.
	a. Come to discussions prepared, having read or studied required material; explicitly draw on that preparation by referring to evidence on the topic, text, or issue to probe and reflect on ideas under discussion.	a. Come to discussions prepared, having read or researched material under study; explicitly draw on that preparation by referring to evidence on the topic, text, or issue to probe and reflect on ideas under discussion.	a. Come to discussions prepared, having read or researched material under study; explicitly draw on that preparation by referring to evidence on the topic, text, or issue to probe and reflect on ideas under discussion.	a. Come to discussions prepared, having read and researched material under study; explicitly draw on that preparation by referring to evidence from texts and other research on the topic or issue to stimulate a thoughtful, well-reasoned exchange of ideas.	a. Come to discussions prepared, having read and researched material under study; explicitly draw on that preparation by referring to evidence from texts and other research on the topic or issue to stimulate a thoughtful, well-reasoned exchange of ideas.
	b. Follow rules for collegial discussions, set specific goals and deadlines, and define individual roles as needed.	b. Follow rules for collegial discussions, track progress toward specific goals and deadlines, and define individual roles as needed.	b. Follow rules for collegial discussions and decision-making, track progress toward specific goals and deadlines, and define individual roles as needed.	b. Work with peers to set rules for collegial discussions and decision-making (e.g., informal consensus, taking votes on key issues, presentation of alternate views), clear	b. Work with peers to promote civil, democratic discussions and decision-making, set clear goals and deadlines, and establish individual roles as needed.

(Continued)

Figure 2.4 (Continued)

Grade 6	Grade 7	Grade 8	Grades 9–10	Grades 11–12
c. Pose and respond to specific questions with elaboration and detail by making comments that contribute to the topic, text, or issue under discussion. d. Review the key ideas expressed and demonstrate understanding of multiple perspectives through reflection and paraphrasing.	c. Pose questions that elicit elaboration and respond to others' questions and comments with relevant observations and ideas that bring the discussion back on topic as needed. d. Acknowledge new information expressed by others and, when warranted, modify their own views.	c. Pose questions that connect the ideas of several speakers and respond to others' questions and comments with relevant evidence, observations, and ideas. d. Acknowledge new information expressed by others, and, when warranted, qualify or justify their own views in light of the evidence presented.	goals and deadlines, and individual roles as needed. c. Propel conversations by posing and responding to questions that relate the current discussion to broader themes or larger ideas; actively incorporate others into the discussion; and clarify, verify, or challenge ideas and conclusions. d. Respond thoughtfully to diverse perspectives, summarize points of agreement and disagreement, and, when warranted, qualify or justify their own views and understanding and make new connections in light of the evidence and reasoning presented.	c. Propel conversations by posing and responding to questions that probe reasoning and evidence; ensure a hearing for a full range of positions on a topic or issue; clarify, verify, or challenge ideas and conclusions; and promote divergent and creative perspectives. d. Respond thoughtfully to diverse perspectives; synthesize comments, claims, and evidence made on all sides of an issue; resolve contradictions when possible; and determine what additional information or research is required to deepen the investigation or complete the task.

	Grade 6	Grade 7	Grade 8	Grades 9–10	Grades 11–12
4	Present claims and findings, sequencing ideas logically and using pertinent descriptions, facts, and details to accentuate main ideas or themes; use appropriate eye contact, adequate volume, and clear pronunciation.	Present claims and findings, emphasizing salient points in a focused, coherent manner with pertinent descriptions, facts, details, and examples; use appropriate eye contact, adequate volume, and clear pronunciation.	Present claims and findings, emphasizing salient points in a focused, coherent manner with relevant evidence, sound valid reasoning, and well-chosen details; use appropriate eye contact, adequate volume, and clear pronunciation.	Present information, findings, and supporting evidence clearly, concisely, and logically such that listeners can follow the line of reasoning and the organization, development, substance, and style are appropriate to purpose, audience, and task.	Present information, findings, and supporting evidence, conveying a clear and distinct perspective, such that listeners can follow the line of reasoning, alternative or opposing perspectives are addressed, and the organization, development, substance, and style are appropriate to purpose, audience, and a range of formal and informal tasks.
6	Adapt speech to a variety of contexts and tasks, demonstrating command of formal English when indicated or appropriate.		Adapt speech to a variety of contexts and tasks, demonstrating command of formal English when indicated or appropriate.		

Using Text-Dependent Questions About *What the Text Says*

Helping students figure out what the text says requires attention to two main clusters of content:

- General understanding

- Key details

As we have noted, this is a good starting place when students encounter complex texts. Importantly, if students demonstrate their understanding of what the text says early on during a close reading, the teacher should abandon this phase and move to the next one.

Questions About General Understanding

The first questions students consider when reading a new text are those that help them locate the literal level of meaning of the text, especially as it applies to plot and sequence. These elements assist them in accurately identifying the main idea of the piece. Although high school students have been taught main idea since elementary school, it can prove more elusive with complex texts. Many still rely on the simple formulas they learned as young readers, namely, finding a sentence that explicitly states the main idea—all the better if it contains a phrase such as, "The purpose of this article is to . . ." But many texts written for older readers don't contain easily identified sentences like this. A central theme or idea may not immediately make itself known. Questions that focus on the general understanding—the gist—are the place to begin.

> The first questions students consider when reading a new text are those that help them locate the literal level of meaning of the text, especially as it applies to plot and sequence.

These initial questions guide students to explore the information contained within the text. But teachers are also keeping one eye on the core message, which students may not get to until much later in the discussion. And that's OK. It's tempting to step in too early and tell them, "This text is really about the persistence and partnership of two explorers who faced challenges but were able to overcome obstacles in order to achieve." We get excited and we want them to get excited, too. But in their initial readings of a passage from *View From the Summit*, a memoir by Sir Edmund Hillary (2000), students probably won't identify the source of Hillary's discomfort as he describes receiving a British knighthood while Sherpa Tenzing Norgay did not. The teacher may understand the tension, but students may not. The goal is to not simply tell students this then, but to lay the groundwork so that students will be able to reach this understanding themselves as they delve deeper into the meaning of the text. To help them accomplish this, some of our general understanding questions steer them in this direction. For example,

*How many times in this passage does Hillary describe Norgay's
actions as they advanced toward the summit?*

And as they look back into the text, the teacher can remind students to
list these actions, perhaps even cataloging them for later reference. As
they go deeper, students will begin to understand the injustice of placing
one man's achievement in front of another's. Although the two agreed
that they reached the peak of Everest together, media reports of the time
profiled Hillary as the explorer and Norgay as the carrier of the supplies.
"But we were not leader and led," Norgay wrote. "We were partners"
(Norgay & Ullman, 1955, p. 46). There will be time to get to what the
text means, and this process begins by understanding what the text *says*.

> There will be time to get
> to what the text means,
> and this process begins
> by understanding
> what the text *says*.

Questions for General Understanding in Middle School English

The students in Macro Corbrera's seventh grade class had just about finished their first reading of the text *The People Could Fly* (Hamilton, 1993)
when Paulina said, "Wow! This isn't what I thought it was going to be
about at all. I thought we would be reading about flying people. Like in
a fantasy or something, like really flying."

Several students nodded in agreement. Already accustomed to reading
texts closely, the students set about looking for the central theme or
message of the text. As Marlin noted, "I'm not really sure what the main
idea is. I think it's about slavery."

Mr. Corbrera asked them to begin their conversations with a discussion
in small groups about the story arc. *"Let's start our discussion recapping
what we know happens in the text. Try to retell the story in your own words.
Start with the beginning, and try to recount it in order."*

As they did so, Mr. Corbrera walked around the room listening to his students. As he considered the discussion in each group, he noted that they
had a fairly strong understanding of the text in terms of the sequence
of events that the author used to tell the story. He wanted them to dig a
little deeper, so he interrupted the groups and asked, *"So what's the message here? You all understand the flow of ideas, but think about the message."*

As the students discussed this question, Mr. Corbrera circulated around
the room. Some groups were not quite where he wanted them to be;
others were getting close to the understanding he was looking for. Then
Brandon raised his hand. Mr. Corbrera asked if he needed something, and
Brandon said no, that he thought his group got it. Mr. Corbrera asked the
other groups to listen in while Brandon's group shared their thinking.

Brandon started, saying, "We don't think it's really flying any more.
Maybe the big idea is that you have to remember what the people before
you could do, so that you will try to get that back."

"It's really a folktale, we think," Myeisha added. "So, if it is, it doesn't have to be true. It should help you understand something else, right?"

"Interesting," Mr. Corbrera responded. *"So, if this is a folktale like Myeisha said, what is it that we should be able to understand? Maybe that's a better question for us to talk about. Go ahead and discuss that with your groups."*

As Mr. Corbrera listened in to several groups, he was pleased to hear their discussions about what they should understand. The groups focused on the abuses of slave owners and the ways that people had to cope with it. They also talked about the story as one that built hope for people, noting the ending where the author said that people love freedom and talking about it.

Questions for General Understanding in High School English

"Romance at short notice was her specialty."

The students in Nancy's ninth grade English class looked up at her in mild shock. They had just finished an initial reading of the 1914 short story "The Open Window" by Saki (H. H. Munro). The last line is a surprising ending to the piece, but it's the term *romance* that throws them. In the past, Nancy had pretaught the archaic meaning of the word, which was used to describe imaginative thought, not the more contemporary meaning that has made it synonymous with emotional attachment. But this year she had not pretaught it, because she realized that telling her students the meaning of the word gave away the ending of the story and removed the productive struggle students need to engage in as they learn.

"I can see you're looking at me like I just did something terrible to you, but I really didn't. It's Saki who did it," she chuckled. *"Let's start with discussing what we know about what occurred. That should help us figure out what that last line means."* And with that, Nancy began posing questions related to the general understanding of the text. For the next 10 minutes or so, she led the class in a discussion about the sequence of events and what the author tells his readers about the characters. She revisited the purpose she had established at the beginning of the lesson in order to guide the discussion—to analyze how an author uses elements of characterization to portray the protagonist and antagonist in a short story. *"This is a study in character,"* she reminded them. A series of text-dependent questions she had prepared in advance directed them to also examine the plot:

- *Who are the main characters?*

- *What is the sequence of events that occur in the story?*

Nancy prompted students as needed to provide evidence when it wasn't already furnished so that others in the class could locate the information in the text and follow the discussion. Although they had not yet identified the meaning of the short story's ending, these questions helped them to organize their thinking to determine what they did know. *"Don't forget to mark up the text,"* she reminded them. *"Your annotations will be useful later when you write an analysis about this story."*

To build on their initial understanding, she posed questions designed to shift their attention to the source: *What is the title? Who is the author? What type of text is it? When was it written?* Quick discussion of these points led them to some new conclusions. They noted that the author went by a pen name and that the story was published at the turn of the last century.

"So it's not only that it took place a long time ago. It was written a long time ago, too," said Alexis as others nodded in agreement.

"What about the title?" Nancy asked. Ernesto stated that titles are usually chosen carefully by the author, and he was speculating about whether the setting was more important than he had realized the first time through the story. *"It sounds like you're ready to read it again,"* Nancy said. *"This time, make sure you're annotating on the text when you find examples related to direct and indirect characterization."*

Questions for General Understanding
in Middle School Social Studies

As part of their investigation about the Civil War, the students in Leslie Robinson's eighth grade social studies class read the text, "Narrative of the Life of Frederick Douglass." They understood a lot of the factual information related to slavery as well as general information about the Civil War, but Ms. Robinson wanted her students to gain an understanding of the perspective of a person who lived during this time. As she often said, "History is a story well told."

She provided her students with several paragraphs from the text so that they could annotate directly on it. As she distributed the text, she asked them to *"try to identify Douglass's message."* This question about general understanding provided them with a concrete task and focus as they did their initial reading of the text.

A quick look at the students' annotations revealed their ability to underline key ideas as well as to identify words and phrases that were confusing. In this case, students grasped the message of the text from their initial reading and discussions. To ensure that this was the case, Ms. Robinson asked her students to *summarize Douglass's message in five or fewer sentences.* She read over their shoulders as they did so, noting that her students understood that Douglass was focused on the value of learning to read as well as the danger of him doing so at that time in history.

Ms. Robinson asks her students to summarize Douglass's message in five or fewer sentences.

Questions for General Understanding in High School Social Studies

In Javier Vaca's US history class, students read a lot of primary source documents. They had developed the habit of analyzing texts, always looking at the source as well as the context in which the text was written. When they initially read Franklin D. Roosevelt's Inaugural Address from March 4, 1933, they applied those same skills. As they commonly did with primary source documents, they began their reading focused on the main message of the text.

"As you read this speech for the first time, focus on FDR's message. Ask yourself, what is he trying to tell the people? Remember that we always read considering the source and the context," Mr. Vaca said.

Listening in to one group, Mr. Vaca noted that they focused on the "good neighbor" policy. As Ashlee said, "I think that the big idea here is that Americans have to come together to solve the problems of their time. He's really asking for help from regular people."

"I agree," John added, "because he says the 'great army of our people' and he isn't talking about the Army. It's all of the people in the US have to get together to fix this. Lots of people don't have food to eat. There are all of those lines for food."

"And they don't have a lot of jobs. People need work so that they can support their family. It's kinda like now, how we hear 'where have all the jobs gone?'" Brandi added.

Having visited a few groups, Mr. Vaca decided to call the class back together. He signaled for them to finish their conversations and said, *"I'm going to ask for one person from each group to summarize the general ideas in the text in one sentence. Reach agreement about that and then I'll randomly call on folks to respond."* When Jovan was called on, his group had agreed on the following, "Solving America's problems in 1933 would take everyone's help."

Questions for General Understanding in Middle School Science

The sixth grade students in Paula Choi's class were starting a unit of study on geology. Unlike in the past, when she had explained the field of geology and showed them several videos of geologists at work, Ms. Choi decided to begin the unit with a reading from the *U-X-L Encyclopedia of Science (Nagel, 2007).*

First, she asked her students to *"take an initial read through the text, focusing on the flow of information."* Pointing to her annotation instructions chart, she said, *"You can annotate on this round, or not. It's really up to you. It's a new unit, so there will probably be some confusing terms. That's okay. Remember, we're focused on the big ideas in the text. If you find a big idea, you can underline it. But don't worry if you don't find any big ideas this first time through. You know that we'll dig deeper into this text and come out the other side really understanding it."*

As they finished reading, Ms. Choi asked them a fairly literal question, *"What are the two main branches of geology?"*

The students quickly got out their pencils and went to look for that information. To a student, they all identified both *physical geology* and *historical geology* from the text. Ms. Choi then asked them to summarize what each of these meant in the margins of the text so that she could determine their level of understanding. As Fernando did so, he commented, "See, we got this. It ain't so scary." When asked what he meant, he responded, "I useta just give up 'cuz I didn't know where to start. Now I got more confidence and Ms. Choi makes it understandable."

As they completed the task, Ms. Choi created a t-chart on the board and asked for volunteers to identify characteristics of each major branch. Each group was allowed to add one item to either side of the chart until they ran out of ideas.

As Ms. Choi noted, "I also want them using the terminology from the text. It's important to me that they can find information, understand that information, and then use that information. I used a t-chart to check their understanding before taking them a bit deeper into this introductory text. We'll still do a lot of other things in this unit, including watching several videos and having a visit from a real geologist, but I think that beginning with a text and building their knowledge from there is important."

Questions for General Understanding in High School Science

The students in Brad Neilson's biology class were focused on natural selection. He knew that this was a difficult concept and that students often oversimplified or overgeneralized it. His students had been studying this topic for several weeks when he invited them to read a section from Chapter 4 of Darwin's *Origin of the Species*. As they began to read, he said to his students, *"I have a lot of questions about this text. There's so much information packed into it! It will give us tons to talk about. But I don't want to force your conversation, so I made a list of the questions that came to my mind. You can talk about these, or any general understanding questions that your group has. Don't limit yourself to the questions that I have, but make sure that you talk about your understanding of the text.*" Then he revealed his questions:

- *Who is the author of the text, and what topic is he discussing?*

- *What questions does Darwin ask in the first paragraph of the excerpt? How do these help to introduce the purpose of the text?*

- *Why is the term* domestication *so important to Darwin's discussion? What does it mean?*

- *How does Darwin define natural selection?*

- *What analogy does Darwin use in the second paragraph? How does it illustrate natural selection?*

- *In Paragraph 2, Darwin discusses the effects of immigration on a population. Does he support this influx of new inhabitants? What is the alternative he suggests?*

- *Does Darwin see natural selection as something helpful to humankind? How do you know?*

Interestingly, different groups started at different places. One group began with the question about population, with Mohammed saying, "I think we should talk about population because we already learned about that in stats."

Dalasia agreed, adding, "I don't think Darwin supports immigration because he says 'by checking immigration and consequently competition will give time for any new variety to be slowly improved' and I think that means that they should try to stop immigration so that it doesn't stop the natural selection process, but I'm not 100% on that."

Another group focused on the definition of natural selection. "I think that this is the same definition that is used today. It's basically saying that organisms that are a better fit for their environment will survive," Neil said.

"I agree with you," Randy added. "As long as you add that they have to reproduce, because it's the offspring that really have the change, right?"

Questions About Key Details

Each text contains details that are essential to understanding the broader meaning of the text. We don't just mean interesting details, but rather those that are linked to the main idea or central theme. Students sometimes have difficulty in sorting out the difference between key details and merely interesting ones. Text-dependent questions about the key details guide students toward an understanding of the differences between the two. The *text type* drives the type of key details readers are seeking. In a narrative text type, the key details are linked to the dramatic structure: What is the exposition, the major conflict, the rising action, climax, and resolution? In an informational piece, the key details are attached to the organizational patterns, such as problem–solution, cause and effect, compare–contrast, and so on. These narrative and expository text structures are not always apparent to students and are explored more completely when the conversation moves forward to examining how a text *works*. Therefore, the questions about key details ask students about the "five Ws"—*who, what, when, where,* and *why*. Related key detail questions ask students the "how" questions—*how much? How many?*

Questions About Key Details in Middle School English

As he usually does, Mr. Corbrera has a number of key detail questions ready for his students as they read and discuss the short story, "The People Could Fly" from the book of the same title (Hamilton, 1993). He knows that he may not need to use all of the questions he has prepared, but having them at the ready guides his interactions with students, especially when they are not able to figure out the answers.

He starts with a where-and-when question: *"Where and when does this story take place?"* The students talk with each other and quickly identify the answer. Then he focuses their attention on the characters, saying, *"Let's talk about the people in this folktale. Who are the main characters? But maybe even more important, what role does each character play in the story?"*

The students immediately turn their attention to Toby, the character who is able to "fly," after having been a slave.

"It says that Toby is an old man, right here [Cole points to a line in the text]. He helps Sarah," Cole says.

They then turn their attention to Sarah, the Overseer, and the Master. They discuss each of them, pausing when Victor says, "Some of them have names, but others just have jobs."

Hearing this, Mr. Corbrera pauses the conversations and asks Victor to share his comment with the rest of the class. After Victor speaks, Mr. Corbrera asks the class, *"So, what do we think about this detail? Why might the author do that? And what is the effect that it has on us as readers?"*

Samantha, turning to her group says, "We totally missed that. WOW. The cruel people who own the slaves don't get names." Noah adds, "What's it called. Like maybe irony? It's turned around because the people in power don't get names but the people who don't have power do get names."

As their conversations about the characters in the text slow down, Mr. Corbrera asks his students the final key detail questions: *What is*

> Students sometimes have difficulty in sorting out the difference between key details and merely interesting ones.

the conflict, and how does the setting impact the conflict? Again, they turn their attention to the text, but this time the students are rereading and annotating, looking for information about the setting and the conflict. They have deepened their interactions with the text and with each other, and they understand the text better as a result.

Questions About Key Details in High School English

In the past, Nancy would have had students do the character analysis independently. But that would have reduced the opportunity to coconstruct knowledge, and it would have resulted in some students doing well, but too many others still struggling.

The text-dependent questions posed to the class shifted to focusing on key details. Nancy asked students to read "The Open Window" again, this time with an eye toward key details that would yield insights into the characters of Vera and Mr. Nuttel. The class had been studying methods of direct and indirect characterization, such as name analysis, attitude, and the reaction of one character to another. As the class finished, Nancy introduced two character analysis tools, one for each of the main characters (see Figure 2.5). In the past, Nancy would have distributed this for students to use independently. But that would have reduced the opportunity to coconstruct knowledge, and it would have resulted in some students doing well, but too many others still struggling.

"Let's start by looking for some of those key details as they relate to characterization," Nancy said. *"Keep in mind we're looking for evidence, too. Let's start by talking about the physical descriptions Saki gave us for Vera and Mr. Nuttel."*

Students are especially intrigued by the name analysis of the two. One student notes that *ver-* is a Latin derivation meaning *truth,* ironic since Vera tells a huge lie. Another states that Framton Nuttel's last name makes him think of the word *nutty,* and the character is indeed psychologically frail.

"You know, his first name sounds like frame, like when you set someone up. And the aunt's name is Mrs. Sappington, like she's a sap for a story!" Kealin says.

Throughout the conversation, Nancy prompts students to use textual evidence as well as to write down the evidence being discussed.

The students haven't yet settled on the meaning of the ending, but Nancy knows they're moving in the right direction. This initial general understanding and these key detail questions aren't the end of the learning, but they are building a foundation of shared knowledge. As she steers the discussion toward a closer examination of how the text works—namely through its use of vocabulary and text structure—she's confident they'll close in on the meaning.

Figure 2.5   Character Analysis Planning Tool for Key Details

Title and Author of Text: _____

Character's Name: _____

Method of Characterization	Examples and Quotes	What This Reveals About the Character
Physical Description		
Name Analysis		
Attitude		
Dialogue		
Thoughts		
Reactions of Others		
Action or Incident		
Physical or Emotional Setting		

Available for download from **www.corwin.com/textdependentquestions**

Questions About Key Details in Middle School Social Studies

The students in Ms. Robinson's social studies class have a fairly strong understanding of the text, so she decides to ask them two questions to further check their understanding.

"You all really got the big message from the text," she says, *"so let's see how the details help us understand it a bit more. Let's talk about two things. First, where in the text does Douglass explain his motivation for learning? And second, what obstacles does Douglass face in seeking education? Let's go back into the text and look for this information. It may not be right there, on one specific line, but these are important details that will help us understand the overall point the author is trying to make."*

Maya begins the conversation for her group. "Douglas explains his motivation for learning right here. He wants to be able to read and understand the world."

"But it's not easy because he can get in a lot of trouble," David adds. "He has to find someone who will teach him to read; that's the biggest thing. And then he has to figure out how to pay them, so he gives the boys bread because they are so poor, but they can read. So they really trade food for teaching."

The text type drives the type of key details readers are seeking.

Questions About Key Details in High School Social Studies

Mr. Vaca wants his students to focus on some specifics from the text, as they will need to use these details for their analysis of the effectiveness of the plans that FDR enacted.

"What specifically does FDR tell Americans what the government will do to help them through the Great Depression?" he asks them.

The students return to the text and begin highlighting their findings. They discuss the role of the government in helping people get jobs.

"He thinks that the government has to think about the missing jobs like they are going to war," Omar says, "They really have to fight so that people can get jobs and have a better life."

Ashlee adds that the government should also work on keeping people in their houses and owning the farms. "It says right here that they have to stop the foreclosures. That means that the bank takes back the house because the people can't pay. That's also just like today, like we saw on Student News [video broadcast]. But FDR says that the government can help people by dealing with the foreclosures, but he really doesn't say how that will happen," she notes.

"Yeah, because next he says that the things that they have done in the past didn't work," Brian continues. "It says [Brian points to a line on his copy of the text] that the efforts are 'scattered, uneconomical, and unequal.' So, it's like he's saying that the government should not be scattered and not equal. That's what he wants the government to do, to get it together to help people."

Questions About Key Details in Middle School Science

The key details that Ms. Choi was looking for as her students read the encyclopedia entry about geology centered on deepening their understanding of the two main branches they had learned about on their initial read of the text. Referring to their t-chart, Ms. Choi said, *"Let's look for some confirming evidence from the text. I'd like us to really understand these areas of geology. What are the four branches of study for physical geologists?"*

The students easily found this information in the second paragraph of the text. "I think that *petrology* must be about studying rocks because the sentence has two words, *mineralogy* and *petrology,* and then it says that there are two topics that they study, minerals and rocks," Stephanie added to her group's conversation. "So *mineralogy* is probably minerals, because they start the same; so then *petrology* would have to be rocks, but we can Google it to be sure."

Ms. Choi then turned their attention to the other branch asking, *"What are the two areas of historical geology discussed in the article?"*

Again the students got to work, determining the key details from the text. As Ms. Choi ended this part of the lesson, she said, *"I know that there are a lot of new vocabulary words in this reading. We are going to know all of them in a few weeks, but just think about how many you already know because you're reading like scientists."*

Questions About Key Details in High School Science

The students in Mr. Neilson's biology class, having engaged in an extended discussion about their general understanding of the Darwin text, were ready for an exploration of the key details in the text.

"I know there's still a lot to unearth here, and it's going to take us a while to really get a deep understanding of this. To do so, we're going to look for some key details. It will help us figure out what we know and don't know."

The students looked relieved. It is a challenging piece of text, and they appreciated their teacher's acknowledgment of that fact.

He started their discussion with the following question, *"According to Darwin, how does nature 'choose' which traits to perpetuate and which to eradicate?"*

They quickly answered this question, so Mr. Neilson turned their attention to the relationships between organisms, asking, *"How does Darwin describe the relationship between all organisms? What effect does this have on the purpose of his text?"*

Again, the students were quick to respond, landing on the phrase "infinitely complex and close-fitting." Mr. Neilson then tried a more challenging question, *"If a trait is not 'useful' or 'injurious,' what happens to it?"*

While the students are able to locate the appropriate portion of the text due to Mr. Neilson's use of these terms in his question, they are not sure what Darwin means by "fluctuating element," and they are unfamiliar with the term *polymorphic*. The teacher knows that in order for them to more fully understand this key detail, he will need to shift their attention to a discussion of how the text works, especially in terms of vocabulary.

QUESTION •YOURSELF

This chapter has focused on the role of literal questions as a starting place for close reading. We have made the case that general understanding and key detail questions can be used later in the lesson to return to specific information necessary to understand more nuanced information in a text. We have focused on the differences between general understanding and the key details that are important in gaining that understanding.

Now, we invite you to practice yourself. In Figure 2.6, we have included General Eisenhower's speech to the troops on June 6, 1944, a text you can use to apply what you have learned.

First, take a minute or two and read the speech. Then turn your attention to writing questions that you can develop to encourage students to analyze *what the text says*. Remember that this phase is focused on *general understanding* and *key details*. What is it that students should know about this text before you invite them to explore the ways in which the text *works* (which will be the focus of our next chapter)?

Before you begin, you might like to skim the italicized questions in the teachers' lessons, above. If you'd like to check yourself, the questions that Ms. Thayre developed for General Eisenhower's speech can be found on this book's companion website at www.corwin.com/textdependentquestions.

Next, try applying this technique to develop questions that you will use with your own students.

Figure 2.6   General Dwight D. Eisenhower's D-Day Invasion Statement to Soldiers, Sailors, and Airmen of the Allied Expeditionary Force, June 6, 1944

Soldiers, Sailors, and Airmen of the Allied Expeditionary Force!

You are about to embark upon the Great Crusade, toward which we have striven these many months. The eyes of the world are upon you. The hopes and prayers of liberty-loving people everywhere march with you. In company with our brave Allies and brothers-in-arms on other Fronts, you will bring about the destruction of the German war machine, the elimination of Nazi tyranny over the oppressed peoples of Europe, and security for ourselves in a free world. Your task will not be an easy one. Your enemy is well trained, well equipped and battle hardened. He will fight savagely. But this is the year 1944! Much has happened since the Nazi triumphs of 1940–41. The United Nations have inflicted upon the Germans great defeats, in open battle, man-to-man. Our air offensive has seriously reduced their strength in the air and their capacity to wage war on the ground. Our Home Fronts have given us an overwhelming superiority in weapons and munitions of war, and placed at our disposal great reserves of trained fighting men. The tide has turned! The free men of the world are marching together to Victory! I have full confidence in your courage and devotion to duty and skill in battle. We will accept nothing less than full Victory! Good luck! And let us beseech the blessing of Almighty God upon this great and noble undertaking.

SIGNED: Dwight D. Eisenhower

Source: D-day statement to soldiers, sailors, and airmen of the Allied Expeditionary Force, 6/44, Collection DDE-EPRE: Eisenhower, Dwight D: Papers, Pre-Presidential, 1916–1952; Dwight D. Eisenhower Library; National Archives and Records Administration.

Available for download from **www.corwin.com/textdependentquestions**

Videos

To read a QR code, you must have a smartphone or tablet with a camera. We recommend that you download a QR code reader app that is made specifically for your phone or tablet brand.

Videos can also be accessed at
www.corwin.com/textdependentquestions

Video 2.1 Oscar Corrigan's seventh grade social studies students silently read and annotate a passage from *Things Fall Apart* before discussing the main points as a class.

Video 2.2 Will Mellman's seventh grade science class reads an article on ulcers to gather a general understanding of the content before making annotations during their second close read.

Video 2.3 Javier Vaca introduces Eisenhower's "Message to the Troops" to his eleventh grade U.S. history class to support their studies of World War II.

Video 2.4 Heather Anderson leads her tenth grade English class in a discussion of Maya Angelou's poem "Phenomenal Woman," using annotations to focus their understanding of the poem's message.

Video 2.5 Marisol Thayre's eleventh grade English class annotates Susan Bordo's "The Empire of Images in Our World of Bodies," using their citations to discuss the general meaning.

Video 2.6 Kim Elliot's tenth grade biology class discusses the link between DNA and cancer after they perform a close read of "Untangling the Roots of Cancer."

HOW DOES THE TEXT **WORK**?

A bridge is a powerful symbol for most of us. It connotes movement from one place to another. It offers reliable passage across an otherwise difficult divide. It marks a path for travel. When we encounter a bridge, we cross it. The urge to do so is deeply rooted in our nature. Metaphorically, bridges represent transitions, paths, or connections. And this is exactly what questions focused on *how the text works* do for students.

Attention to how a text works can provide students with a cognitive bridge as they travel from the literal meaning (*what the text says*) to the inferential (*what the text means*). The journey from literal to inferential understanding requires analysis, and the divide between the two can be rocky. In fact, more than a few students can lose their way without a clear path and a good guide. Text-dependent questions cast a light on the vocabulary, structure, and craft used by a writer to convey a message.

To borrow a term introduced by Adler and Van Doren (1972), questions about how the text works allow us to "x-ray the book" (p. 75). These questions prompt students to look beyond what is at the surface in order

Questions about how the text works allow us to "x-ray the book" (Adler and Van Doren, 1972).

to more closely examine the internal workings of the text. If determining *what the text says* is analogous to inspection, then figuring out *how the text works* is similar to investigation. Consider what a crime scene investigator does. After inspecting the scene and determining that the incident cannot be easily explained, she begins to collect evidence. She uses these samples to reconstruct what has occurred. She knows what to look for (the footage from a security camera, a set of footprints near a broken window) and keeps her eyes open for more subtle trace evidence that she can find using special techniques, such as dusting for fingerprints. These practices help her to reconstruct what might have happened leading up to the crime. She's not ready to formulate conclusions, but this investigation is an essential step in her process toward understanding what happened.

An Invitation to Read Closely: *Structural*-Level Questions

Analytic reading requires in part that the reader take the text apart and then reassemble it. By probing the parts, readers can begin to understand the whole. While it is true that the whole text is more than the sum of its parts, the practice of unearthing components that are likely to be important is critical to understanding the text as a whole. But simply making piles of parts is insufficient. That would be deconstruction without reconstruction. The analysis must also include how the parts fit into the whole. The first is a pile of bricks, while the second is a complete house (Adler & Van Doren, 1972).

> Discussion about vocabulary, text structure, and author's craft serves as the bridge to understanding the text as a whole.

Discussion about vocabulary, text structure, and author's craft serves as the bridge to understanding the text as a whole. The text-dependent questions for these discussions bear some functional similarities to adjunct questions, which are written questions that are interspersed throughout a text in order to draw the reader's attention to an element of the passage. Several studies have demonstrated positive effects on the comprehension of older readers who are provided adjunct questions (e.g., Chi & Bassock, 1989; Peverly & Wood, 2001). Their usefulness lies in their ability to shift a reader's attention to an element of the text the reader may have overlooked, especially in the case of students termed *low structure builders* (Callender & McDaniel, 2007). *Structure building* is a construct proposed by Gernsbacher (1991) that describes comprehension as a process that

involves building a coherent structure out of the presented information. This process involves laying a foundation with the initial information that is read and mapping the new information onto the existing structure. When information is encountered that is not conceptually related to the existing structure . . . the reader shifts and builds a new substructure. This is done repeatedly throughout the text resulting in a mental representation, or structure of the text. (Callender & McDaniel, 2007, p. 340)

Poor structure builders have a difficult time assembling these substructures into a coherent whole. How can we help? Add the power of discussion to the concept of interspersing questions throughout a reading in order to aid comprehension. Nystrand's (2006) analysis of 150 years of research on the effects of discussion on reading comprehension confirmed what many teachers already realize: "The relative ineffectiveness of recitation and other monologic practices in teaching reading comprehension, compared to discussion and instructional conversation, [means that] meaning is realized only in the process of active, responsive understanding" (p. 400). In other words, naming the piles (recitation) does little to enable structure building. Discussion in small and large groups aids students in assembling the substructures in order to understand the piece.

> Discussion in small and large groups aids students in assembling the substructures in order to understand the piece.

Why Students Need This Type of Questioning

Elements that underpin a text include its *expository or literary structures and features,* and *vocabulary words and phrases.* These components are intentionally selected by skilled writers to convey experience, information, or formal argument. Think of these as the bones of the text, as they hold up the ideas and concepts presented. These elements organize a text and properly channel the flow of information such that the reader can follow its internal logic.

But it is this framework that often eludes adolescent writers. These elements may seem invisible to them, because when the elements are skillfully utilized they are a backdrop to the action. In some instances, they are deliberately subtle. Take signal words for example. Most students learn in elementary school that signal words let readers know the organizing text structure, in the same way that flags mark out the course for a downhill skier. Sets of signal words, such as *first, then, next,* and *last* are used to organize sequenced text; the presence of an *if . . . then* pairing means it is a problem–solution text structure. But some of these more obvious signal words give way in middle and high school texts to more subtle forms. In their places, words like *simultaneously* and *previously* signal not only a chronology, but one that has an altered time order. A problem may be described as a *dilemma,* and its solution may not be discussed until many paragraphs or even chapters later.

The text structures utilized in secondary-level texts expand as well. The simple story grammar used in elementary texts gives way to the dramatic structure used in many forms of literature. Middle and high school students are asked to locate events that signal the rising action, the climax, and the denouement. Science texts use deductive and inductive reasoning, while other texts utilize Toulmin's elements of argument (1954)—claim, grounds, warrant, backing, rebuttal, and qualification. Structure elements such as these unfold over sentences, not single words.

Text-dependent questions focus students on the organizational structures and word choices that organize the text. But they also make more apparent what it is the writer is *doing*, something collectively referred to as *author's craft*. Skilled writers select organizational structures and make word choices to serve their purposes in the same way that a builder selects materials to construct a house. Who will live there? What weather conditions must the house be able to endure? Even skilled readers have difficulty employing the elements of good writing, in part because they may not be consciously attending to them. Questions that shift students' attention to the inner workings of a text can have the cumulative effect of raising their consciousness as writers. Hansen (2001) notes that when students read as writers, they make decisions about how they themselves will enact these same craft moves.

> Text-dependent questions focus students on the structures and word choices that organize the text. But they also make more apparent what it is the writer is *doing*, something collectively referred to as *author's craft*.

Consider the discussion of the spare stage directions in the play *Our Town* (Wilder, 1938/2003). In small groups, the eleventh grade students in Bethany Rodrigo's English class are discussing the play, which they have both read and watched over the past week. They are now returning to the printed text version. *"Let's keep going with this analysis,"* Ms. Rodrigo says. *"We keep getting directions about the sound being used all throughout the play. What are some examples, and how does that affect the meaning? Select one act to help narrow your search and talk about it in your small groups before we have a whole class discussion."*

Patrice and her group decide on Act 2 and begin to catalog the sounds featured. They locate directions about the sound of a newspaper being delivered on a front porch, the sounds of young people talking, a choir singing, and an organ playing "The Wedding March." Patrice turns the list so everyone in the group can see it, and they begin to discuss what the sound directions might mean.

> **Joe:** We know the set's almost not there at all. You have to use your imagination.
>
> **Sandra:** Yeah, like most of the props are imaginary, even taking a drink of water from an invisible glass.
>
> **Patrice:** So if Wilder's taking the time to put in these details, it's for a reason. 'Cause he hardly put in much detail at all, other than the fact that there's almost nothing on the stage.

Sandra: 'Cause it's like a sense, right? Like sound is a sense, even though we can't see all the other things they're using in the play.

Joe: Oh, yeah, remember when we were learning about how writers use senses so it gets you to feel something. What was that called?

Patrice: RENNS model.

Joe: Yeah, yeah, RENNS model.

Patrice: That's got me thinking, so let's look at the list again to see what they've got in common. [The group studies the list.]

Sandra: So one thing they've got in common is that the sounds are really known, like everyone would know these sounds.

Joe: So that's like the model we learned about details in writing. That a writer's gonna pick a sensory detail that is familiar, because then it reminds you of lots of personal memories.

Patrice: That makes sense . . . ha ha joke! Like the wedding music, that's real emotional and practically everyone who hears it is going to have their own memories. So do we agree that Wilder's using sound as a way to trigger our own personal memories?

Ms. Rodrigo knows that the deeper meaning of the text still needs to be mined in more detail. But her use of questions that focus on *how the text works* are allowing her students to link their knowledge of structure and craft to their understanding of the play and the ways that writers write. And she knows that these questions allow her to assess her students' developing understanding of the standards she has been teaching.

Students discuss how the stage directions in *Our Town* affect the play's meaning.

How Examining *How the Text Works* Addresses the STANDARDS

Reading Standards

The cluster of reading standards entitled "craft and structure" lie at the heart of this second cognitive path. **Standard 4** focuses on words and phrases, while **standard 5** addresses structures at the sentence level and across the text. **Standard 6** examines how authors establish a point of view. In middle school, words and phrases in literary and informational texts are explored for figurative, connotative, and technical meanings, and students are introduced to literary terms such as *mood, tone, allusion,* and *analogy.* At the high school level, students move from specific words and phrases to their cumulative effect on a piece. The intent of **standard 5** is to draw back a bit further from words and phrases to examine how text structures affect meaning and style. These structures include the use of literary devices such as flashback and foreshadowing, as well as the method used to present a formal argument over the span of a longer piece of text. **Standard 6** concerns itself with how point of view is established within and across characters or people. Once again, the purpose is more than simply identifying a device. Rather, the intent is to link craft and method to meaning. See Figure 3.1 for the grade-specific standards for grades 6–12.

These same **standards (4, 5,** and **6)** articulate a comparable vision for literacy in history/social studies, science, and the technical subjects.

Figure 3.1   ELA Reading Standards That Focus on *How the Text Works*

Standard (Grade)	Literary	Informational
4 (6)	Determine the meaning of words and phrases as they are used in a text, including figurative and connotative meanings; analyze the impact of a specific word choice on meaning and tone. Determine the meaning of words and phrases on meaning and tone.	Determine the meaning of words and phrases as they are used in a text, including figurative, connotative, and technical meanings.
4 (7)	Determine the meaning of words and phrases as they are used in a text, including figurative and connotative meanings; analyze the impact of rhymes and other repetitions of sounds (e.g., alliteration) on a specific verse or stanza of a poem or section of a story or drama.	Determine the meaning of words and phrases as they are used in a text, including figurative, connotative, and technical meanings; analyze the impact of a specific word choice on meaning and tone.
4 (8)	Determine the meaning of words and phrases as they are used in a text, including figurative and connotative meanings; analyze the impact of specific word choices on meaning and tone, including analogies or allusions to other texts.	Determine the meaning of words and phrases as they are used in a text, including figurative, connotative, and technical meanings; analyze the impact of specific word choices on meaning and tone, including analogies or allusions to other texts.

Standard (Grade)	Literary	Informational
4 (9–10)	Determine the meaning of words and phrases as they are used in the text, including figurative and connotative meanings; analyze the cumulative impact of specific word choices on meaning and tone (e.g., how the language evokes a sense of time and place; how it sets a formal or informal tone).	Determine the meaning of words and phrases as they are used in a text, including figurative, connotative, and technical meanings; analyze the cumulative impact of specific word choices on meaning and tone (e.g., how the language of a court opinion differs from that of a newspaper).
4 (11–12)	Determine the meaning of words and phrases as they are used in the text, including figurative and connotative meanings; analyze the impact of specific word choices on meaning and tone, including words with multiple meanings or language that is particularly fresh, engaging, or beautiful. (Include Shakespeare as well as other authors.)	Determine the meaning of words and phrases as they are used in a text, including figurative, connotative, and technical meanings; analyze how an author uses and refines the meaning of a key term or terms over the course of a text (e.g., how Madison defines *faction* in *Federalist* No. 10).
5 (6)	Analyze how a particular sentence, chapter, scene, or stanza fits into the overall structure of a text and contributes to the development of the theme, setting, or plot.	Analyze how a particular sentence, paragraph, chapter, or section fits into the overall structure of a text and contributes to the development of the ideas.
5 (7)	Analyze how a drama's or poem's form or structure (e.g., soliloquy, sonnet) contributes to its meaning.	Analyze the structure an author uses to organize a text, including how the major sections contribute to the whole and to the development of the ideas.
5 (8)	Compare and contrast the structure of two or more texts and analyze how the differing structure of each text contributes to its meaning and style.	Analyze in detail the structure of a specific paragraph in a text, including the role of particular sentences in developing and refining a key concept.
5 (9–10)	Analyze how an author's choices concerning how to structure a text, order events within it (e.g., parallel plots), and manipulate time (e.g., pacing, flashbacks) create such effects as mystery, tension, or surprise.	Analyze in detail how an author's ideas or claims are developed and refined by particular sentences, paragraphs, or larger portions of a text (e.g., a section or chapter).
5 (11–12)	Analyze how an author's choices concerning how to structure specific parts of a text (e.g., the choice of where to begin or end a story, the choice to provide a comedic or tragic resolution) contribute to its overall structure and meaning as well as its aesthetic impact.	Analyze and evaluate the effectiveness of the structure an author uses in his or her exposition or argument, including whether the structure makes points clear, convincing, and engaging.
6 (6)	Explain how an author develops the point of view of the narrator or speaker in a text.	Determine an author's point of view or purpose in a text and explain how it is conveyed in the text.
6 (7)	Analyze how an author develops and contrasts the points of view of different characters or narrators in a text.	Determine an author's point of view or purpose in a text and analyze how the author distinguishes his or her position from that of others.

(Continued)

Figure 3.1 (Continued)

Standard (Grade)	Literary	Informational
6 (8)	Analyze how differences in the points of view of the characters and the audience or reader (e.g., created through the use of dramatic irony) create such effects as suspense or humor.	Determine an author's point of view or purpose in a text and analyze how the author acknowledges and responds to conflicting evidence or viewpoints.
6 (9–10)	Analyze a particular point of view or cultural experience reflected in a work of literature from outside the United States, drawing on a wide reading of world literature.	Determine an author's point of view or purpose in a text and analyze how an author uses rhetoric to advance that point of view or purpose.
6 (11–12)	Analyze a case in which grasping point of view requires distinguishing what is directly stated in a text from what is really meant (e.g., satire, sarcasm, irony, or understatement).	Determine an author's point of view or purpose in a text in which the rhetoric is particularly effective, analyzing how style and content contribute to the power, persuasiveness, or beauty of the text.
10 (6)	By the end of the year, read and comprehend literature, including stories, dramas, and poems, in the grades 6–8 text complexity band proficiently, with scaffolding as needed at the high end of the range.	By the end of the year, read and comprehend literary nonfiction in the grades 6–8 text complexity band proficiently, with scaffolding as needed at the high end of the range.
10 (7)	By the end of the year, read and comprehend literature, including stories, dramas, and poems, in the grades 6–8 text complexity band proficiently, with scaffolding as needed at the high end of the range.	By the end of the year, read and comprehend literary nonfiction in the grades 6–8 text complexity band proficiently, with scaffolding as needed at the high end of the range.
10 (8)	By the end of the year, read and comprehend literature, including stories, dramas, and poems, at the high end of grades 6–8 text complexity band independently and proficiently.	By the end of the year, read and comprehend literary nonfiction at the high end of the grades 6–8 text complexity band independently and proficiently.
10 (9–10)	By the end of grade 9, read and comprehend literature, including stories, dramas, and poems, in the grades 9–10 text complexity band proficiently, with scaffolding as needed at the high end of the range. By the end of grade 10, read and comprehend literature, including stories, dramas, and poems, at the high end of the grades 9–10 text complexity band independently and proficiently.	By the end of grade 9, read and comprehend literary nonfiction in the grades 9–10 text complexity band proficiently, with scaffolding as needed at the high end of the range. By the end of grade 10, read and comprehend literary nonfiction at the high end of the grades 9–10 text complexity band independently and proficiently.
10 (11–12)	By the end of grade 11, read and comprehend literature, including stories, dramas, and poems, in the grades 11–CCR text complexity band proficiently, with scaffolding as needed at the high end of the range. By the end of grade 12, read and comprehend literature, including stories, dramas, and poems, at the high end of the grades 11–CCR text complexity band independently and proficiently.	By the end of grade 11, read and comprehend literary nonfiction in the grades 11–CCR text complexity band proficiently, with scaffolding as needed at the high end of the range. By the end of grade 12, read and comprehend literary nonfiction at the high end of the grades 11–CCR text complexity band independently and proficiently.

Vocabulary terms are critical in these disciplines, especially as secondary students encounter an increasing volume of technical vocabulary. **Standard 5** in history/social studies describes text structure somewhat differently from the framework widely used in English and science. In history, text structures are described as *sequential, comparative,* and *causal.* These correlate to the ways in which historical information is presented and analyzed. For instance, is the text an account of the event written as a firsthand account? Or is it a text meant to persuade, and therefore comparing two ideologies? Or is it an explanation of a decision, using a causal structure to present a rationale? **Standard 6** casts a discipline-specific light on the subject of point of view. For instance, middle school students should look for loaded language in texts, while high school students are considering when information is strategically omitted in order to gain support. A table of the literacy standards for these disciplines can be located in Figure 3.2.

Figure 3.2 History, Science, and Technical Subjects Reading Standards That Focus on *How the Text Works*

Standard (Grade band)	History/Social Studies	Sciences and Technical Subjects
4 (6–8)	Determine the meaning of words and phrases as they are used in a text, including vocabulary specific to domains related to history/social studies.	Determine the meaning of symbols, key terms, and other domain-specific words and phrases as they are used in a specific scientific or technical context relevant to grades 6–8 texts and topics.
4 (9–10)	Determine the meaning of words and phrases as they are used in a text, including vocabulary describing political, social, or economic aspects of history/social studies.	Determine the meaning of symbols, key terms, and other domain-specific words and phrases as they are used in a specific scientific or technical context relevant to grades 9–10 texts and topics.
4 (11–12)	Determine the meaning of words and phrases as they are used in a text, including analyzing how an author uses and refines the meaning of a key term over the course of a text (e.g., how Madison defines *faction* in *Federalist* No. 10).	Determine the meaning of symbols, key terms, and other domain-specific words and phrases as they are used in a specific scientific or technical context relevant to grades 11–12 texts and topics.
5 (6–8)	Describe how a text presents information (e.g., sequentially, comparatively, causally).	Analyze the structure an author uses to organize a text, including how the major sections contribute to the whole and to an understanding of the topic.
5 (9–10)	Analyze how a text uses structure to emphasize key points or advance an explanation or analysis.	Analyze the structure of the relationships among concepts in a text, including relationships among key terms (e.g., *force, friction, reaction force, energy*).

(Continued)

Figure 3.2 (Continued)

Standard (Grade band)	History/Social Studies	Sciences and Technical Subjects
5 (11–12)	Analyze in detail how a complex primary source is structured, including how key sentences, paragraphs, and larger portions of the text contribute to the whole.	Analyze how the text structures information or ideas into categories or hierarchies, demonstrating understanding of the information or ideas.
6 (6–8)	Identify aspects of a text that reveal an author's point of view or purpose (e.g., loaded language, inclusion or avoidance of particular facts).	Analyze the author's purpose in providing an explanation, describing a procedure, or discussing an experiment in a text.
6 (9–10)	Compare the point of view of two or more authors for how they treat the same or similar topics, including which details they include and emphasize in their respective accounts.	Analyze the author's purpose in providing an explanation, describing a procedure, or discussing an experiment in a text, defining the question the author seeks to address.
6 (11–12)	Evaluate authors' differing points of view on the same historical event or issue by assessing the authors' claims, reasoning, and evidence.	Analyze the author's purpose in providing an explanation, describing a procedure, or discussing an experiment in a text, identifying important issues that remain unresolved.
10 (6–8)	By the end of grade 8, read and comprehend history/social studies texts in the grades 6–8 text complexity band independently and proficiently.	By the end of grade 8, read and comprehend science/technical texts in the grades 6–8 text complexity band independently and proficiently.
10 (9–10)	By the end of grade 10, read and comprehend history/social studies texts in the grades 9–10 text complexity band independently and proficiently.	By the end of grade 10, read and comprehend science/technical texts in the grades 9–10 text complexity band independently and proficiently.
10 (11–12)	By the end of grade 12, read and comprehend history/social studies texts in the grades 11–CCR text complexity band independently and proficiently.	By the end of grade 12, read and comprehend science/technical texts in the grades 11–CCR text complexity band independently and proficiently.

Sixth grade social studies students in Christina Engel's class discussed an excerpt from a primary source document featured in their textbook. The passage was from a letter written by Pliny the Younger recounting the death of his uncle, Pliny the Elder, at the eruption of Vesuvius in 79 AD. During text-based discussion about what the text says, the students discovered that the letter was written to a Roman historian as an account of the uncle's death while the uncle was trying to rescue survivors. Ms. Engel shifted attention to the chronology. *"Pliny the Younger is writing this account sequentially, but we also need to be mindful of the geographical and time details that help us understand what occurred. So let's use a map and figure out what happened and when it happened on the last day of Pliny the Elder's life."*

Using a map of the area, the students traced Pliny's travel by ship from Misenum, on the northwest area of the bay where his naval fleet was stationed, to Pompeii 20 or 30 miles away. *"Let's look closer to figure out what the time span is,"* Ms. Engel said to her students. *"Are we talking about hours, days, or weeks?"* Samuel found the information that stated that Pliny the Elder first saw the plume arising from Vesuvius in the early afternoon, and Alexis pointed out that near the end of the letter, the writer said, "Elsewhere there was daylight by this time, but they were still in darkness, blacker and denser than any ordinary night" and that this information comes right before the writer discloses that Pliny the Elder had died. "So we're probably only talking about a few hours," said Riley.

"So let's take a step back from this so we can figure out what we know so far from our discussion," said the teacher. *"Pliny the Elder, who is this famous naval commander and scholar, is enjoying a sunny summer afternoon in his villa when he sees the volcano erupt. He could have sent others, but he immediately decides he's going to investigate, because he's a scholar. He sails across the bay and runs into town to find out what's going on. But once he gets there he knows he has to help. A few hours later he's dead. As we look more into this letter, let's keep in mind how drastically this man's life took an unexpected turn in one afternoon, and why Pliny the Younger uses the word* courageous *to describe his uncle."*

Language Standards

While reading spotlights one mode of literacy, language encompasses all: reading, writing, speaking, and listening. The language standards that hone in on discovering *how a text works* flow directly from those discussed in the previous section on reading. The middle school versions of **standard 3** describe the importance of listening, reading, and writing for clarity and consistency. In high school, the grade band standards turn to an understanding of how language functions and how context influences its purpose. **Standards 4** and **6** are clustered around vocabulary acquisition and use. Collectively, these standards require students to use structural and contextual analysis to resolve unknown words and phrases, turning to resources as needed in pursuit of new vocabulary. **Standard 5** closely parallels the reading standards described in the previous section. A table of the targeted language standards for middle and high school can be found in Figure 3.3.

Students in Mark Johannsen's seventh grade English class were engaged in a weeklong interdisciplinary unit cotaught by science teacher Art Inoue. In Mr. Inoue's class, students examined contributing factors that led to the Dust Bowl that engulfed much of the southwestern United States in the 1930s. In Mr. Johannsen's class, students were engaged in the study of the popular culture of the time, especially songs, movies, and radio shows. They had read a brief biographical article about humorist Will Rogers, one of the most popular entertainers of the time, and had viewed several short video clips of his performances. (See www.cmgww.com/historic/rogers/about/biography.html for these items.)

Figure 3.3 Language Standards That Focus on *How the Text Works*

	Grade 6	Grade 7	Grade 8	Grades 9–10	Grades 11–12
3	Use knowledge of language and its conventions when writing, speaking, reading, or listening. a. Vary sentence patterns for meaning, reader/listener interest, and style. b. Maintain consistency in style and tone.	Use knowledge of language and its conventions when writing, speaking, reading, or listening. a. Choose language that expresses ideas precisely and concisely, recognizing and eliminating wordiness and redundancy.	Use knowledge of language and its conventions when writing, speaking, reading, or listening. a. Use verbs in the active and passive voice and in the conditional and subjunctive mood to achieve particular effects (e.g., emphasizing the actor or the action; expressing uncertainty or describing a state contrary to fact).	Apply knowledge of language to understand how language functions in different contexts, to make effective choices for meaning or style, and to comprehend more fully when reading or listening.	Apply knowledge of language to understand how language functions in different contexts, to make effective choices for meaning or style, and to comprehend more fully when reading or listening.
4	Determine or clarify the meaning of unknown and multiple-meaning words and phrases based on grade 6 reading and content, choosing flexibly from a range of strategies. a. Use context (e.g., the overall meaning of a sentence or paragraph; a word's position or function in a sentence) as a clue to the meaning of a word or phrase.	Determine or clarify the meaning of unknown and multiple-meaning words and phrases based on grade 7 reading and content, choosing flexibly from a range of strategies. a. Use context (e.g., the overall meaning of a sentence or paragraph; a word's position or function in a sentence) as a clue to the meaning of a word or phrase.	Determine or clarify the meaning of unknown and multiple-meaning words and phrases based on grade 8 reading and content, choosing flexibly from a range of strategies. a. Use context (e.g., the overall meaning of a sentence or paragraph; a word's position or function in a sentence) as a clue to the meaning of a word or phrase.	Determine or clarify the meaning of unknown and multiple-meaning words and phrases based on grades 9–10 reading and content, choosing flexibly from a range of strategies. a. Use context (e.g., the overall meaning of a sentence, paragraph, or text; a word's position or function in a sentence) as a clue to the meaning of a word or phrase.	Determine or clarify the meaning of unknown and multiple-meaning words and phrases based on grades 11–12 reading and content, choosing flexibly from a range of strategies. a. Use context (e.g., the overall meaning of a sentence, paragraph, or text; a word's position or function in a sentence) as a clue to the meaning of a word or phrase.

Grade 6	Grade 7	Grade 8	Grades 9–10	Grades 11–12
b. Use common, grade-appropriate Greek or Latin affixes and roots as clues to the meaning of a word (e.g., audience, auditory, audible).	b. Use common, grade-appropriate Greek or Latin affixes and roots as clues to the meaning of a word (e.g., belligerent, bellicose, rebel).	b. Use common, grade-appropriate Greek or Latin affixes and roots as clues to the meaning of a word (e.g., precede, recede, secede).	b. Identify and correctly use patterns of word changes that indicate different meanings or parts of speech (e.g., analyze, analysis, analytical, advocate, advocacy).	b. Identify and correctly use patterns of word changes that indicate different meanings or parts of speech (e.g., conceive, conception, conceivable).
c. Consult reference materials (e.g., dictionaries, glossaries, thesauruses), both print and digital, to find the pronunciation of a word or determine or clarify its precise meaning or its part of speech.	c. Consult general and specialized reference materials (e.g., dictionaries, glossaries, thesauruses), both print and digital, to find the pronunciation of a word or determine or clarify its precise meaning or its part of speech.	c. Consult general and specialized reference materials (e.g., dictionaries, glossaries, thesauruses), both print and digital, to find the pronunciation of a word or determine or clarify its precise meaning or its part of speech.	c. Consult general and specialized reference materials (e.g., dictionaries, glossaries, thesauruses), both print and digital, to find the pronunciation of a word or determine or clarify its precise meaning, its part of speech, or its etymology.	c. Consult general and specialized reference materials (e.g., dictionaries, glossaries, thesauruses), both print and digital, to find the pronunciation of a word or determine or clarify its precise meaning, its part of speech, its etymology, or its standard usage.
d. Verify the preliminary determination of the meaning of a word or phrase (e.g., by checking the inferred meaning in context or in a dictionary).	d. Verify the preliminary determination of the meaning of a word or phrase (e.g., by checking the inferred meaning in context or in a dictionary).	d. Verify the preliminary determination of the meaning of a word or phrase (e.g., by checking the inferred meaning in context or in a dictionary).	d. Verify the preliminary determination of the meaning of a word or phrase (e.g., by checking the inferred meaning in context or in a dictionary).	d. Verify the preliminary determination of the meaning of a word or phrase (e.g., by checking the inferred meaning in context or in a dictionary).

(Continued)

Figure 3.3 (Continued)

	Grade 6	Grade 7	Grade 8	Grades 9–10	Grades 11–12
5	Demonstrate understanding of figurative language, word relationships, and nuances in word meanings. a. Interpret figures of speech (e.g., personification) in context. b. Use the relationship between particular words (e.g., cause/effect, part/whole, item/category) to better understand each of the words. c. Distinguish among the connotations (associations) of words with similar denotations (definitions) (e.g., stingy, scrimping, economical, unwasteful, thrifty).	Demonstrate understanding of figurative language, word relationships, and nuances in word meanings. a. Interpret figures of speech (e.g., literary, biblical, and mythological allusions) in context. b. Use the relationship between particular words (e.g., synonym/antonym, analogy) to better understand each of the words. c. Distinguish among the connotations (associations) of words with similar denotations (definitions) (e.g., refined, respectful, polite, diplomatic, condescending).	Demonstrate understanding of figurative language, word relationships, and nuances in word meanings. a. Interpret figures of speech (e.g. verbal irony, puns) in context. b. Use the relationship between particular words to better understand each of the words. c. Distinguish among the connotations (associations) of words with similar denotations (definitions) (e.g., bullheaded, willful, firm, persistent, resolute).	Demonstrate understanding of figurative language, word relationships, and nuances in word meanings. a. Interpret figures of speech (e.g., euphemism, oxymoron) in context and analyze their role in the text. b. Analyze nuances in the meaning of words with similar denotations.	Demonstrate understanding of figurative language, word relationships, and nuances in word meanings. a. Interpret figures of speech (e.g., hyperbole, paradox) in context and analyze their role in the text. b. Analyze nuances in the meaning of words with similar denotations.
6	Acquire and use accurately grade-appropriate general academic and domain-specific words and phrases; gather vocabulary knowledge when considering a word or phrase important to comprehension or expression.		Acquire and use accurately general academic and domain-specific words and phrases, sufficient for reading, writing, speaking, and listening at the college and career readiness level; demonstrate independence in gathering vocabulary knowledge when considering a word or phrase important to comprehension or expression.		

"We've watched Will Rogers perform, and now we're going to look back into his biography," said Mr. Johannsen. *"You've got a transcript of the videos we watched on your tables. I'm interested in how he used language, because he really did say some pretty politically charged things, like calling the US Congress 'the national joke factory.' Look back into the biography. What are some words and phrases the author uses to describe Rogers's language?"*

Students identified several examples, including *folksy* and *no-nonsense*. "*Simple language* gets used a couple of times," said Olivia. *"I'm so glad you saw that! Take a look at one of the sentences that discusses* simple language. *Look at the context, because the author is making a connection to Rogers's success,"* said Mr. Johannsen. They read to themselves, "His simple language and country roots appealed to audiences, who saw him as one of their own" (*Biography*, n.d., ¶5). During discussion about this point, Mr. Johannsen reminds them to continue to annotate. *"We've been drilling down to get to the descriptions of his use of language. Now let's look for evidence of his appeal to his audiences."*

Speaking and Listening Standards

The standards profiled previously in Chapter 2 remain the same when discussing how a text works. As with other aspects of a close reading process, it is discussion that elevates this from rudimentary independent work to true discourse. Text-based discussion provides learners with the opportunity to hone their listening skills in small and large groups, and participate as coconstructors of knowledge, rather than simple question-and-answer exchanges that rarely evolve past recitation and recall. Figure 3.4 contains a list of the speaking and listening standards addressed in text-based discussions of *how the text works*.

Figure 3.4 Speaking and Listening Standards That Focus on *How the Text Works*

	Grade 6	Grade 7	Grade 8	Grades 9–10	Grades 11–12
1	Engage effectively in a range of collaborative discussions (one-on-one, in groups, and teacher-led) with diverse partners on grade 6 topics, texts, and issues, building on others' ideas and expressing their own clearly. a. Come to discussions prepared, having read or studied required material; explicitly draw on that preparation by referring to evidence on the topic, text, or issue to probe and reflect on ideas under discussion. b. Follow rules for collegial discussions, set specific goals and deadlines, and define individual roles as needed.	Engage effectively in a range of collaborative discussions (one-on-one, in groups, and teacher-led) with diverse partners on grade 7 topics, texts, and issues, building on others' ideas and expressing their own clearly. a. Come to discussions prepared, having read or researched material under study; explicitly draw on that preparation by referring to evidence on the topic, text, or issue to probe and reflect on ideas under discussion. b. Follow rules for collegial discussions, track progress toward specific goals and deadlines, and define individual roles as needed.	Engage effectively in a range of collaborative discussions (one-on-one, in groups, and teacher-led) with diverse partners on grade 8 topics, texts, and issues, building on others' ideas and expressing their own clearly. a. Come to discussions prepared, having read or researched material under study; explicitly draw on that preparation by referring to evidence on the topic, text, or issue to probe and reflect on ideas under discussion. b. Follow rules for collegial discussions and decision-making, track progress toward specific goals and	Initiate and participate effectively in a range of collaborative discussions (one-on-one, in groups, and teacher-led) with diverse partners on grades 9–10 topics, texts, and issues, building on others' ideas and expressing their own clearly and persuasively. a. Come to discussions prepared, having read and researched material under study; explicitly draw on that preparation by referring to evidence from texts and other research on the topic or issue to stimulate a thoughtful, well-reasoned exchange of ideas. b. Work with peers to set rules for collegial discussions and decision-making (e.g., informal consensus, taking votes on key issues,	Initiate and participate effectively in a range of collaborative discussions (one-on-one, in groups, and teacher-led) with diverse partners on grades 11–12 topics, texts, and issues, building on others' ideas and expressing their own clearly and persuasively. a. Come to discussions prepared, having read and researched material under study; explicitly draw on that preparation by referring to evidence from texts and other research on the topic or issue to stimulate a thoughtful, well-reasoned exchange of ideas. b. Work with peers to promote civil, democratic discussions and decision-making, set clear goals and deadlines, and

Grade 6	Grade 7	Grade 8	Grades 9–10	Grades 11–12
c. Pose and respond to specific questions with elaboration and detail by making comments that contribute to the topic, text, or issue under discussion. d. Review the key ideas expressed and demonstrate understanding of multiple perspectives through reflection and paraphrasing.	c. Pose questions that elicit elaboration and respond to others' questions and comments with relevant observations and ideas that bring the discussion back on topic as needed. d. Acknowledge new information expressed by others and, when warranted, modify their own views.	deadlines, and define individual roles as needed. c. Pose questions that connect the ideas of several speakers and respond to others' questions and comments with relevant evidence, observations, and ideas. d. Acknowledge new information expressed by others, and, when warranted, qualify or justify their own views in light of the evidence presented.	presentation of alternate views), clear goals and deadlines, and individual roles as needed. c. Propel conversations by posing and responding to questions that relate the current discussion to broader themes or larger ideas; actively incorporate others into the discussion; and clarify, verify, or challenge ideas and conclusions. d. Respond thoughtfully to diverse perspectives, summarize points of agreement and disagreement, and, when warranted, qualify or justify their own views and understanding and make new connections in light of the evidence and reasoning presented.	establish individual roles as needed. c. Propel conversations by posing and responding to questions that probe reasoning and evidence; ensure a hearing for a full range of positions on a topic or issue; clarify, verify, or challenge ideas and conclusions; and promote divergent and creative perspectives. d. Respond thoughtfully to diverse perspectives; synthesize comments, claims, and evidence made on all sides of an issue; resolve contradictions when possible; and determine what additional information or research is required to deepen the investigation or complete the task.

(Continued)

Figure 3.4 (Continued)

	Grade 6	Grade 7	Grade 8	Grades 9–10	Grades 11–12
4	Present claims and findings, sequencing ideas logically and using pertinent descriptions, facts, and details to accentuate main ideas or themes; use appropriate eye contact, adequate volume, and clear pronunciation.	Present claims and findings, emphasizing salient points in a focused, coherent manner with pertinent descriptions, facts, details, and examples; use appropriate eye contact, adequate volume, and clear pronunciation.	Present claims and findings, emphasizing salient points in a focused, coherent manner with relevant evidence, sound valid reasoning, and well-chosen details; use appropriate eye contact, adequate volume, and clear pronunciation.	Present information, findings, and supporting evidence clearly, concisely, and logically such that listeners can follow the line of reasoning and the organization, development, substance, and style are appropriate to purpose, audience, and task.	Present information, findings, and supporting evidence, conveying a clear and distinct perspective, such that listeners can follow the line of reasoning, alternative or opposing perspectives are addressed, and the organization, development, substance, and style are appropriate to purpose, audience, and a range of formal and informal tasks.
6	Adapt speech to a variety of contexts and tasks, demonstrating command of formal English when indicated or appropriate.		Adapt speech to a variety of contexts and tasks, demonstrating command of formal English when indicated or appropriate.		

Viewed collectively, text-dependent questions about the vocabulary, text structure, and author's craft build a bridge for students to mentally traverse as they move from what the text says to what the text means. The critical thinking needed to get to levels 3 and 4 in the Depth of Knowledge framework (see Chapter 1) does not come easily. In fact, our experience has been that readers may balk at some of these questions, because they are more accustomed to focusing on the literal-level meaning of the text. When teachers press for evidence from the text to support answers to questions that focus on *how the text works*, students must consider the structures that the author used to create the text, which in turn leads to deeper understanding of the text.

Using Text-Dependent Questions About *How the Text Works*

Helping students figure out how the text works requires attention to three main clusters of content:

- Vocabulary

- Text structures

- Author's craft

That's not to say that all texts are complex in these ways or that teachers have to ask questions in each of these areas. It is to say that teachers can analyze the texts for their internal workings, considering vocabulary, text structure, and author's craft, to determine the specific questions that they can ask to help students deepen their understanding of the text or to assess students' developing proficiency with the standards.

Questions About Vocabulary

One significant predictor of reading comprehension is vocabulary (Baumann, Kame'enui, & Ash, 2003). Simply said, if a reader knows the meaning of the words, the text is more likely to be understood. That doesn't mean that students should already know all of the words and phrases before they read a complex text. Students learn a lot of words and phrases from the reading that they do (White, Graves, & Slater, 1990). Mason, Stahl, Au, and Herman (2003) estimate that a student can learn about 2,250 new words per year while reading. Interestingly, these same researchers estimate that students can learn between 300–500 words through systematic instruction. As Adams (1990) noted,

> While affirming the value of classroom instruction in vocabulary, we must also recognize its limitations. By our best estimates,

the growth in recognition vocabulary of the school age child typically exceeds 3,000 words per year, or more than eight per day. This order of growth cannot be ascribed to their classroom instruction, nor could it be attained through any feasible program of classroom instruction. (p. 172)

Close reading of complex texts is one of the activities in which students can learn a lot of words. Of course, wide independent reading is another activity in which students can learn a lot of words, and we would be remiss if we did not point out that teachers have to carefully select the words that they are going to directly teach, given that students don't learn a lot of words this way.

We are not suggesting that close reading becomes a time for vocabulary instruction. We are suggesting that there be time for direct and systematic vocabulary instruction but that it occurs outside of the close reading lesson. During close readings, the text-dependent questions that teachers ask allow students to practice and apply their word-solving skills. As noted in language **standard 4**, students should be able to "determine or clarify the meaning of unknown and multiple-meaning words and phrases by using context clues, analyzing meaningful word parts, and consulting general and specialized reference materials, as appropriate" (CCSSI, 2010a, p. 25). Solving for unknown words is one of the habits that students need to develop if they are going to be successful with reading closely.

This starts with an identification of the terms that may trip up students. If there are words that cannot be easily solved, the teacher may simply provide students with a definition on the bottom of the page. For example, during their reading of *Kipling and I* (Colon, 1993), Kelly Johnson provided her students with a margin note that included the definition of *gilded frame*. She decided that it wasn't a very important word for students to focus on, and she knew that the context and structural clues were not helpful. Providing students with access to the meaning of that phrase while they were reading and rereading the text allowed them to focus on the meaning of the text, and there were plenty of other words and phrases that deserved her students' cognitive attention.

Alternatively, on their third read of Oscar Wilde's preface to *The Picture of Dorian Grey* (Wilde, 1891/1992), Marisol Thayre invited her students to use their iPads to find the meaning of several words, including *realism*, *Caliban* [a Shakespearean character known for his coarse and crude ways], and *romanticism*. As they used this resource, the meaning of the text became clearer. As Ms. Thayre said,

> Teachers have to carefully select the words that they are going to directly teach, given that students don't learn a lot of words this way.

By the time we get out the iPads to find the meanings of words, the students have a lot of knowledge from the text, and they're looking for definitions that make sense. It's really more inquiry based than me just telling them the meaning of the words, hoping that they'll remember them and be able to use the definitions. And, if I really think about it, it's what I do when I read. I have to figure out the meaning of the text, and sometimes that means I have to reread and figure out the words the author is using. I like to tell my students that in college I used to read with a dictionary next to me. Now I read with my phone handy.

Students use their iPads to find the meaning of several words.

As we have noted, the text-dependent questions should focus on both words and phrases. Sometimes it's worth the time to focus on individual words, as was the case in Ms. Thayre's class. Other times, it's important to consider phrases, as was the case in Ms. Johnson's class. Confusion does not exist only at the word level, and the standards are specific in the attention to words and phrases, as well as to students' ability to "demonstrate understanding of figurative language, word relationships, and nuances in word meanings" (CCSSI, 2010a, p. 25). Just think how easy each word in the idiom "hit the books" is, but simply understanding each word will not result in students understanding that they should be studying.

Knowledge of the vocabulary deepens the reader's understanding of the text, and not only through definition. When Ms. Thayre's students first read the preface to *The Picture of Dorian Gray*, their initial understanding of the following sentences was limited: "The nineteenth century dislike of Realism is the rage of Caliban seeing his own face in a glass. The nineteenth century dislike of Romanticism is the rage of Caliban not seeing his own face in a glass." In other words, Wilde was commenting on readers' distress at seeing themselves portrayed as flawed (realism), but equally disliked it when they *couldn't* see themselves in more abstract art (romanticism). Ms. Thayre had her students return to the preface a few weeks later, after they had finished the novel. "Now when they reread it, they recognized more clearly that Oscar Wilde was satirizing British society, especially the bourgeois middle class. The story itself is what contextualized the meaning of those terms, and they had a greater appreciation for his sharp wit," she said.

> Knowledge of the vocabulary deepens the reader's understanding of the text, and not only through definition.

Questions About Vocabulary in Middle School English

Mr. Corbrera's analysis of *The People Could Fly* (Hamilton, 1993) suggested that vocabulary would not be a significant barrier for his students. They learned a great deal about slavery as part of their fifth grade social studies curriculum, so terms like *slavery*, *master*, and *overseer* were known to them. As he expected, they read the text with ease and were able to discuss their general understanding and the key details of the text. Mr. Corbrera was interested in exploring a few phrases from the text, namely "Say he was a hard lump of clay. A hard, glinty coal." (p. 167) So he asked his students to discuss what it meant.

"Let's take apart this phrase. And let's start with 'he.' Who is 'he'?"

As the groups discussed this, Mr. Corbrera noted that one of the groups thought it was referring to a character named Toby, but the others correctly identified the master as the person referred to in the sentence. Mr. Corbrera asked one of the groups with the correct answer (the master) to explain the thinking behind their decision.

"I think it's the owner because of the sentence before where it says the owner called him the master. So then he should be the master," Bradley said.

Cara, a member of another group, raised her hand, offering, "And the sentence after where it says 'his overseer' so it would be the owner, that's the 'he' because he has the guy to watch over them. That's what the context clues say to me."

Mr. Corbrera, satisfied that they understood the pronoun referent, followed up with the question, "*So what does it mean that the slave owner was 'a hard lump of clay'? Or 'a hard, glinty coal'?*"

As the students discussed their responses, Mr. Corbrera joined the group that had the incorrect response to the first question. He interrupted their conversation and asked if the pronoun referent made sense to them, and what the phrase meant. The students in the group indicated that they did now understand it referred to the owner, and that the phrase meant that he wasn't emotional or kind. As Mauricio said, "He doesn't care at all about those people. He just wants the work done and he doesn't care that they are hurt or sick. He's just hard, like they don't even matter."

Questions About Vocabulary in High School English

Nancy's ninth grade students returned to the short story "The Open Window" by Saki the following class. She knew the word *romance* in the story's last sentence was still puzzling to students and key to unlocking the meaning of the story: "Romance at short notice was her specialty." But she wasn't ready to take that on quite yet. Instead, she wanted the discussion to shift to a turning point early in the story. The phrase *letters of introduction* didn't offer much in the way of contextual clues. After inquiring as to whether anyone was familiar with the term (no one was), she briefly explained that they were commonly used before the invention of telecommunications as a way of vouching for a stranger. *"Now go back into the story and reread the beginning, stopping after Mr. Nuttel says, 'Only her name and address.' This time, I want you to use what I just told you about letters of introduction to get a glimpse of how Vera's mind is working. What's she up to?"*

As they read the passage, several students began to nod and smile to themselves. "She's pretty sneaky," said Alexis. "Vera knows about him because of the letters of introduction, but Framton doesn't know anything about her or her family."

Several minutes of discussion ensued about how Vera saw an opportunity to tell a lie. *"Now let's look again at the last sentence: 'Romance at short notice was her specialty.' How does this square with what you are already thinking about Vera?"*

Kealin was stuck on *romance*, "because there isn't any," but Nancy encouraged him to look at another phrase—*short notice*.

Chris added his thoughts. "She's quick, like she just jumped on the chance to tell the lie without missing a beat. She told the lie on short notice . . . wait, is that romance?"

Nancy told them they were definitely on the right track.

Questions About Vocabulary in Middle School Social Studies

The students in Ms. Robinson's eighth grade social studies class had circled several words in the text they were reading, *The Narrative Life of Frederick Douglass* (1845/1995). She had already told them that *stratagem* meant a strategy that was deceptive and that *slumbering* was a light sleep, like dozing, or to lie and do nothing. She expected that her students would not immediately know the meaning of *discontented*, *depravity*, and *unutterable*, but was not worried about those terms, as they did not distract from students' understanding of the text. To check their understanding of the text through vocabulary, Ms. Robinson asked her students, *"What various stratagems did Frederick use?"*

The students talked about his practice with the book he found and the kids he had teach him in trade for food.

She then turned their attention to the word *discontent,* saying *"Remember that Mr. Auld tells his wife that reading will make Frederick discontented and unhappy. In the final paragraph, he uses the word* discontentment. *What happened? The text says, 'that very discontentment which Master Hugh had predicted.' Talk about that with your group."*

Roland started the conversation for his group. "I think it's saying that learning to read was a problem for him. Not that the learning was hard, but that once he knew how to read, he wanted more freedom. Like the text says, 'It opened my eyes to the horrible pit, but to no ladder upon which to get out."

"I agree with you," Paulina said, "because it says that it was a torment, and that means that it was bad suffering and bothering,"

Immediately, Jayson added, "And it says 'sting my soul,' and that sounds like it really hurt. Because then later he says that it was the thinking that tormented him. Because he could read, but wasn't allowed to. And then he knew that there was another life besides being a slave but he didn't know how to get free."

Questions About Vocabulary in High School Social Studies

The FDR inaugural speech has a lot of very difficult vocabulary words, including *induction, candor, impels, withered, grim, optimist, resolutely, sanctity,* and *temper.* Given that students read this text well into the semester, their habits with annotation were already strong. As part of their interaction with the text, they circled words and phrases that were confusing to them. Mr. Vaca made notes about the words and phrases that his students circled on his copy of the text. He noted that every student circled *impels,* so he decided to talk about that word first, saying *"I want to read a sentence to you. 'I will address them with a candor and a decision, which the present situation of our Nation impels.'"*

Immediately several students said "Oh!"

Jose added to that. "When you said it out loud, I got it. It's to make someone do something. I was reading it im-pels, and it didn't make sense. It's impels. Like our vocabulary word from last semester, compel, to force it. So, he's saying that the situation of the nation is making him make some decisions, right?"

Mr. Vaca then asked students to review the words they had circled and to discuss them at the table. *"Make sure that the people in your group all have the same knowledge about vocabulary. We've read this twice, so now let's make sure that the words are solid. If there are words that no one in your group knows, please write them on a card, and I'll come by to collect the cards."*

Sarah, turning to her group, asked, "So, which words do we all need? I don't know what *sanctity* is for sure."

Michael added, "Yeah, that one. And *withered*?"

"So, for *withered*, I think it means that they shrunk, like got smaller and wrinkled up. See, the paragraph is about difficulties," Sarah replied. "And then he says that 'values have shrunken' but that 'taxes have risen.' So leaves don't rise, they turn brown, shrivel up, and fall off. I think that's what he wants people to think about. That the American situation is like dead leaves falling off the tree,"

"That's cool, because then he could say that the leaves will grow back with the right conditions," Michael added.

The conversations among the groups of students continued as they negotiated the meaning of several words, with Sarah's group writing *sanctity* on a card, because none of the members of their group understood that word. Mr. Vaca knew that he would have to come back around to the vocabulary again on a subsequent reading to ensure that students were applying their knowledge of words and phrases to the text, but time was nearly up for the day, and he wanted to check their understanding, so he asked students to write a response to the following prompt:

"What is the situation in America such that Roosevelt must address the nation with candor? What does he impel the people of the nation to do?"

Questions About Vocabulary in Middle School Science

Ms. Choi's students were well on their way to understanding the text about geology. They had already identified the main characteristic of each branch of geology and some of the major terms associated with each branch. Given that they would be learning a great deal more about geology over the course of several weeks, Ms. Choi wanted to focus some of the instructional time on the specific words that were associated with each branch, asking her students *"What words are associated with physical processes? Let's make sure that we know what the terms mean and how they are used by scientists."*

Students identified *volcanic eruptions*, *landslides*, *earthquakes*, and *floods* as the physical processes. As they did so, they discussed the terms with their groups. For example, Mariam said, "All of these change what the land looks like. A volcano can cover the land with lava and an earthquake can split the land."

On their papers, students were asked to explain the terms with brief notes. Ms. Choi would collect their papers later to determine if there were any vocabulary terms that needed additional instruction. Before doing so, she asked her students *"What do geologists do? Take a look at the verbs and see what you think."*

Angela, looking back to the text, responded to her group, "I see the word *study*. So one of the things that geologists do is study, like they study rocks, volcanoes, and fossils."

"And they 'monitor and predict earthquakes and volcanoes,' it says right here," Julian added.

"Yeah, and one more thing," Robert commented, "They figure out the ages and the types of rock that are in different places in the world. I didn't think I was going to like this, but it would be kinda cool to be a geologist and go around the world looking at how the world changes."

Questions About Vocabulary in High School Science

As part of their discussion of *The Origin of the Species*, the students in Mr. Nielsen's class focused on a key vocabulary term that had implications for their understanding of the text.

"If a trait is not useful or injurious, what happens to it?" Mr. Nielson asked his students.

The question itself, and the terms within the question, were not very complex, but students' responses to the question allowed Mr. Nielson to determine whether or not his students understood Darwin's perspective on variations and natural selection. The students struggled with this question for some time, looking for a specific line in the text that would answer this question. As they discussed the text, they began to focus on the final sentences of the selection.

As an example, Ivette said, "I think he is using variations for traits. We can't figure it out, because we're looking for trait. But the end says, 'Variations neither useful nor injurious would not be affected by natural selection.' So I think that means that the traits that are not useful or injurious, then nothing changes for natural selection."

Marco agreed. "Yeah, so if the trait doesn't help or hurt, then the species should continue like it was, basically reproducing without noticing the variation, right? The trait would be there, but it wouldn't favor one over another."

After a pause, Justine said, "Yeah, I see that, but then it says something else. It says that it would be a 'fluctuating element,' so I think it might mean that it could sometimes have an influence but not always. I'm kinda confused by that last part."

"And the very end says that it's polymorphic. I have that word in my notes from last week. Remember talking about how a species could maintain a variety of forms? So, is he saying that there can be many traits in a species, and that some of them aren't doing anything right now, but they might in the future?" Ivette asked. In listening to their responses, Mr. Neilson knew that his students were developing their understanding of the text.

Questions About Structure

The opening sections of this chapter contain a great deal of information about the importance of considering text structures in planning close reading lessons. By the time students reach middle and high school classrooms, they should be familiar with the basic dramatic structure of many narrative texts (e.g., rising action, climax, falling action, and resolution) as well as common informational text structures, such as compare and contrast, problem and solution, cause and effect, sequence, and description. (See Figure 3.5 for a list of common informational text structures.) As texts become more complex, so do their structures. Often, these narrative texts involve complex plots, with numerous characters that complicate the protagonist and antagonist roles, as well as intricate dialogue and sophisticated narrative elements. (Narrative elements

Figure 3.5   Common Text Structures

Text Structure	Definition
Compare–contrast	A text that describes the similarities and differences among two or more things, places, events, ideas, people, or other factors.
Problem–solution	A text that identifies an issue and how the issue is solved. Often the solution becomes another problem.
Cause–effect	A text that explains how or why something happened, in terms of both the root cause and the impact of that cause.
Chronological/sequence/temporal	This text presents information as a process or in order of time or sequence.
Descriptive	This text provides details that could be a list or outline.

Available for download from **www.corwin.com/textdependentquestions**

are covered more thoroughly in the next section.) Increasingly complex informational texts use multiple text structures across paragraphs rather than solely focusing on a cause and effect, for example. In addition, these informational texts often differ based on the discipline in which they were developed. For example, scientific texts often rely on generalization and classification, whereas historical texts beg for corroboration and contextualization.

As texts become more complex, so do their structures.

Questions About Structure in Middle School English

Mr. Corbrera's students understood that their text, *The People Could Fly* (Hamilton, 1993), was a folktale, and they had talked about the structure the author used, including a chronological telling of the events. They also had discussed how the reading experience was different when the author used dialogue versus when the narrator took over.

As Victor noted, "I like it when the people talk. It seems more real."

To which Arif added, "Yeah, me too, but if you don't have the narrator, you don't get the other perspective, only what the characters could know."

Given that this text was not complex in the area of structure, and his students had previously discussed the structure in their groups, Mr. Corbrera did not feel the need to ask them any other questions.

Questions About Structure in High School English

"Let's look at the structure of the story for a moment," Nancy began. *"You're onto the fact that Vera could tell a lie on short notice, like when Framton Nuttel told Vera he didn't know anything about the family. Can you go back into the story and see where her lies are occurring? Be sure to annotate them on your copies of the text."*

As her students reread, Nancy observed where they were marking their papers, as she was hoping they'd locate the second big lie Vera tells. She asked them to discuss it at their tables.

"She tells one set of lies about the uncles being dead, but then she's got another set of lies she tells to her aunt after Mr. Nuttel runs away," Ernesto said.

Amal laughed. "She turned right around and told this big made-up story to her aunt and didn't even get nervous or anything! You know when I lie, I always feel like my face is getting hot and everyone can tell. But not Vera!"

Nancy brought the groups back to a whole class discussion. *"The text structure's pretty easy to follow—it's told in chronological order. But Munro's got an interesting story-within-a-story going on as well. What did you notice when you went back to the text to locate the lies?"*

The class discussed the two lies, and Amal used the word *boldfaced* to describe them. Nancy picked up on this. "You're right, Amal. They are boldfaced lies. *Now look at the last sentence again*: 'Romance at short notice was her specialty.' *We already unpacked* short notice. *What's her specialty?"*

Amal answered immediately. "She can tell a lie at the drop of a hat and everyone believes her."

Questions About Structure in Middle School Social Studies

As part of their discussion about what the text meant, Ms. Robinson's students discussed the fact that this was told in first person and provided the perspective of Frederick Douglass himself. So Ms. Robinson knew that she did not need to ask her students about point of view or perspective. Instead, she wanted to remind students of their genre studies from earlier in the year, so she asked them, *"What genre is this and how do you know? You might want to use your notes from English."*

"I think it's a biography, because it's about a person's life and it tells about problems or obstacles the person had to deal with," Andrew said. "And, like on the checklist, it has important events from history and talks about people who influenced the person. So, biography."

"I disagree because it was written by Frederick Douglass, so it is a special kind of biography. It's an autobiography," Sumaya commented.

"I agree with Sumaya, because it says 'I,' not 'he.' But it's also like a biography, because it tells the events in the order that they happened and has a lot of details," Anthony added.

As the groups finished analyzing the text, Ms. Robinson said, *"I know that this isn't English, but I think it's important that we understand text types, because they are used in history. In history, we talk about sources, and this is an example of a source that was written by the person who experienced a time in history. That doesn't make it more true than other sources, but understanding the type of text we're analyzing helps us think about the context in which it was written and the source itself."*

Questions About Structure in High School Social Studies

The students in Mr. Vaca's class knew from the title that the text they were reading was a speech and that it was, more specifically, a presidential inaugural address. Like Ms. Robinson, Mr. Vaca wanted his students to read primary source documents as historians do, specifically engaging in the following practices (Wineburg, Martin, & Monte-Sano, 2011):

1. *Sourcing:* Analyzing the author's point of view, when and why a document was written, and the credibility of the source

2. *Contextualization:* Considering the setting and identifying what else was happening historically or socially at that time

3. *Corroboration:* Considering what other pieces of evidence say or analyzing another version of the same event

It is important for students to understand what the text says, but this is not sufficient to ensure that they read like historians. The second (and third) phase of close reading allows students to develop their historical thinking skills.

With these goals in mind, Mr. Vaca focused his students on more than the literal level of understanding when they first encountered the text. It is important for students to understand what the text says, but this is not sufficient to ensure that they read like historians. The second (and third) phase of close reading allows students to develop their historical thinking skills.

Questions about the structure of the text can help students understand the *source* of the text and consider some aspects of the *context* of the text. In Mr. Vaca's classroom, in which students were reading the FDR inaugural address, he asked his students *"From your read of the text, and your analysis of the structure, what can you say about the source, President Roosevelt? I'd like you to start with reviewing the text and making some additional margin notes or annotations about this, and then talk with your groups."*

After they had reviewed the text again, Brianna started, saying "I think he's credible, because he just became the president of the US. There are a lot of problems, and he is saying what the problems are and what he thinks should happen. The speech is said so that people can understand his point of view. And he's making sure they know that he understands what the problems are."

"I think it's pretty obvious why this was written—now he's the president, and people expect him to give the speech when he's elected," Russell added. "I agree with Brianna, because it says what his point of view is. And I think we have to remember that he won, so his party won, so the speech is really also saying that these other things were not done by the president before. He even says 'Only a foolish optimist can deny the dark realities of the moment,' so the text also has some negative comments about people who do not agree with him."

"I think that the structure is like this," Andrea adds. "First, he says that he is going to tell the truth, because the nation needs it. Then he names the problems and tries to convince people. If they don't agree, he says they are foolish, like Russell said. Then he offers his plan and asks people to be a 'good neighbor' and help. I think that's how he builds his credibility."

Questions About Structure in Middle School Science

Ms. Choi's students understood the branches of geology from their text and could identify terms associated with physical processes. As a quick check, *Ms. Choi asked her students to talk about the point of view of the text and why the author might have chosen that perspective.*

Jorge was the first to speak in his group. "I think it's called third person."

Monica agreed. "I agree with you because it doesn't say 'I' or 'you' and that would be weird anyway because it is from the encyclopedia, so it should be just facts, not on what some person believes."

"Yeah, because it's supposed to be accurate and truthful and not just some ideas or a story. But it could be the truth in first person, right?" Jorge added.

"I think that it's more professional in third person," Jeff commented. "What did Ms. Choi call it?"

"An authority. It makes you sound more like an authority," Monica responded.

Ms. Choi wanted to be sure that her students read the text scientifically as well. *"As we know from many weeks ago,"* she said to them, *"scientists look for generalizations about, and classification of, the physical and biological world. How does this author help us generalize the information? And how does he classify information? I ask this because you'll need to be able to do this in your own scientific writing, and you can learn how by examining how other writers create explanatory texts."*

"That's easy," Alden said. "We already did classify. See? [He points to their t-chart.] The way that this was written told us the classifications. That's what we gotta do when we write our reports."

"I'm not sure, but I think that we can generalize this, because it always works this way. Like, when it's an earthquake, it's a process that can change the land, or geography. Same with the earthquake or landslide. They also change the land. So we can generalize that these things can make a change in what the land looks like on the surface," Kristen added.

"Now take that one step further," Ms. Choi said. *"You're on a roll. Draw a quick graphic organizer that shows how you're visualizing this information. There's a couple different ways. All I want to see right now is how you're organizing this information in your heads."*

Ms. Choi asked them to do this because she saw that the text was dense and didn't have some of the text features that often augment science texts. As she checked in with groups, she saw some students making bubble webs, while others made tables. Ms. Choi would be returning to these informal organizers again later in the lesson.

Questions About Structure in High School Science

As part of their reading of *The Origin of the Species* (Darwin, 1859/2003), the students in Mr. Nielsen's class were asked about the structure of the text. As Mr. Nielsen said, *"You probably aren't used to being asked about text structure in science, but I think it's important that we develop our understanding of different writing styles used by scientists and people who write about science. We've looked at research reports, scientific articles, and popular press texts about science. This time, we're looking at a text from someone who is proposing a theory. In doing so, the author has to think about his or her readers and how to make the content accessible to them. So, let's start with the analogy Darwin uses in Paragraph 2. How does that help the reader understand the concept of natural selection?"*

This question provided students with an opportunity to return to the text and reread the second paragraph. They easily found the analogy: a country undergoing some physical change. As they talked, the students noted that physical changes could be caused by many different factors and that the type of influence that was applied determined the changes that resulted.

Anna summed up the conversation her group had, saying "I don't think anymore that he's saying natural selection is good or bad, like I used to. I think that he's saying that there are influences and they create change. Like an earthquake would cause a different change than a drought. I think he's also saying that some changes can change the number of species involved and that just the number itself can make for more or less variation and ability to survive."

Mr. Nielsen then turned their attention to an earlier part of the text. *"Darwin uses a series of questions in the first paragraph of the selection. What are they, and what is the purpose of this strategy?"*

"I think that the questions are a good strategy," Jonathan commented. "They help me think about what the author will answer, and they are probably the questions that the author expected people to be asking. I think that the questions are important, because that's what scientists do: They ask a lot of questions and then figure out how to find the answers to those questions. I put the questions in my notes when we read this the first time because I think that they help the reader."

Questions About Author's Craft

Craft is that which separates good writing from bad writing and effective arguments from ineffective ones. We all know writers who exhibit exceptional craft and writers who are amateurs. Developing students' understanding of author's craft helps them understand texts more deeply. For example, if the author uses sarcasm that is missed by the reader, part of the message, or the impact of that message, is lost. But perhaps even more important, questions about the author's craft have the potential for impacting the writing students do. When they understand the impact that various craft moves have on the reader, novice writers begin to incorporate those moves in their own compositions.

There is a wide range of tools at an individual author's disposal. These include these literary and poetic devices (which can overlap):

- Genres and the specific features of these genres

- The ways in which specific words and phrases contribute to mood and tone

- The role of the narrator

- Sentence length and rhythm

- Text features, such as charts, figures, and diagrams

Questions about the author's craft have the potential for impacting the writing students do.

Some of these are presented in Figure 3.6. For example, the way an author uses a narrator can contribute to understanding or confusion. Edgar Allen Poe was famous for using an unreliable narrator in his short stories, adding a great deal of confusion. Zusak (2005) used Death as the narrator in *The Book Thief* and provided the narrator with omniscient understanding of the historical events as well as the human condition. In *Out of the Dust* (Hesse, 1997), the narrator is 13-year-old Billie Jo, and the story is told entirely in first person, using open verse. These are conscious choices that authors make, choices that readers must contend with.

Some genres are more familiar or consumable than others. As any reader of the Rilke letters (1929/1993) can attest, an epistolary (story told through letters) is complex. Similarly, readers have to take note when an author explodes the moment to slow down the action through the use of extensive details. Sometimes authors use sentence structure and length to engender physical response. For example, Cisneros (1991) uses long sentences in "Salvador, Late or Early" to leave the reader breathless, whereas the short dialogue in Hemingway's novels conveys urgency.

Informational text often contains supporting photographs, captions, and diagrams. Imagine reading almost anything from a *National Geographic* magazine issue without the stunning visuals and detailed maps. These text features are a part of the author's craft as sure as the written text, as they are integral to the presentation of information. Readers can be challenged to integrate information when it is presented across multiple elements, such as illustrations, end papers, and such. Even the design can convey meaning. For example, the lettering used to ink the text in the graphic novel *Maus* (Spiegelman, 1986) conveys a sense of place and time, especially in the rendering of the letter *s*, which bears a strong resemblance to the typeface used by the Nazi SS, represented by the cats in the piece.

As we have noted, attention to author's craft facilitates students' understanding of the text as well as their ability to compose increasingly sophisticated prose, narrations, and informative texts. Text-dependent questions about such elements can shift students' focus to the moves a writer makes, and over time spill into the students' own writing.

Questions About Author's Craft in Middle School English

Mr. Corbrera focused on the authors' use of literary devices as his students explored *The People Could Fly* (Hamilton, 1993). He started with the question, *"What literary or poetic devices does the author use, and what do they do for you as a reader?"*

David started the conversation in his group, saying, "I think that the author uses similes, like when she says 'And they flew like blackbirds over the fields,' because they really didn't fly and they aren't blackbirds."

"Yeah, I guess so, but I think 'as light as a feather' is a better simile. She really wasn't light. She was still human," Julio said.

David added, "Oh, and she 'flew like an eagle.' Like really fast, but not really, because this is a fable, and it's not really true; it's just to teach a lesson."

Elizabeth, who had been quiet as David and Julio talked, jumped into the conversation. "I think you have it right; there are a lot of similes that the author uses, but remember Mr. Corbrera wanted us to talk about what they did for us. I think that they help us understand the folktale. I don't think that it's a fable, because the animals don't talk and it's not really so much about a lesson. It's more about a story that has been told by lots of people over and over."

Figure 3.6 Sample of Author's Craft Components

Literary Devices	Allegory
	Allusion
	Cliffhanger
	Flashback
	Foreshadowing
	Imagery
	Irony and satire
	Point of view
	Time lapse
	Tone and mood
Unique Structures	Writing in diary or journal style
	Quotes or famous sayings
	Using dates or unique ways to identify chapters
	Enumerating an argument
	Prologue and epilogue/coda
Poetic Devices	Alliteration
	Hyperbole
	Metaphor
	Onomatopoeia
	Personification
	Repetition
	Simile
	Symbolism
Text Features	Charts
	Diagrams
	Figures
	Illustrations
	Boldface or italicized words
	Font
Narration	First person, second person, third person
	Limited, omniscient, unreliable

Available for download from **www.corwin.com/textdependentquestions**

"Oh, yeah, I agree with you," David says. "I got confused. It's not a fable."

"And you're right that we should be talking about how the similes help us understand. I think that they let us think about things we know about so that that we can see it in our minds. Like I know that eagles fly fast, so I can picture that Sarah was going really fast, so the Overseer couldn't catch her," Julie added.

The conversation continued with discussion about the role of literary and poetic devices and how the devices are used by the author, what they mean, and how they facilitate understanding.

Questions About Author's Craft in High School English

"Yesterday we talked about the methods of indirect and direct characterization used by the author to give us some insight about Vera and Mr. Nuttel," said Nancy. *"Let's return to those characterization sheets for the next part of our discussion. In what ways does Munro use his author's craft to round out his characters so quickly?"*

For the next 10 minutes or so, the class discusses evidence of indirect and direct characterization, including the characters' names, Mr. Nuttel's thoughts, and the reactions of others. *"Now let's go a bit further. How do the title and the setting factor into this discussion?"*

In small groups, the students discuss the title, while Nancy prompts their thinking. *"What images and feelings come to mind when you see an open window?"*

"Well, I think of a fresh breeze, like when the room is stuffy and hot and you open the window," Alexis said.

"And an open window is something you can go through, like it's a way to get to the outside where it's going to be more open," Kealin added.

After allowing the table discussions to progress for several minutes, Nancy spoke. *"Welcome back to all of you. I was listening in on your conversations, and I heard lots of associations with an open window."*

As they offered their ideas, Nancy recorded their insights on a document camera. Soon the list included words and phrases such as *cool, breezy,* and *refreshing.* She encouraged them to think about what abstract concepts the words represented. Then terms like *freedom* and *not hiding anything* appeared.

She circled the last one. *"That's a really interesting idea. Is there anything in this story that suggests there's nothing to hide?"*

The students agreed that the story was just the opposite, and Nancy reminded them to turn back in their notebooks to earlier in the semester when they reviewed literary devices. *"What's that device called when an author says one thing but means the opposite?"* At this point the students were circling around irony. In the remaining portion of the lesson, together they located and discussed evidence of irony in the short story.

Questions About Author's Craft in Middle School Social Studies

Ms. Robinson's students had demonstrated fairly sophisticated analysis of the text structure of *The Narrative Life of Frederick Douglass* (1845/1995) and had explored the role of the narrator and first person perspectives. In other words, they had engaged in the type of thinking that Wineburg, Martin, and Monte-Sano (2011) suggest around sourcing. They understood the perspective of the author and his biases. They also understood the context in which the piece was written, as they had been studying this period of history for several weeks and had made connections early on during their discussion about what the text says and about the way enslaved people were treated. What they hadn't discussed was why the text was written. Ms. Robinson showed her students the biographical information from the book, which they read. They learned that the author's real name was Frederick Augustus Washington Bailey, that he didn't know for sure when he was born (probably 1817 or 1818), and that in 1838 he escaped from slavery and went to New York City. In that second text, they focused on a couple of lines:

> In 1841 he addressed a convention of the Massachusetts Anti-Slavery Society in Nantucket and so greatly impressed the group that they immediately employed him as an agent. He was such an impressive orator that numerous persons doubted if he had ever been a slave, so he wrote *Narrative of the Life of Frederick Douglass.* (www.gutenberg.org/files/23/23-h/23-h.htm#link2H_PREF)

Ms. Robinson asked her students, *"So, now that you have a bit more of the context, let's focus on the reasons that Douglass wrote the text we're reading and how that influences our thinking and our understanding."*

"That explains a lot," Luke said, "I wondered why he seemed to be talking to people, but it's because they don't really believe him, so part of this is about making them believe."

Araceli added, "And that's probably why he has so many details. The details make it more believable, because people could check on the details to see if they are true."

"I totally get it now," Tyler commented, "There was a line that was bugging me: 'From that moment, I understood the pathway from slavery to freedom.' He needed to tell people that were reading his book, or listening to him, who didn't believe him, that he was going to be free and that it was there in his mind even before he could really read. Learning to read made it stronger, but he was planning to escape for a long time."

Questions About Author's Craft in High School Social Studies

In an effort to get them to focus on the author's craft, Mr. Vaca asked the students in his history class, *"How does FDR describe the policy of the good neighbor?"*

The question seems literal, because the answer is summarized in a paragraph within the speech, but it is designed to lead students deeper. The students were quick to respond to this question and correctly identified the information from the speech that describes FDR's qualities of a good neighbor.

He then took the question further. *"Why does the author call the people an army, if they are supposed to be good neighbors?"*

His students were confused for a bit. They began rereading without him asking them to do so. They were quiet, pensive, and completely absorbed in the task and finding the answer. Why would neighbors be called an army? Suddenly Zach's hand shot up, and he practically yelled, "I got it!"

Mr. Vaca responded, "Well we usually talk in our groups first, but I can tell that this is really important. Zach, whatcha got?"

Zach thanked Mr. Vaca and explained. "So, here it is. Earlier in the speech, in Paragraph 4, he says that we need a war, but not a war against other countries. He's saying that we have to treat the problems in the US like they are an enemy and that we are at war. It says 'treating the task as we would treat the emergency of a war,' and that task is getting people to work and getting out of the Depression."

"I see your point that he wants to treat the crisis like a war," Mr. Vaca responded, *"and it's logical that the war would need an army. But what about being a good neighbor? How does that fit with a war? Could you talk with each other? Think about what Zach said and the role of the good neighbor policy."*

Josiah, turning to his partner Melissa, said, "I think that he's saying that Americans needed to be good neighbors and stay out of everyone else's business, because we have enough problems here at home. We have to fight the war about getting the economy moving and getting people back to work."

In response, Melissa said, "I think you're on the right track, but I think it's even more than that. He is saying that people are more connected—interconnected—than they have ever been before. When we think of the army, it's not just about fighting, it's also about working together for the common good. It's about having a united force, and it's about having the discipline to get the job done."

Questions About Author's Craft in Middle School Science

Ms. Choi's students explored the way in which the author put the text together in another way. She asked them to identify the ways they knew the piece was written for students, not geologists. When they had difficulty coming up with any evidence, she drew their attention back to the chart they had developed earlier listing all the items geologists studied.

Fernando took the first tentative steps. "So, like, there's lots of examples?" It was really more a question than a statement, but Ms. Choi recognized a spark of an idea. *"Fernando is speculating, which I love, and he's wondering whether examples might be a method the writer is using,"* she said. *"Time to mark on your text,"* she said. *"Can you locate examples?"*

As she visited each group, she saw the momentum pick up as they began noticing examples peppered throughout the text. *"Now let me interrupt your process for a moment to ask another question. What do those examples do for you as a science student?"*

Seated in another group, Alden said, "When I hear examples, it helps me understand an idea. I think that's what the author's doing."

Mariam moved Alden's idea a bit further forward. "It's like when I don't know the name of something, but then you give me examples of the idea, then it draws kind of a picture."

"Illustrates it. Illustrates the idea," Alden said, finishing her thought.

In another group across the room, Robert made the connection to English content. "We learned about exemplification, like using examples so the person who's reading knows what you're talking about."

Ms. Choi was pleased with the direction of the discussions, and she interrupted briefly one more time. *"This idea of examples is really catching on with all of you. Now add those examples into that graphic organizer you developed. That's the mark of a good science writer, by the way. Lots of examples to illustrate abstract ideas."*

Questions About Author's Craft in High School Science

The students in Mr. Nielsen's science class had a lot to think about in terms of the author's craft. They knew who the author was, when he lived, and what he believed. But they needed to understand more than that. Their exploration of sections of *The Origin of the Species* (Darwin, 1859/2003) required that they consider the impact that the text has on the reader, as they would be producing their own texts in which they would present information about their fruit fly experiments.

"Where in the text does Darwin parallel the human process of selection with that of nature? What effect does this have on the text?" Mr. Nielsen asked.

Sebastian found the section pretty quickly and noted, "When he made it parallel, it made the text more believable, because we can see this in nature, so it probably also applies to humans."

Dakota agreed, adding, "I agree with you, because in Paragraph 1, he says that there is a relationship between all 'organic beings to each other and to their physical conditions of life.' Like you said, it's a parallel process, and people should be able to understand it better if isn't just unique to humans.

Mr..Nielsen then turned their attention to another aspect of the author's craft, his attitude. *"How does Darwin's example of an island or country in Paragraph 2 reveal his attitude toward natural selection?"*

Dakota and Sebastian talked with their group members, and they noted that Darwin's attitude is authoritative, and he seems somewhat impressed with what he has learned. As Dakota said, "So, he talks like he really knows his stuff, and the reader gets that. He is an authority. But really, I think he's kinda impressed. Like he's figured something important out. He talks about the barriers and how one tree could change the whole system. But he acts like readers already know that, because he says, 'let it be remembered.' Then he goes on to say what we should expect, in the second paragraph—that 'some of the original inhabitants were in some manner modified,' and then he shows that they are modified. I think he's impressed, with himself and with nature."

QUESTION •YOURSELF

This chapter has focused on questions that push students deeper into their analysis of the text, specifically as they explore the role of vocabulary words and phrases, text structures, and author's craft. As we have noted, not all texts need this level of scrutiny, and not all facets of the question *how does the text work* apply to all texts. Having said that, it is important to ensure that students have explored the inner workings of a complex text before they are required to figure out its meaning and how this text fits into a broader schema of content knowledge.

Now we invite you to test yourself. We have included the poem "Jabberwocky" by Lewis Carroll to practice what you have learned in this chapter. Take a few minutes to read this text in Figure 3.7. Then turn your attention to questions that you can develop to encourage students to determine *how the text works*. Remember that this phase is focused on vocabulary, text structure, and author's craft. What is it that students should understand about the inner workings of this text before you invite them to explore what it *means,* which will be the focus of our next chapter?

Before you begin, you might like to skim the italicized questions in the teachers' lessons, above. If you'd like to check yourself, the questions that Ms. Thayre developed can be found on Corwin's companion website at www.corwin.com/textdependentquestions. Next, apply this technique to develop questions for a short piece that you will use with your own students.

Figure 3.7 "Jabberwocky" by Lewis Carroll

'Twas brillig, and the slithy toves
Did gyre and gimble in the wabe:
All mimsy were the borogoves,
And the mome raths outgrabe.

"Beware the Jabberwock, my son!
The jaws that bite, the claws that catch!
Beware the Jubjub bird, and shun
The frumious Bandersnatch!"

He took his vorpal sword in hand:
Long time the manxome foe he sought—
So rested he by the Tumtum tree,
And stood awhile in thought.

And, as in uffish thought he stood,
The Jabberwock, with eyes of flame,
Came whiffling through the tulgey wood,
And burbled as it came!

One, two! One, two! And through and through
The vorpal blade went snicker-snack!
He left it dead, and with its head
He went galumphing back.

"And, hast thou slain the Jabberwock?
Come to my arms, my beamish boy!
O frabjous day! Callooh! Callay!"
He chortled in his joy.

'Twas brillig, and the slithy toves
Did gyre and gimble in the wabe;
All mimsy were the borogoves,
And the mome raths outgrabe.

Source: Through the Looking-Glass and What Alice Found There by Lewis Carroll, © 1872

Available for download from **www.corwin.com/textdependentquestions**

Videos

To read a QR code, you must have a smartphone or tablet with a camera. We recommend that you download a QR code reader app that is made specifically for your phone or tablet brand.

Videos can also be accessed at
www.corwin.com/textdependentquestions

Video 3.1 Students in Oscar Corrigan's seventh grade social studies class dive into the deeper meaning of *Things Fall Apart* by analyzing the vocabulary and complex phrases used throughout the text.

Video 3.2 Students in Will Mellman's seventh grade science class discuss clues and word choice in a text about ulcers to understand the author's purpose for the piece.

Video 3.3 Javier Vaca's eleventh grade U.S. history class discusses the use of various words and phrases in Eisenhower's "Message to the Troops" before determining the audience and author's purpose for the text.

Video 3.4 The students in Heather Anderson's tenth grade English class discuss the word "phenomenal" to focus on vocabulary before analyzing punctuation and stanza diction in the poem "Phenomenal Woman" by Maya Angelou.

Video 3.5 Marisol Thayre's eleventh grade English class discusses the meaning of pedagogy and how the author uses it to influence the readers interpretation of the images used in a piece on body image by Susan Bordo.

Video 3.6 Students in Kim Elliot's tenth grade biology class determine why the author of "Untangling the Roots of Cancer" compares cancer cells to plants and how various phrases resonate throughout the article.

4

WHAT DOES THE TEXT *MEAN*?

The habit of reading closely begins with inspection of the text in order to develop a solid foundation in what it says—the literal meaning. It continues with investigation, as the reader analyzes the parts of the text to gain a sense of how the text works. But deep reading doesn't stop there. Skilled readers are able to consolidate. They see how the parts relate to the whole, and vice versa.

As humans, we interpret information in order to understand our world. We look at the sky, take note of the temperature, consider the time of year, and make a decision about whether or not we'll need an umbrella. A choreographer interprets a musical composition, giving thought to the tone and tempo, the length of the piece, and the purpose of the musical message in order to create a dance. In both cases, interpretation requires understanding the details while at the same time weighing them against the whole. Much like putting a jigsaw puzzle together, interpretation requires simultaneously looking at the pieces while imagining the whole. (Try putting a jigsaw puzzle together with the pieces turned upside down. It can be done, but it's much more difficult.)

In reading, *inferencing* is the ability to make meaning and arrive at conclusions using textual clues rather than explicitly stated information. There are several dimensions of inferencing as it applies to reading comprehension: lexical, predictive, and elaborative.

Making lexical inferences requires the reader to make an informed judgment about the meaning of an ambiguous word using grammatical, contextual, and structural cues (e.g., determining whether the word *read* is a noun or verb, and whether it is past tense or present tense). Lexical inferencing is often addressed through discussion about vocabulary, which we described in detail in the previous chapter. Additionally, a reader uses her predictive inferencing skills to form a plausible hypothesis, such as whether a character reading *Frankenstein* might have trouble sleeping later that night. A third facet, elaborative inferencing, takes place when a reader fills in unstated information to provide more detail, such as imagining the way the character looked as she read a terrifying passage in Shelley's novel.

> Inferences are cognitively demanding and are not automatic. In other words, they must be nurtured.

All of these inferences are cognitively demanding and are not automatic. In other words, they must be nurtured. In the last chapter we spotlighted the analytic reading needed to understand the organizational parts of a text. In this chapter, we discuss how readers synthesize and interpret the parts while considering the whole piece. This is an essential step on the way to deeply understanding a text.

Three Types of Inferencing

- **Lexical:** Making an informed judgment about the meaning of an ambiguous word, using grammatical, contextual, and structural cues
- **Predictive:** Forming a plausible hypothesis
- **Elaborative:** Filling in unstated information

An Invitation to Read Closely: *Inferential*-Level Questions

We ask students inferential questions in order to gauge their ability to draw upon information that isn't stated explicitly in the text. The texts older students read require them to marshal a great deal of background knowledge about topics and concepts. Think of what these texts present as a kind of shorthand—the writer assumes that the reader possesses a certain level of knowledge. Take a look at the textbooks you used at the beginning of your teacher preparation program. It's likely that those texts were written with much more in the way of explanations of terms and practices, examples, and embedded definitions than a book about teaching that you would choose to read now. Even more important, the instructional routines discussed, now fully integrated into your professional practice, were introduced in novice terms. These textbooks were useful at the very beginning of your teaching career, but now that you are a seasoned teacher, they may no longer provide you enough nuanced information for refining your skills today.

Texts written for students who are acquiring new knowledge usually have a relatively high degree of text cohesion. Cohesion is the way text is held together. Easier texts have a high degree of cohesion in that they make cause and effect relationships explicit (*because it rained, Sue got wet*), and they make reference to ideas, events, or objects (*Sue got wet on her way to work in the city*). Those two phrases have a high degree of cohesion at the local level, because you know where Sue was headed (to the city), why she was headed there (to work), that she got wet, and that it happened because it was raining. But any other details may need to be inferred across a longer passage. What is Sue's work, and how does she feel about it? Did she get wet because she is careless, caught by surprise, or depressed?

Now let's make it more complex. Cohesion runs across paragraphs and passages, not just within them. Consider this paragraph from Chapter 6 of *Silent Spring* (Carson, 1962):

> One of the most tragic examples of our unthinking bludgeoning of the landscape is to be seen in the sagebrush lands of the West, where a vast campaign is on to destroy the sage and to substitute grasslands. If ever an enterprise needed to be illuminated with a sense of history and meaning of the landscape, it is this. For here the natural landscape is eloquent of the interplay of forces that have created it. It is spread before us like the pages of an open book in which we can read why the land is what it is, and why we should preserve its integrity. But the pages lie unread. (p. 64)

There is less cohesion within the paragraph, especially because it refers to several concepts within a few sentences: it mentions geographical features (the West, sagebrush and grasslands), it states a claim (unthinking bludgeoning), and uses an analogy (comparing the land to the pages of a book). There is reference to *we* and *our*, but it isn't stated explicitly who that might involve. It has few connective words and phrases that would link sentence ideas together (e.g., *because of, due to*). In *Silent Spring*, the paragraph just before this one discussed vegetation as part of the web of life and named the weed killer business as having a negative impact on the environment. The paragraph following this one discusses the tectonic activity millions of years ago that resulted in the Rocky Mountain range. The writer expects the reader to be able to keep up as she shifts from one concept to another to formulate a complex thesis.

Inferencing is largely dependent on one's ability to develop a cohesive thread when the author does not explicitly furnish one. It requires the reader to use background knowledge in a measured way, without going too far astray of the text. There's a lot of mental discipline needed in order to form inferences that are useful and logical but not misleading. Not every inference is a good one.

Inferencing is largely dependent on one's ability to develop a cohesive thread when the author does not explicitly furnish one. It requires the reader to use background knowledge in a measured way, without going too far astray of the text.

Sixth grade social studies teacher Sandy Bradshaw saw this happen when her students used their background knowledge a bit too vigorously during a reading of a passage about participants in the ancient Olympic games. While the piece primarily discussed the fact that participants had to be not only athletic but also male and wealthy, her students initially wanted to focus on a single sentence that stated that females were barred as competitors and spectators. She used a number of prompts and cues to steer them back to the text, to no avail. "I noticed that we all got stuck on this idea that women couldn't participate. And that stands out to us, right, because we did all that work with Athens and Sparta, and we compared women's rights," she told them.

Ms. Bradshaw recognized that in this instance, their recently constructed background knowledge about the role of women in ancient Greece trumped their ability to make textual inferences that would help them identify the central meaning of the reading. Her continued instruction, including modeling and thinking aloud, assisted them in properly using both their background knowledge and the information in the text to make the correct inference about the roles of wealth, status, and gender as conditions for participation.

Why Students Need This Type of Questioning

A stereotype about adolescents is that they are quick to judge. As seen in the previous example, they latch on to an idea and run with it, whether it is accurate or not. In the worst cases, the trope is that adolescent judgment is superficial and lacks substance. Wander into a conversation in the restroom at school, or take a look at postings on social media, and it's easy to see why many believe that outward appearances and status are all that matter to teens. But all of us who are secondary educators know that our students are far more complex. They can be incredibly insightful and breathtakingly wise. But when we lower our expectations about their ability to contribute to meaningful dialogue, they in turn lower their expectations about themselves. When we expect them to behave as silly beings, they oblige. And then they retreat from us. We pigeonhole them at our own peril when we don't provide for them the forums they need to be profound: to experiment with ideas, to be wrong and survive the experience, to be intellectually resilient.

Text-dependent questions that require students to synthesize and interpret information communicate your expectation about their cognitive capabilities. None of us intentionally pose questions to others that we don't believe they can answer. Questions that require a higher degree of cognition signal your respect for their intellect. However, this phase of a close reading lesson serves another purpose, as it builds the habit of

This phase of a close reading lesson serves another purpose, as it builds the habit of taking the time to comprehend before making judgments or criticisms.

taking the time to comprehend before making judgments or criticisms. The tendency to skip over this step in order to make a judgment isn't confined to adolescence. We as adults indulge in this far too often. Self-help gurus remind us the "seek first to understand, then to be understood" (Covey, 2004, p. 235). In terms of reading, Adler and Van Doren (1972) call it "intellectual etiquette. . . . Do not say you agree [or] disagree . . . until you can say 'I understand'" (p. 164).

Text-dependent questions that focus on *what a text means* include those that cause readers to explore the *author's purpose* (stated or implied) and to examine them further for hidden or subversive intentions. In some cases, the writer's relationship to the topic provides insight into his or her motivation. For instance, an article written by a lobbyist for the pharmaceutical industry should be questioned if the topic is eliminating regulatory standards for prescription medications. In literary texts, the role of the narrator demands attention. Why is Holden Caulfield, the narrator of *The Catcher in the Rye* (Salinger, 1951) so cynical about the world? Is he a reliable narrator, or do we understand that his limited point of view is impinged upon by his age, experiences, tendency to lie, and confinement in a mental institution?

The meaning of a text extends to its connection to other works. The works of writers may take on an added dimension when readers consider the writer's biographical information, such as examining both the life and the literary works of Maya Angelou to more fully understand *I Know Why the Caged Bird Sings* (1969). An informational piece on the construction of the Panama Canal may be more fully understood when contextualized with primary source documents from the presidential administration of Theodore Roosevelt and the malaria program headed by US Army medical director John W. Ross. Text-dependent questions that draw on multiple sources require students to utilize critical thinking skills to make inferences within and across texts, and to consolidate ideas and concepts learned in one or more of the disciplines.

Students examine multiple texts using their critical thinking skills before consolidating their ideas.

How Examining *What the Text Means* Addresses the STANDARDS

Reading Standards

The verbs used in reading **standard 7** say it all: *compare, contrast, evaluate, analyze*. As students solidify their understanding of *what the text says* and begin to grasp *how the text works*, they are poised to drill deeper to locate the underlying currents of the piece. Nonprint media provide an added dimension, as students are asked to apply their knowledge of multiple literacies to understand how light, sound, and motion offer nonlinguistic representational knowledge. Film studies, drama, and audio recordings provide students with a means to compare and contrast how a story is variously interpreted depending on the medium. **Standard 9** expands textual knowledge by asking students to think across texts, events, topics, themes, and time periods. A chart detailing the reading standards related to text meaning can be found in Figure 4.1.

Figure 4.1   ELA Reading Standards That Focus on *What the Text Means*

Standard (Grade)	Literary	Informational
7 (6)	Compare and contrast the experience of reading a story, drama, or poem to listening to or viewing an audio, video, or live version of the text, including contrasting what they "see" and "hear" when reading the text to what they perceive when they listen or watch.	Integrate information presented in different media or formats (e.g., visually, quantitatively) as well as in words to develop a coherent understanding of a topic or issue.
7 (7)	Compare and contrast a written story, drama, or poem to its audio, filmed, staged, or multimedia version, analyzing the effects of techniques unique to each medium (e.g., lighting, sound, color, or camera focus and angles in a film).	Compare and contrast a text to an audio, video, or multimedia version of the text, analyzing each medium's portrayal of the subject (e.g., how the delivery of a speech affects the impact of the words).
7 (8)	Analyze the extent to which a filmed or live production of a story or drama stays faithful to or departs from the text or script, evaluating the choices made by the director or actors.	Evaluate the advantages and disadvantages of using different mediums (e.g., print or digital text, video, multimedia) to present a particular topic or idea.
7 (9–10)	Analyze the representation of a subject or a key scene in two different artistic mediums, including what is emphasized or absent in each treatment (e.g., Auden's "Musée des Beaux Arts" and Breughel's *Landscape with the Fall of Icarus*).	Analyze various accounts of a subject told in different mediums (e.g., a person's life story in both print and multimedia), determining which details are emphasized in each account.
7 (11–12)	Analyze multiple interpretations of a story, drama, or poem (e.g., recorded or live production of a play or recorded novel or poetry), evaluating how each version interprets the source text. (Include at least one play by Shakespeare and one play by an American dramatist.)	Integrate and evaluate multiple sources of information presented in different media or formats (e.g., visually, quantitatively) as well as in words in order to address a question or solve a problem.

Standard (Grade)	Literary	Informational
9 (6)	Compare and contrast texts in different forms or genres (e.g., stories and poems; historical novels and fantasy stories) in terms of their approaches to similar themes and topics.	Compare and contrast one author's presentation of events with that of another (e.g., a memoir written by and a biography on the same person).
9 (7)	Compare and contrast a fictional portrayal of a time, place, or character and a historical account of the same period as a means of understanding how authors of fiction use or alter history.	Analyze how two or more authors writing about the same topic shape their presentations of key information by emphasizing different evidence or advancing different interpretations of facts.
9 (8)	Analyze how a modern work of fiction draws on themes, patterns of events, or character types from myths, traditional stories, or religious works such as the Bible, including describing how the material is rendered new.	Analyze a case in which two or more texts provide conflicting information on the same topic and identify where the texts disagree on matters of fact or interpretation.
9 (9–10)	Analyze how an author draws on and transforms source material in a specific work (e.g., how Shakespeare treats a theme or topic from Ovid or the Bible or how a later author draws on a play by Shakespeare).	Analyze seminal U.S. documents of historical and literary significance (e.g., Washington's Farewell Address, the Gettysburg Address, Roosevelt's Four Freedoms speech, King's "Letter from Birmingham Jail"), including how they address related themes and concepts.
9 (11–12)	Demonstrate knowledge of eighteenth-, nineteenth- and early-twentieth-century foundational works of American literature, including how two or more texts from the same period treat similar themes or topics.	Analyze seventeenth-, eighteenth-, and nineteenth-century foundational U.S. documents of historical and literary significance (including The Declaration of Independence, the Preamble to the Constitution, the Bill of Rights, and Lincoln's Second Inaugural Address) for their themes, purposes, and rhetorical features.
10 (6)	By the end of the year, read and comprehend literature, including stories, dramas, and poems, in the grades 6–8 text complexity band proficiently, with scaffolding as needed at the high end of the range.	By the end of the year, read and comprehend literary nonfiction in the grades 6–8 text complexity band proficiently, with scaffolding as needed at the high end of the range.
10 (7)	By the end of the year, read and comprehend literature, including stories, dramas, and poems, in the grades 6–8 text complexity band proficiently, with scaffolding as needed at the high end of the range.	By the end of the year, read and comprehend literary nonfiction in the grades 6–8 text complexity band proficiently, with scaffolding as needed at the high end of the range.
10 (8)	By the end of the year, read and comprehend literature, including stories, dramas, and poems, at the high end of grades 6–8 text complexity band independently and proficiently.	By the end of the year, read and comprehend literary nonfiction at the high end of the grades 6–8 text complexity band independently and proficiently.
10 (9–10)	By the end of grade 9, read and comprehend literature, including stories, dramas, and poems, in the grades 9–10 text complexity band proficiently, with scaffolding as needed at the high end of the range.	By the end of grade 9, read and comprehend literary nonfiction in the grades 9–10 text complexity band proficiently, with scaffolding as needed at the high end of the range.

(Continued)

Figure 4.1 (Continued)

Standard (Grade)	Literary	Informational
	By the end of grade 10, read and comprehend literature, including stories, dramas, and poems, at the high end of the grades 9–10 text complexity band independently and proficiently.	By the end of grade 10, read and comprehend literary nonfiction at the high end of the grades 9–10 text complexity band independently and proficiently.
10 (11–12)	By the end of grade 11, read and comprehend literature, including stories, dramas, and poems, in the grades 11–CCR text complexity band proficiently, with scaffolding as needed at the high end of the range. By the end of grade 12, read and comprehend literature, including stories, dramas, and poems, at the high end of the grades 11–CCR text complexity band independently and proficiently.	By the end of grade 11, read and comprehend literary nonfiction in the grades 11–CCR text complexity band proficiently, with scaffolding as needed at the high end of the range. By the end of grade 12, read and comprehend literary nonfiction at the high end of the grades 11–CCR text complexity band independently and proficiently.

Students in Lily Antrim's ninth grade humanities class analyzed the portrayal of beauty and fitness in the media. They read articles about the practice of retouching the photographs of models and viewed *Seventeen* magazine's no-Photoshop pledge, as well as articles alternately in support of or criticizing the policy. "This is part of our study of the use of persuasive techniques in advertising," said Ms. Antrim. "They're looking at examples of how manipulation of visual images influences our perceptions." Her students must read and view across documents and videos in order to draw conclusions.

Literacy **standard 7** performs a similar function in history, social sciences, and the technical subjects. In **standard 9**, regarding multiple texts, some discipline-related differences emerge. Middle school history students compare and contrast primary and secondary source texts, while in science they examine how experiments and demonstrations augment textual readings. The grade-specific standards can be found in Figure 4.2. Students compare and contrast informational displays of data to understand concepts; an example would be discussing technical diagrams and accompanying text explaining how Bernoulli's principle explains how air flows over and under an airplane wing so it can fly.

Martin Robbins, a seventh grade science teacher, used digital resources from the National Drought Mitigation Center at the University of Nebraska–Lincoln (http://drought.unl.edu) so his students could research drought conditions in regions throughout the United States. "The data visualizations are excellent," said Mr. Robbins. "They have maps to report ground water storage and climographs [monthly average temperatures and precipitation] as well as state plans for drought planning." His students used information from these and other maps to draw conclusions about the relationship between drought status and state policies. "They have to move between several data sources, and they're learning that there's a difference between being prepared for a drought and waiting for a drought to occur before there's a response," said the science teacher. "So when they read the state websites, they have to consider

Figure 4.2 History, Science, and Technical Subjects Reading Standards That Focus on *What the Text Means*

Standard (Grade band)	History/Social Studies	Sciences and Technical Subjects
7 (6–8)	Integrate visual information (e.g., in charts, graphs, photographs, videos, or maps) with other information in print and digital texts.	Integrate quantitative or technical information expressed in words in a text with a version of that information expressed visually (e.g., in a flowchart, diagram, model, graph, or table).
7 (9–10)	Integrate quantitative or technical analysis (e.g., charts, research data) with qualitative analysis in print or digital text.	Translate quantitative or technical information expressed in words in a text into visual form (e.g., a table or chart) and translate information expressed visually or mathematically (e.g., in an equation) into words.
7 (11–12)	Integrate and evaluate multiple sources of information presented in diverse formats and media (e.g., visually, quantitatively, as well as in words) in order to address a question or solve a problem.	Integrate and evaluate multiple sources of information presented in diverse formats and media (e.g., quantitative data, video, multimedia) in order to address a question or solve a problem.
9 (6–8)	Analyze the relationship between a primary and secondary source on the same topic.	Compare and contrast the information gained from experiments, simulations, video, or multimedia sources with that gained from reading a text on the same topic.
9 (9–10)	Compare and contrast treatments of the same topic in several primary and secondary sources.	Compare and contrast findings presented in a text to those from other sources (including their own experiments), noting when the findings support or contradict previous explanations or accounts.
9 (11–12)	Integrate information from diverse sources, both primary and secondary, into a coherent understanding of an idea or event, noting discrepancies among sources.	Synthesize information from a range of sources (e.g., texts, experiments, simulations) into a coherent understanding of a process, phenomenon, or concept, resolving conflicting information when possible.
10 (6–8)	By the end of grade 8, read and comprehend history/social studies texts in the grades 6–8 text complexity band independently and proficiently.	By the end of grade 8, read and comprehend science/technical texts in the grades 6–8 text complexity band independently and proficiently.
10 (9–10)	By the end of grade 10, read and comprehend history/social studies texts in the grades 9–10 text complexity band independently and proficiently.	By the end of grade 10, read and comprehend science/technical texts in the grades 9–10 text complexity band independently and proficiently.
10 (11–12)	By the end of grade 12, read and comprehend history/social studies texts in the grades 11–CCR text complexity band independently and proficiently.	By the end of grade 12, read and comprehend science/technical texts in the grades 11–CCR text complexity band independently and proficiently.

the state's drought status as well. The kids are surprised to find out that some states are showing clear signs that a drought is going on yet don't have much of a plan in place at all," said Mr. Robbins. "This is really developing their ability to recognize patterns and spot trends using scientific data."

There's quite a bit of inferencing that must occur in Mr. Robbins's class if his students are to be successful. They must engage in predictive inferencing based on the information they are collecting. For instance, given data sets that suggest a state is in the early stages of a drought, their predictive inferencing should cause them to expect that the state would have some plan developing or enacted. This kind of predictive inferencing parallels the inductive reasoning used within the scientific method, especially in gathering observational data and analyzing them in order to draw a conclusion.

Language Standards

As discussion plays such a key role in exploring *what the text means*, the opportunities to apply the conventions of the English language are plentiful (**standard 1**). In addition, discussion of the power of language should foster students' understanding of its functions in different contexts (**standard 3**) and its vocabulary (**standard 3**). The grades 11–12 expression of **standard 1** is especially intriguing, as students wrestle with the application of language and its variants. In the language of historical study, it calls for an examination of the use of loaded language in political thought, and parallels the rhetorical modes of *ethos* and *pathos* by considering the writer's credibility and use of emotional terms to influence perceptions. Students in Beth Hilliard's government class confronted just such an issue in their discussion about the use of the terms *freedom fighter*, *terrorist*, and *guerrilla* in several news reports about a conflict. "It really ended up being a great discussion about the use of these words and how they situate the writer's viewpoint," she said. She asked her students to examine the news accounts more closely to determine why each of these words would have been selected by the writer. "They eventually agreed that who was being attacked mattered. Was it civilians or military? That was a determinant for deciding whether a group should be described as terrorists or not. But they also said that identifying the difference between *freedom fighter* and *guerrilla* was harder, as this distinction was more of an indicator of the writer's political stance," she said. A table displaying these targeted language standards can be found in Figure 4.3.

Speaking and Listening Standards

The standards are replete with opportunities for expanding speaking and listening skills through extended discussion, and **standards 1, 4,** and **6** have been reviewed in previous chapters. But **standards 2** and **3** are of particular note in the context of determining text meaning. (Figure 4.4 on page 110 lists the grade-specific speaking and listening standards.)

Standard 2 in speaking and listening aligns with reading **standard 7**'s emphasis on using diverse texts, media, and visual displays. To be clear, analysis of nonprint media is similar to analysis of print media (*What does the text say? How does the text work?*), but we have chosen to spotlight diverse

Figure 4.3 Language Standards That Focus on *What the Text Means*

	Grade 6	Grade 7	Grade 8	Grades 9–10	Grades 11–12
1	Demonstrate command of the conventions of standard English grammar and usage when writing or speaking.	Demonstrate command of the conventions of standard English grammar and usage when writing or speaking.	Demonstrate command of the conventions of standard English grammar and usage when writing or speaking.	Demonstrate command of the conventions of standard English grammar and usage when writing or speaking.	Demonstrate command of the conventions of standard English grammar and usage when writing or speaking.
	a. Ensure that pronouns are in the proper case (subjective, objective, possessive).	a. Explain the function of phrases and clauses in general and their function in specific sentences.	a. Explain the function of verbals (gerunds, participles, infinitives) in general and their function in particular sentences.	a. Use parallel structure.	a. Apply the understanding that usage is a matter of convention, can change over time, and is sometimes contested.
	b. Use intensive pronouns (e.g., myself, ourselves).	b. Choose among simple, compound, complex, and compound-complex sentences to signal differing relationships among ideas.	b. Form and use verbs in the active and passive voice.	b. Use various types of phrases (noun, verb, adjectival, adverbial, participial, prepositional, absolute) and clauses (independent; dependent; noun, relative, adverbial) to convey specific meanings and add variety and interest to writing or presentations.	b. Resolve issues of complex or contested usage, consulting references (e.g., *Merriam-Webster's Dictionary of English Usage*, *Garner's Modern American Usage*) as needed.
	c. Recognize and correct inappropriate shifts in pronoun number and person.	c. Place phrases and clauses within a sentence, recognizing and correcting misplaced and dangling modifiers.	c. Form and use verbs in the indicative, imperative, interrogative, conditional, and subjunctive mood.		
	d. Recognize and correct vague pronouns (i.e., ones with unclear or ambiguous antecedents).		d. Recognize and correct inappropriate shifts in verb voice and mood.		
	e. Recognize variations from standard English in their own and others' writing and speaking, and identify and use strategies to improve expression in conventional language.				

(Continued)

Figure 4.3 (Continued)

	Grade 6	Grade 7	Grade 8	Grades 9–10	Grades 11–12
3	Use knowledge of language and its conventions when writing, speaking, reading, or listening. a. Vary sentence patterns for meaning, reader/listener interest, and style. b. Maintain consistency in style and tone.	Use knowledge of language and its conventions when writing, speaking, reading, or listening. a. Choose language that expresses ideas precisely and concisely, recognizing and eliminating wordiness and redundancy.	Use knowledge of language and its conventions when writing, speaking, reading, or listening. a. Use verbs in the active and passive voice and in the conditional and subjunctive mood to achieve particular effects (e.g., emphasizing the actor or the action; expressing uncertainty or describing a state contrary to fact).	Apply knowledge of language to understand how language functions in different contexts, to make effective choices for meaning or style, and to comprehend more fully when reading or listening.	Apply knowledge of language to understand how language functions in different contexts, to make effective choices for meaning or style, and to comprehend more fully when reading or listening.
6	Acquire and use accurately grade-appropriate general academic and domain specific words and phrases; gather vocabulary knowledge when considering a word or phrase important to comprehension or expression.		Acquire and use accurately general academic and domain-specific words and phrases, sufficient for reading, writing, speaking, and listening at the college and career readiness level; demonstrate independence in gathering vocabulary knowledge when considering a word or phrase important to comprehension or expression.		

formats in this chapter precisely because these often offer a path for further contextualizing content. Take poetry, for example. While it lives on a page, it comes alive through spoken word. We often use audio recordings of poets reciting their poems to better understand the meaning. A favorite of ours is Carl Sandburg's 1944 performance of "Grass," a poem originally written during World War I (Paschen & Mosby, 2001). In his reading, he includes Stalingrad in his list of battlefields dating back to Gettysburg. Students are initially startled as they hear him deviate from the original printed poem in their hands. The text-dependent question that follows is obvious: "Why would Sandburg add that place?" The discussion that follows moves from figuring out where Stalingrad (now Volgograd) is to understanding that each battlefield selected by the poet marked a turning point in a war, but with catastrophic loss of human life.

As the discussion deepens, students gain an understanding of the deeper meaning of Sandburg's message. The more obvious one is that we soon forget the cost of war, as battlefields are transformed into peaceful military cemeteries. The poet's addition in the spoken version adds another layer of meaning, as students gain a keener sense that Sandburg's purpose was also to comment on the inevitability of war. Their discussion moves to an analysis of Sandburg himself, who at the time of the audio recording had already won the first of three Pulitzer Prizes, thus relying on the ethos of credibility and authority as an award-winning poet.

Standard 3 in speaking and listening offers more direction on the role of logic and reasoning. In the same way that reading **standard 8** requires students to locate and analyze reasoning within a text, speaking and listening **standard 3** requires effective speakers and listeners to adhere to a logical progression in their discussions. These include backing claims by furnishing credible evidence and appealing to the emotions of others when it is suitable. **Standard 4** (discussed in previous chapters) reflects the demands on the speaker, but **standard 3** asks them to use their listening skills to detect when and where these occur.

Students in Jeff Tsei's eighth grade science class viewed several short videos demonstrating principles of wave energy. They viewed several explaining why the Tacoma Narrows Bridge (often called "Galloping Gertie") collapsed in 1940 due to design flaws that led to oscillations that caused it to bounce and twist wildly before eventually crumbling. Mr. Tsei paused after each video and then asked students to view it again, this time considering the sequence of information and the scientific rationale. Students worked together to detail the information given in each video and identify facts that might have been excluded.

"So one problem is that there's only one video that says they knew it was a problem on the day it opened," said Misael.

Another member of his group, Ellie, said, "In one of the videos, they didn't talk at all about the wind. But in another, the narrator said it was a factor. It seems to me like the wind information should be part of all the videos; they should not just be film clips of the bridge moving." In this case, these students are applying their elaborative inferencing skills to identify what information is missing.

Figure 4.4 Speaking and Listening Standards That Focus on *What the Text Means*

Grade 6	Grade 7	Grade 8	Grades 9–10	Grades 11–12
1 Engage effectively in a range of collaborative discussions (one-on-one, in groups, and teacher-led) with diverse partners on grade 6 topics, texts, and issues, building on others' ideas and expressing their own clearly.	Engage effectively in a range of collaborative discussions (one-on-one, in groups, and teacher-led) with diverse partners on grade 7 topics, texts, and issues, building on others' ideas and expressing their own clearly.	Engage effectively in a range of collaborative discussions (one-on-one, in groups, and teacher-led) with diverse partners on grade 8 topics, texts, and issues, building on others' ideas and expressing their own clearly.	Initiate and participate effectively in a range of collaborative discussions (one-on-one, in groups, and teacher-led) with diverse partners on grades 9–10 topics, texts, and issues, building on others' ideas and expressing their own clearly and persuasively.	Initiate and participate effectively in a range of collaborative discussions (one-on-one, in groups, and teacher-led) with diverse partners on grades 11–12 topics, texts, and issues, building on others' ideas and expressing their own clearly and persuasively.
a. Come to discussions prepared, having read or studied required material; explicitly draw on that preparation by referring to evidence on the topic, text, or issue to probe and reflect on ideas under discussion.	a. Come to discussions prepared, having read or researched material under study; explicitly draw on that preparation by referring to evidence on the topic, text, or issue to probe and reflect on ideas under discussion.	a. Come to discussions prepared, having read or researched material under study; explicitly draw on that preparation by referring to evidence on the topic, text, or issue to probe and reflect on ideas under discussion.	a. Come to discussions prepared, having read and researched material under study; explicitly draw on that preparation by referring to evidence from texts and other research on the topic or issue to stimulate a thoughtful, well-reasoned exchange of ideas.	a. Come to discussions prepared, having read and researched material under study; explicitly draw on that preparation by referring to evidence from texts and other research on the topic or issue to stimulate a thoughtful, well-reasoned exchange of ideas.
b. Follow rules for collegial discussions, set specific goals and deadlines, and define individual roles as needed.	b. Follow rules for collegial discussions, track progress toward specific goals and deadlines, and define individual roles as needed.	b. Follow rules for collegial discussions and decision-making, track progress toward specific goals and deadlines, and define individual roles as needed.	b. Work with peers to set rules for collegial discussions and decision-making (e.g., informal consensus, taking votes on key issues, presentation of alternate views), clear goals and deadlines, and individual roles as needed.	b. Work with peers to promote civil, democratic discussions and decision-making, set clear goals and deadlines, and establish individual roles as needed.
c. Pose and respond to specific questions				c. Propel conversations by posing and responding to questions that probe reasoning and evidence; ensure a

	Grade 6	Grade 7	Grade 8	Grades 9–10	Grades 11–12
	with elaboration and detail by making comments that contribute to the topic, text, or issue under discussion. d. Review the key ideas expressed and demonstrate understanding of multiple perspectives through reflection and paraphrasing.	c. Pose questions that elicit elaboration and respond to others' questions and comments with relevant observations and ideas that bring the discussion back on topic as needed. d. Acknowledge new information expressed by others and, when warranted, modify their own views.	c. Pose questions that connect the ideas of several speakers and respond to others' questions and comments with relevant evidence, observations, and ideas. d. Acknowledge new information expressed by others, and, when warranted, qualify or justify their own views in light of the evidence presented.	c. Propel conversations by posing and responding to questions that relate the current discussion to broader themes or larger ideas; actively incorporate others into the discussion; and clarify, verify, or challenge ideas and conclusions. d. Respond thoughtfully to diverse perspectives, summarize points of agreement and disagreement, and, when warranted, qualify or justify their own views and understanding and make new connections in light of the evidence and reasoning presented.	hearing for a full range of positions on a topic or issue; clarify, verify, or challenge ideas and conclusions; and promote divergent and creative perspectives. d. Respond thoughtfully to diverse perspectives; synthesize comments, claims, and evidence made on all sides of an issue; resolve contradictions when possible; and determine what additional information or research is required to deepen the investigation or complete the task.
2	Interpret information presented in diverse media and formats (e.g., visually, quantitatively, orally) and explain how it contributes to a topic, text, or issue under study.	Analyze the main ideas and supporting details presented in diverse media and formats (e.g., visually, quantitatively, orally) and explain how the ideas clarify a topic, text, or issue under study.	Analyze the purpose of information presented in diverse media and formats (e.g., visually, quantitatively, orally) and evaluate the motives (e.g., social, commercial, political) behind its presentation.	Integrate multiple sources of information presented in diverse media or formats (e.g., visually, quantitatively, orally), evaluating the credibility and accuracy of each source.	Integrate multiple sources of information presented in diverse formats and media (e.g., visually, quantitatively, orally) in order to make informed decisions and solve problems, evaluating the credibility and accuracy of each source and noting any discrepancies among the data.

(Continued)

Figure 4.4 (Continued)

	Grade 6	Grade 7	Grade 8	Grades 9–10	Grades 11–12
3	Delineate a speaker's argument and specific claims, distinguishing claims that are supported by reasons and evidence from claims that are not.	Delineate a speaker's argument and specific claims, evaluating the soundness of the reasoning and the relevance and sufficiency of the evidence.	Delineate a speaker's argument and specific claims, evaluating the soundness of the reasoning and relevance and sufficiency of the evidence and identifying when irrelevant evidence is introduced.	Evaluate a speaker's point of view, reasoning, and use of evidence and rhetoric, identifying any fallacious reasoning or exaggerated or distorted evidence.	Evaluate a speaker's point of view, reasoning, and use of evidence and rhetoric, assessing the stance, premises, links among ideas, word choice, points of emphasis, and tone used.
4	Present claims and findings, sequencing ideas logically and using pertinent descriptions, facts, and details to accentuate main ideas or themes; use appropriate eye contact, adequate volume, and clear pronunciation.	Present claims and findings, emphasizing salient points in a focused, coherent manner with pertinent descriptions, facts, details, and examples; use appropriate eye contact, adequate volume, and clear pronunciation.	Present claims and findings, emphasizing salient points in a focused, coherent manner with relevant evidence, sound valid reasoning, and well-chosen details; use appropriate eye contact, adequate volume, and clear pronunciation.	Present information, findings, and supporting evidence clearly, concisely, and logically such that listeners can follow the line of reasoning and the organization, development, substance, and style are appropriate to purpose, audience, and task.	Present information, findings, and supporting evidence, conveying a clear and distinct perspective, such that listeners can follow the line of reasoning, alternative or opposing perspectives are addressed, and the organization, development, substance, and style are appropriate to purpose, audience, and a range of formal and informal tasks.
6	Adapt speech to a variety of contexts and tasks, demonstrating command of formal English when indicated or appropriate.		Adapt speech to a variety of contexts and tasks, demonstrating command of formal English when indicated or appropriate.		Adapt speech to a variety of contexts and tasks, demonstrating command of formal English when indicated or appropriate.

Using Text-Dependent Questions
About *What the Text Means*

As noted in previous chapters, the text-dependent questions we develop in advance of a discussion can ensure that students' awareness of a text's meaning deepens over time. As we move beyond questions about vocabulary and text structure and locating explicitly stated information, we transition students into a heavier reliance on inferences. They are further challenged to use evidence and reasoning in their discussions. Because of this, lessons about *what the text means* may take longer and will be punctuated by periods of silence as students think closely. You may discover that you're only posing a few of these questions, because it takes students longer to draw conclusions. Our experience is that this phase of instruction results in more extended, longer student responses and more conversation across the room. We always view those moments when students stop talking to us and begin talking to one another as a sign of success.

> Lessons about *what the text means* may take longer and will be punctuated by periods of silence as students think closely.

Understanding a text more deeply allows students to make logical inferences from the text. Authors *imply* and readers *infer*. To infer, students must understand the author's purpose and how a given text relates to other texts. In the following sections, we focus on helping students figure out *what the text means* by attending to two main elements of texts:

- Author's purpose

- Intertextual connections

But inferencing doesn't end there. In Chapter 5, we focus our attention on students' use of the text to accomplish other tasks. It's in this fourth phase that logical inferences that include text evidence are realized.

Questions for Determining the Author's Purpose

Writers write for a host of reasons, some of which parallel the purposes of the three major text types: to convey an experience, to inform or explain, and to argue a position. When we pose text-dependent questions about the author's purpose, we don't purport to delve into the deep psychological motivations of the writer. But we do examine the text carefully for stated purposes and seek to contextualize the writing using what we know about the time and circumstances of its creation. It is helpful when the writer states, "The purpose of the study was to . . . ," because it makes the process more transparent. Statements such as this typically appear in scientific research articles but rarely appear outside of these documents. Instead, as is often the case in narrative texts, the reader usually has to dig around a bit more to glean this information.

The author's purpose can often be inferred through examination of several features of the text. Below are three ways you can teach students to do this.

Consider Point of View. Each writer shines a unique light on a topic, and with that comes a unique set of biases. Biases are not inherently negative; our attitudes, experiences, and perspectives are what make all of us interesting. In the case of some texts, the bias is inconsequential. For instance, an informational text explaining the process of cell division is probably not going to offer much at all in the way of bias. But an explanation of cell division within a position paper on when life begins can include an examination of whether the information presented is accurate and complete. The author's point of view is less important in a text like *The Hunger Games* (Collins, 2010), but it could influence understanding in a narrative text that is based on experiences an author has had, as is the case in *Stuck in Neutral* (Trueman, 2000), a text told from the perspective of an adolescent who has a significant disability and believes his father wants to kill him. In the latter case, the author notes that he wrote the book because of a lawsuit in Canada and his own experience as the parent of child with a disability.

Identify the Format. A blog post cannot be understood solely for its content; it must also be understood through the platform, in this case, the Internet. That author's purpose is further contextualized based on the hosting website. Does it appear on the website of a respected organization or on one with a poor reputation? Printed text deserves the same inspection. Does it appear in a well-regarded magazine, or is it featured in a publication underwritten by a special interest group? Similarly, a poem must be analyzed in its format, which would differ from a short story or memoir.

Consider How the Author Wants the Reader to React. Every written and verbal communication contains the rhetoric of human thought. The Greek philosopher Aristotle described three modes of rhetoric as methods of persuasion:

- *Ethos* appeals to the credibility of the writer or speaker, including his or her likability, authority, and character.

- *Pathos* appeals to the emotions of the listener or reader.

- *Logos* appeals to formal reasoning and logic, including inductive and deductive reasoning, and the use of facts and statistics.

We challenge middle and high school students to consciously seek the use of these modes of persuasion in the texts they read, as they influence our thoughts about a subject. As students learn to analyze texts for their modes of persuasion, they begin to incorporate these moves in their own writing. In English, students look at persuasive techniques in advertising, while in history they may analyze editorial cartoons. But these modes of rhetoric run through all texts, and skilled writers utilize the most effective proportions of each to develop a compelling case.

Look again at the passage from *Silent Spring* (Carson, 1962) on page 99. This paragraph primarily uses pathos as the form of persuasion, with statements such as "tragic examples of our unthinking bludgeoning of the landscape" and further personifying it by stating that the landscape is *eloquent* and possessing *integrity* (p. 64). How does Carson want us to react? She wants us to see the land as noble and pure, and to evoke in us a sense of stewardship to protect an ecosystem. Her use of pathos works well in forwarding her claims. Carson could have written a very different book, relying on fact and statistics alone. Her purpose wasn't only to inform; it was to act. Her use of pathos throughout the book was meant to move us to action. By analyzing the arguments and modes of persuasion, we can glean the author's purpose.

Questions for Determining the
Author's Purpose in Middle School English

The students in Mr. Corbrera's seventh grade English class had discussed a great deal about the text, *The People Could Fly* (Hamilton, 1993), but they had not talked about the metaphor of flying to freedom and what it meant for the people who could not fly. He asked students to consider why the author of this folktale would give the power to fly only to some people.

"Then people might believe it more," Carlos responded. "Because in a folktale, it's supposed to explain why things are the way they are. So, if there were people who were still slaves, then everyone couldn't fly away. Because then the people who were still there wouldn't tell the story anymore because they would think that it was totally wrong."

"Folktales usually have magic," Liana added, "but I agree with Carlos that everyone couldn't have the magic, because then all of the people would have flown away and there wouldn't be slaves."

Mr. Corbrera responded to the conversations the groups had. *"What I hear you all saying is that the author made a choice about what to include and that having everyone fly wouldn't really work. As you were talking, I was thinking about the details that the author includes that guide our emotional responses. What emotions do you believe that the author intended us to experience and why?"*

"It's depressing and sad. The people are getting hit with the whip all the time, and they have to work all day until it's dark," Caitlin responded.

"Yeah, I agree," Noah added. "The baby is just crying because it's hungry and then they whip it."

Victor commented, "But I also think that there is hope, because a lot of the people get away. I think that this is supposed to help people get through the bad things that are happening to them as slaves."

Mr. Corbrera interrupted the group conversation. *"As you have all said, there's a lot of emotion going on in this text. Make sure that you update your annotations so that you have your thoughts recorded. That will help you a lot when you want to quote from the text or review your ideas."*

He paused to provide them time to do so, and then said, *"There's this one line that has me thinking. It says, 'They must wait for a chance to run'* (Hamilton, 1993, p. 171). *What do you think the author's intent is with that line? What does it mean and what can you infer from that line?"*

"Toby stayed until all the people who could fly had gone," Mauricio said. "The people who were left had to escape themselves. So, I think that this is the hope part. I think it's telling people that there are others waiting for them and that they have to wait for a chance to run away."

Questions for Determining the Author's Purpose in High School English

The students had found evidence of irony in "The Open Window" as they discussed author's craft, which made the transition to author's purpose seamless. *"So why would Saki write this? How does his use of irony give us a clue about his purpose?"* Nancy asked them.

The question was difficult for them, and in seeing this she realized they needed more time to process. *"Start with conversation at your tables first. Why would Saki write this?"*

Chris was the first to float an idea with his group. "Irony can be a way to make fun of something," he said, to which Kealin added, "Or somebody, but who's he making fun of?"

For several minutes the group discussed whether he was making fun of any of the characters, but they were unsatisfied with these possibilities. The subsequent large group discussion unfolded, and the class was soon echoing a similar sentiment—yes, the author was using irony to poke fun, but at whom?

Nancy posed another question to guide their thinking. *"I'd like you to look at the date of publication and the setting of the story. Keep in mind that irony is always situated in a certain context and time."*

This appeared to spark some understanding, as the students reconsidered the audience. "It's the turn of the century, and the people in the story are kinda fancy," said Amal. "You know, with the letter of introduction and the French window and everything."

Alexis nodded in agreement. "They'd be the people he's making fun of, like he's sort of irritated with them."

Now Ernesto joined in. "But I don't really think he's irritated, but more like they're just a little full of themselves, and he's telling them that they can be easily tricked by a little girl."

The class resumed its discussion, as Nancy monitored their understanding. They were moving closer to understanding that Saki is making fun of 19th century manners of the middle class, but she realized that they would need more information to get there. She anticipated that when they watched a short video of the story, they'd grasp this concept more firmly.

Questions for Determining the
Author's Purpose in Middle School Social Studies

Following their discussion of the question, *"How does Frederick Douglass's use of language create a convincing picture of slavery's horrors?'* the students in Ms. Robinson's history class were ready to tackle the unstated messages in the narrative. She started this deeper investigation of the text by asking them about a line that they had previously discussed.

"I'd like us to go back to a line in the text that we talked about before. It says, 'I envied my fellow slaves for their stupidity.' We know that he was learning to read and that the prediction that he would become discontented had come true. But what do you think is the purpose of that statement? In other words, why did Frederick Douglass say that he envied people who could not read?"

As the groups talked, they seemed to focus on the idea that reading made him realize how bad his life really was. As Andrew said, "So, it's like reading made him understand that it was really, really bad. So, he makes the point that it was easier to be stupid and not know how bad your life really is, but before that it says, 'In moments of agony,' so I don't think he means it full-on. He's telling us readers that there were times that he thought it would be easier to not know all that he did know, but then it's what got him free and why he was invited to give the speech and then write the book."

"I totally agree," Paulina added. "I think he really is trying to say that it made his life harder, but that he still thinks it was important. Before that line he says, 'At times I feel that learning to read had been a curse rather than a blessing.' So, like Andrew said, it's not all of the time. He does this for effect, to let us know how bad he was being treated, not that he wished that he couldn't read again. That's what I think."

Questions for Determining the
Author's Purpose in High School Social Studies

Mr. Vaca knew that his students understand the purpose of FDR's Inaugural Address, at least at the basic level. He decided to ask them anyway, saying *"We've been discussing the speech that FDR gave as he assumed the presidency. What's the purpose of the speech again? Let's look at his arguments and how he persuaded people to accept his plan."*

Zach turned to his group and said, "I think it's to let people know about the problems and what they can do about them."

Brianna and Russell agreed. "I agree with you, because he directly tells people what the problems are and then what the government and the people are supposed to do about it," Brianna said.

Mr. Vaca then turned their attention to the opening of the next-to-the-last paragraph and asked, *"Why would FDR, toward the end of the speech, say 'If I read the temper of our people correctly'? What do you think is the intent of that line and why?"*

"I'm not sure," Andrea said. "Temper is how people are feeling, like emotionally, right? So is he saying that he checked in with different people? You know, like he took their temperature?" The class laughed. "Not really took their temperature, but you know what I mean."

Josiah responded, "I think it's a little different. I think that he's saying that he knows what the people are thinking and their emotional place. It kinda makes me think that the purpose was to show people that he understood them. It's like he was saying, I know how you're feeling, and this is what you're thinking. It's that ethos appeal. You know, like 'you can believe me because I'm just like you.'"

"Yeah, good point," Andrea added. "He was a rich guy, and he'd want to make sure they knew he thought like the common man. It's like one of those conditional statements. He says if I have this part right, then the rest must be right. So, if I understand the people's thinking, then we need to get together and help each other and 'sacrifice for the good of a common discipline,' and I think that he wants to do that anyway, but if he gets people to think that it's because of their mood, then they might be more willing."

Next Mr. Vaca turned their attention to the final paragraph and said, *"Let's take a look at the final sentence of the first part of his speech. He starts by saying that he has taken a pledge, which he would have done before the speech. We've seen presidents take the oath of office, so we know what that was like. But then he says 'I assume unhesitatingly the leadership of this great army of our people.' What's the purpose of that last sentence?"*

Luis said to his group, "So, I've changed my mind. I thought the purpose of the speech was to talk about the problems and what the country could do about them. But I think it's more. It's about him being the right person to be the leader. He needs the support of the people to get the work done. I think he's showing them, through the logic in his speech, that they should trust him as the leader, because he understands the issues and the people."

"I think you're right," Ashlee said. "I think it's more about persuasion and not so much about information, like I thought when we first started reading this speech. He has to persuade people, Democrats and Republicans, to do what he says so that things can get done."

Questions for Determining the
Author's Purpose in Middle School Science

Ms. Choi's students understood the author's purpose for the geology text. As Jeff said, "This is supposed to provide information."

"I agree with you, because it's from the science encyclopedia, so people would use this if they needed to find some information," Monica said.

"Yeah, that's pretty easy," Fernando commented. "And I think he had to know a lot to write this. Maybe it's also to show people that he knows a lot."

"Yeah, like he's the authority or that he is an expert or something," Monica added.

The students had already studied water and erosion, so Ms. Choi decided to ask them to make some inferences based on what they knew about the text and their previous learning, saying, *"Would a geologist be interested in glaciers?"*

"It's doesn't say that in the text, but I think they would be, because they are interested in mountains and that's where the glaciers are," Angela said.

"I agree with you, because glaciers can change the surface of the earth, and it does say that geologists are interested in that, so they probably would be," Julian commented.

Stephanie added, "I think that the physical geologists could be interested, because it says that they are 'concerned with the processes occurring on or below the surface,' and that is what a glacier does, it can change the surface of the earth."

"I also think that the historical geologists would be interested in glaciers, because they are 'concerned with the chronology of events,'" Mark suggested, "and that means that things that happen in time are interesting to them. And glaciers are really slow, so that would be interesting to people who study history."

Ms. Choi, having listened to several groups discuss the question, thought that her students were able to make inferences from the text and apply what they understood to other fields. To check this, she decided to ask another question, "*Would geologists be interested in space junk? Remember the beginning of the year when we studied all of the materials that were floating around in outer space? Would a geologist be interested in that?*"

"I don't think so, because that really isn't about the surface of the earth and what happens on the earth," Eric said.

Paulina, agreeing, said, "Right. There are other people who study that, not the geologists."

With a smile, Omar added, "Well, yeah, but if that space junk came down to earth and created big holes or something, then I bet they'd be interested."

Questions for Determining the
Author's Purpose in High School Science

The students in Mr. Nielsen's class anticipated the questions about the author's purpose. Given their experience with close reading and the ways in which questions guided their thinking, they often asked each other questions about the text. In his group, Neil asked, "Does Darwin's audience know about natural selection already?"

Pablo was the first to answer. "There are all kinds of text clues that say that people knew about it already. Like for example, he says that he calls it natural selection, which I think means that other people might call it something else."

Ivette disagreed. "I think that his audience doesn't really know much, because he talks directly to them. He asks them questions at the beginning, and I don't think you do that if people already know the answer,"

"But then he acts like he's reminding readers of things they already know. Like it says right here, 'Variations useful to man have undoubtedly occurred.' So, I think that the people reading this had experience, but maybe they didn't think it was because of natural selection," Neil said.

Mr. Nielsen asked another group a question: *"Darwin refers to domestication to explain how genes have been manipulated by humans—why does he do this? Does he have an argument embedded in his explanations?"*

Randy responded, "I think that he does this to show that we have experienced this and that we already understand it. Basically, he says that he is going to remind people of what they already know, but he says it like this: 'Let it be borne in mind.' That means remember this. And then he says that domestication has created a lot of variations, just like nature."

Anna took over at that point. "I think he does this to make a point—that there are variations even when humans are involved in domestication and that some of the traits that we want in domestication get more favor so that the species with that trait gets to reproduce more, and then we have more of that trait in the population. So, if people can do that through domestication, then he makes the argument that nature can also do that.

Picking up where Anna left off, Jonathan said, "Yeah, and that's kinda cool. He tries to explain things, but there is also an argument in there. He really is making a case and backing it up with evidence, but it's a good way to do that. It's like you don't even notice that you're part of the argument, because it just seems like an explanation. So, even though he has it as a question, he has made his case. As he says right here, 'Individuals having any advantage, however slight, over others, would have the best chance of surviving,' and that's the whole argument in this text."

As the groups finished their conversations, Mr. Nielsen asked another question: *"How does the tone of the text reveal the author's relationship to the topic?"*

This question was easy for the students in this biology class. They understood that tone is shaped by words and by the way that the author engages a reader. As Marco said, "It's all about him being an authority. His attitude toward the subject is that he understands it and that he makes his case in a formal way."

"I think he's serious; that's the general tone, and maybe academic and formal," Dalasia added. "I think that this is really important to him, because he uses questions to get the reader to think, and then he basically tries to remind the reader of information that's already known so that he can make his case. It just seems that this is really important to him, and he wants to make sure that the other people understand it."

Students listen to a dramatic reenactment of a complex text they've read.

Questions for Making Intertextual Connections

Texts don't exist in isolation; they are better understood when compared and contrasted with other texts, including those that utilize other media platforms, such as audio recordings, film, and multimedia. In the case of diverse media applications, the target text may be better understood when images are used to augment description. This is often the case with texts that were written long ago and with stories that occur in unfamiliar settings. Seventh grade social studies teacher Elian Cortez used film clips to provide his students with a visual vocabulary that supported their readings about historical events. "It's amazing how much it helps when I use a short clip from a documentary about a time in ancient history," he said. "We're studying ancient China right now, and the textbook has some great photographs for them to view. But I've discovered that a short, well-done reenactment gives them so much more," commented Mr. Cortez. "They get to see people talking, going to market, whatever. It helps them understand unique elements of the time, like the fact that most people walked or rode a horse to get from one place to another. But the wealthy, and the military officers, they would have wagons and oxen. [My students] see that people from long ago have much in common with themselves, like the need to move from one place to another, and that the rich usually have a better ride than the poor."

Intertextual connections are necessary in order for students to translate and integrate information. For instance, in history class, students must discern the difference between primary and secondary source documents and recognize the benefits and drawbacks of each. The details and perspective of an eyewitness account can round out understanding of an event, such as the use of Pliny the Younger's description of the eruption of Mount Vesuvius, recounted in the previous chapter. Of course, his description does not note that the discovery of the well-preserved human and architectural remains in 1748 would advance our contemporary understanding of ancient Roman life. Only a secondary source, such as their textbook or other informational piece, would be able to do so. Each is of value; both become more valuable when used together.

In science, students translate quantitative and visual data into words, and vice versa. Words and images that enable them to make these translations may be found inside of a single text, such as when a chart or diagram is used to represent a complex process. For example, an informational reading on the electromagnetic spectrum is likely to contain a diagram that details the inverse relationship between wavelength and frequency. In addition, the diagram will indicate where gamma rays, x-rays, and ultraviolet, visible, infrared, microwave, and radio waves occur in relation to one another on the spectrum. The accompanying written text will contain more information about measurement units (nanometers) and the transfer of energy. The diagram and textual information are best understood in conjunction with one another, and each has its own demands. In the diagram, color features, the caption, directionality arrows, and a scale provide visual representations of information. Text-based questions about what the diagram means include those that ask students to interpret why the intensity of colors changes (to reflect intensity of wavelengths and frequency), and to comment on the relatively narrow spectrum of visible light. Questions that foster discussion about elaborative inferencing within scientific diagrams increase student comprehension in high school biology (Cromley et al., 2013).

A final dimension for intertextual connections involves the ways in which literary texts are performed across platforms. A common example of this exists in virtually every high school English classroom: the practice of viewing the performance of a Shakespearean play. The reasoning is obvious, as dramas are written to be performed, and students gain a tremendous amount of knowledge from such experiences. Other resources include audio recordings of speeches, and organizations such as the National Archives (www.archives.gov) and the Library of Congress (www.loc.gov) are invaluable for locating these and other multimedia materials.

Eighth grade English teacher Tina Ellsworth used Gwendolyn Brooks's rendition of her poem "We Real Cool" (1960) so that her students could further understand the poet's use of enjambments (line breaks that interrupt a line of text) to emphasize the uncertainty of its otherwise boastful narrators.

"Brooks wants you to read the word 'we' more softly and hesitantly," said the teacher after they listened to the recording several times. *"Why is that a key to understanding this poem?"* asked Ms. Ellsworth.

As the discussed progressed, she shifted their focus to comparing the print version of the 24-word poem with its performance. Several students, including Hamze, heard the cadence in the spoken version of the poem. "It's like a march," he said. "I can see these tough guys taking up all the room on the sidewalk."

In the case of diverse media applications, the target text may be better understood when images are used to augment description. This is often the case with texts that were written long ago and with stories that occur in unfamiliar settings.

"When I read it, I thought they were just tough guys," Arlissa added, "but when I hear [Brooks] say it, it's like they're tough but they're a little scared, too. Maybe they are scaring themselves."

Hamze finished her sentence. "We die soon," he said, repeating the last line of the poem.

Questions for Making Intertextual Connections in Middle School English

"Remember the last text we read by Virginia Hamilton (1993), "Carrying the Running-Aways?" asked Mr. Corbrera. *"Please take out those pages, and let's look at the similarities and differences between the two tales. Let's start by comparing Toby and the man who rows across the river."*

"So, it's kinda obvious but they both help other people," Arif said.

Cara agreed. "Yeah, and they both risk themselves to help."

"If Toby could fly, and the man has the boat, they could both be free way earlier. But they don't go. They stay to help other people," Elizabeth added. "That's an important message, I think, that there were people who helped the slaves."

"Yeah, because it would be good for the people to hear that so that more of them would be willing to help, even if they almost got caught and could get whipped or killed," Arif agreed.

In another group, the students focused on the differences. Marlin and Brandon were talking about the differences in the texts themselves. As Marlin said, "This one is true [Marlin points to his copy of "Carrying the Running-Aways"] because it says that it is a true story and that his name was Arnold Gragston. This one [Marlin points to his copy of *The People Could Fly*] doesn't say that it's true, so we don't know if Toby was real or not."

After several minutes, Mr. Corbrera asked his students to turn their attention to the lessons that both texts could teach people, then and now. As he said, *"We're reading a lot of narratives. Some of these are true and others are folktales. I'd like you to think across all of these texts we've been reading. What's the lesson they're all trying to teach?"*

Brandon said it well. "I think that there are a lot of lessons. For one, people can do really bad things to other people. And for two, when that happens, some people will take a risk to help people. But I think that the main message for me is that people have to write things down so that we can learn from it later. If they didn't write these down, then we wouldn't know about the bad things or the people who made a difference."

Questions for Making Intertextual
Connections in High School English

Nancy's students were moving closer to understanding why Saki, the author of "The Open Window," used irony in the piece. She showed them a nine-minute video performance of the short story, choosing one that was a nearly verbatim rendition of the written version. The costumes, demeanor, and setting became clearer because of the visual information students gained.

When the video was over, Nancy invited them to continue the discussion. *"You were saying that irony can be used to poke fun at someone or something, but you weren't quite sure what. Has that changed for you, now that you've seen the story being performed?"*

The students turned to their table partners, this time more confident. "I could see that they weren't really rich, like they didn't have servants or anything," said Amal.

"They were more regular, like middle class."

"I think he's making fun of all us regular people, 'cause we like to gossip and tell stories about each other just for the fun of it," Alexis remarked.

Nancy listened in on this and several other similar small group conversations. Now satisfied that they had arrived at a new understanding, she reminded them to add the information to their annotations. *"Be sure to mark out your evidence of irony as a literary device,"* she said.

"Now let's turn our attention back to that last line, where it says, 'Romance at short notice was her specialty.' How is romance being used here?" she said.

Several students confirmed that they were now certain that it wasn't about romantic love, and Chris took special note of the actress's smirk at the end. Nancy said, *"So go back into the text, everyone. Chris, you're on it. Where can you find evidence to support that claim?"*

Nancy listed the examples they provided in response: "a very self-possessed young lady" who tells him, "You must try and put up with me."

Kealin noticed for the first time that the phrase "self-possessed young lady" is mentioned a second time when Vera realizes that Nuttel would believe anything she told him, because he didn't know anyone locally.

"There's a third time!" said Amal. "Saki says, 'The child's voice lost its self-possessed note and became falteringly human.'"

"OK, bring it home," Nancy said. *"Vera is good at* what?"

Many of the students were now willing to answer. *Lies, tall tales, fibs,* they replied.

"That's what romance means in this piece!" said Alexis, now relieved. "She can tell a big ol' whopper of a lie on the spur of the moment. And she did it again to her family when Mr. Nuttel ran out the door!"

Nancy felt the momentum as students gained new insight. *"Back to our previous question,"* she said. *"Who is Saki criticizing in a lighthearted way?"*

This time Ernesto answered. "He's telling all of us that we make up stuff about other people for the sake of gossiping, and we're way too willing to believe others just because they've told us a story."

Questions for Making Intertextual
Connections in Middle School Social Studies

Ms. Robinson shared the two-page text about Frederick Douglass from *50 American Heroes Every Kid Should Meet* (Denenberg & Roscoe, 2001) with her students, in part to demonstrate to her students how much they knew about the text and in part to emphasize why reading primary source documents is critical in history. She asked them to read the first two paragraphs of the text:

> Right now, you're doing what for Frederick Douglass was an illegal activity that enabled him to become a free man. You are reading.
>   It was against the law to teach a slave to read and write. If a slave could read, the slave might start to think about ideas like freedom, justice, and fairness. That sounded like trouble to slave owners. But Mrs. Auld didn't know the law when eight-year-old Frederick was given to her family. (p. 40)

Ms. Robinson asked her students to compare the differences in the two texts, saying, *"Remember that we can compare primary and secondary sources to determine if they corroborate, to tell the same story. We can also compare author's perspectives and what each author left out. Talk about the differences you see in these texts."*

Julia started the conversation in her group. "There really is no comparison. It's like they just skipped over a big important thing. It's true that he wasn't supposed to learn to read and that Mrs. Auld started to teach him. But there's so much more. He struggled once he learned and wondered if it was a good idea himself."

"Yeah, right. And he even says that maybe his 'master' was right, that learning to read wasn't a good thing," Tyler added.

"That's true," Luke commented. "But I don't think that was his real purpose. He really wanted to read so that he could get his freedom.

I think it's more about being frustrated that you can read, but then you can't do anything about it."

Julia, having read more of the secondary source, added, "We know he became free, but it says on this page that he ran away when he was 20. I bet there's more to that part of the story. They had to leave out a lot about his life when he was little, so there is probably a lot more to learn about when he was 20 and when he finally ran away."

"Yeah, and I bet that is interesting too. I wonder if he doubted himself when he was free, like he did when he learned to read. It's like, maybe it would be easier again, like when he couldn't read," Luke said.

"I wish we could find out," Julia responded. "I think it probably is true, because he really has to figure out who he is as a person. He was free, but then where did he live and where did he get money to live? Maybe he had some thoughts that there were times when it was easier to be a slave, at least in some parts of your life. But then, he didn't want to go back. Like he didn't stop learning to read, even though he sometimes wished he was like the others who couldn't read."

At that point, Ms. Robinson interrupted the groups. *"I appreciate all of your conversations about the differences between the two texts. Reading primary and secondary sources helps us understand history from a number of perspectives and contexts. But I am interested in the quote that is on page 41. Can you read that to yourself and explain to each other what you think it means, based on your understanding of the two texts we've read?"* The students read the following quote from Frederick Douglass:

> No man can put a chain about the ankle of his fellow man without at last finding the other end fastened about his own neck. (Douglass, 1845/1995, p. 41)

"Well, I think that he's saying that if you try to hold someone down, you end up holding yourself down," Maya said.

"So, I'm thinking that he is saying that humans are all connected and that if you chain up somebody else, you end up being in the chain," Andrew added.

Paulina interrupted. "Yeah, I get it. He's saying that. If you try to control someone by putting a chain on their ankle, you end up trying to control that person and you end up trapped, like having a chain around your own neck. I don't think he means that literal. I think it's more, what do you call it, figurative. It's like he's saying that you'll be weighted down, or trapped, when you try to do that to others."

Questions for Making Intertextual
Connections in High School Social Studies

The students in Mr. Vaca's US History class had completed their reading of FDR's inaugural address up to the point where he notes the pledge was taken and he assumes leadership. Mr. Vaca then shared an excerpt from later in the speech with his students. He projected the following two paragraphs for them to read:

> I am prepared under my constitutional duty to recommend the measures that a stricken nation in the midst of a stricken world may require. These measures, or such other measures as the Congress may build out of its experience and wisdom, I shall seek, within my constitutional authority, to bring to speedy adoption.
>
> But in the event that the Congress shall fail to take one of these two courses, and in the event that the national emergency is still critical, I shall not evade the clear course of duty that will then confront me. I shall ask the Congress for the one remaining instrument to meet the crisis—broad Executive power to wage a war against the emergency, as great as the power that would be given to me if we were in fact invaded by a foreign foe. (in Rosenman, 1938)

"What is the purpose of this information being included in the speech that FDR gave as he assumed the presidency?" Mr. Vaca asked.

William started the conversation in his group. "It sounds like he's going to do what he wants, with support from Congress or not."

"This makes me think about him being a leader," Melissa added. "He doesn't seem like a leader; he's more like a dictator."

"I don't really think he's acting like a dictator," William responded. "I think he's saying that he's going to get the work done and if the Congress can't act, he would like more executive power. It would be interesting to know if he got that extra power. I bet we'll read about that in this unit."

Questions for Making Intertextual
Connections in Middle School Science

Ms. Choi showed her students an excerpt from the Annenberg video *Earth Revealed* (www.learner.org/resources/series78.html?pop=yes&pid=312) and asked them to discuss the difference between the text and the video. In the video, students are introduced to the idea that nearly everything that they use (other than solar energy) comes from the earth and that geologists are key in helping people obtain things from the earth as safely as possible. Following their discussion about the differences,

Ms. Choi asks her students *"to identify places in the video in which physical geology is featured and places in which historical geology is featured."*

The students correctly identify several instances of each, and Ms. Choi moves their conversation to focus on the different topics addressed in the video and the text, saying *"Which of the words in our text did you see or hear in the video? Did you see any visuals that would help you understand the text?"*

"Can we watch that one more time to be sure?" asked Mariam, raising her hand.

Following another viewing of the video, the students discuss the terms that they heard and saw in the video.

"They talked about rocks and minerals and showed a lot of different pictures," Marc said. "But I didn't know that geologists helped to find oil. They said that they had geophones that could listen to the movement, kinda like a seismologist does to predict earthquakes."

Ms. Choi knew that her students got more out of the video as a result of their careful and close reading of the encyclopedic entry.

Questions for Making Intertextual Connections in High School Science

Several students in Mr. Nielsen's class assumed that Darwin's audience already knew a lot of the information contained in the text. As Aden said, "Isn't this obvious? Darwin says, 'Many more individuals are born than can possibly survive,' so those with the strongest systems or the best advantage would be the ones to live."

Mr. Nielsen wanted his students to understand that the ideas had been around for some time, along with the controversies and social unrest that the text caused. To begin this conversation with his students, Mr. Nielsen said, "In 1789, 70 years before *On the Origin of Species* was written, Thomas Robert Malthus wrote (the following was projected from the document camera):

> It does not . . . by any means seem impossible that by an attention to breed, a certain degree of improvement, similar to that among animals, might take place among men. Whether intellect could be communicated may be a matter of doubt; but size, strength, beauty, complexion, and perhaps longevity are in a degree transmissible. . . . As the human race, however, could not be improved in this way without condemning all the bad specimens to celibacy, it is not probable that an attention to breed should ever become general. (Malthus, 1798)

"Where do you see influence from Malthus's work on Darwin's theory of natural selection?" Mr. Nielsen asked.

"See, they already knew a lot of this," Aden said. "Darwin was building on this guy. Like Malthus, Darwin says there can be variations that will cause an improvement."

"Yeah, I see that connection," Jeremy added. "Darwin is definitely building on the idea that some things, like size and strength, could be improved with attention, or as Darwin calls it, *natural selection*, but there's something even bigger in this text. It says that humans really couldn't be improved unless some people didn't get to have kids."

Sebastian interrupted. "And that's what Hitler was trying to do, right? Like he was trying to make sure that people he thought were bad specimens didn't get to reproduce. But the guy who wrote way back in 1798 says that it's shouldn't become general, but it did during World War II."

Later in the class period, Mr. Nielsen asked students to read a different piece of text. As he said, "Consider the following excerpt from the article *10 Examples of Natural Selection* by Diana Bocco (projected for the class to read):

> Many times a species is forced to make changes as a direct result of human progress. Such is the case with the peppered moth (*Biston betularia*). Up until the Industrial Revolution, these moths were typically whitish in color with black spots, although they were found in a variety of shades. As the Industrial Revolution reached its peak, the air in London became full of soot, and the once-white trees and buildings that moths used for camouflage became stained black. The birds began to eat more of the lighter-colored moths because they were more easily spotted than the darker ones. Over the course of a few months, dark moths started appearing in the area and lighter moths became scarce. Once the Industrial Revolution peak passed, lighter moths made a comeback. (www.discovery.com/tv-shows/curiosity/topics/10-examples-natural-selection.htm)

"So class, what specific aspect of natural selection does this illustrate?" asked Mr. Nielsen.

"I think it's differential reproductive success, because only the dark moths were producing more baby moths," Leo said.

"Yeah, I think that's part of it, but I think that there's something that happens before," Dakota added. "I think that it's the predator one, because the birds are eating them and that's why they aren't there. It's not a change that lasts, because remember that the lighter ones came back once the environment changed."

"That's probably right, because it did start with the birds being able to see the moths to eat. That's why there were less of them to reproduce," agreed Leo.

QUESTION • YOURSELF

This chapter has focused on questions that push students even deeper into their analysis of the text, specifically as they explore the role of inferences, author's purpose, and intertextual connections. These deep analyses of texts are possible when students know what the text says and how it works.

Now we invite you to try this yourself. In Figure 4.5 we show an article about the 1854 London cholera epidemic that you can use to practice what you have learned in this chapter. Take a few minutes to read the text below. Then turn your attention to the questions that you can develop to encourage students to determine what the text means. Remember that this phase is focused on making *inferences* and specifically understanding author's *purpose* and *intertextual connections*. What is it that students should understand about this text? How might the data table that follows, or the map that follows that, help them understand the text?

Before you begin, you might like to skim the italicized questions in the teachers' lessons in this chapter. If you'd like to check yourself, the questions that Ms. Thayre developed can be found on Corwin's companion website at www.corwin.com/textdependentquestions. Next, apply this technique to develop questions for a short piece that you will use with your own students.

Figure 4.5 **"Instances of the Communication of Cholera Through the Medium of Polluted Water in the Neighborhood of Broad Street, Golden Square" by John Snow**

The most terrible outbreak of cholera which ever occurred in this kingdom, is probably that which took place in Broad Street, Golden Square, and the adjoining streets, a few weeks ago. Within two hundred and fifty yards of the spot where Cambridge Street joins Broad Street, there were upwards of five hundred fatal attacks of cholera in ten days. The mortality in this limited area probably equals any that was ever caused in this country, even by the plague; and it was much more sudden, as the greater number of cases terminated in a few hours. The mortality would undoubtedly have been much greater had it not been for the flight of the population. Persons in furnished lodgings left first, then other lodgers went away, leaving their furniture to be sent for when they could meet with a place to put it in. Many houses were closed altogether, owing to the death of the proprietors; and, in a great number of instances, the tradesmen

(Continued)

(Continued)

who remained had sent away their families: so that in less than six days from the commencement of the outbreak, the most afflicted streets were deserted by more than three-quarters of their inhabitants.

There were a few cases of cholera in the neighborhood of Broad Street, Golden Square, in the latter part of August; and the so-called outbreak, which commenced in the night between the 31st August and the 1st September, was, as in all similar instances, only a violent increase of the malady. As soon as I became acquainted with the situation and extent of this irruption of cholera, I suspected some contamination of the water of the much-frequented street-pump in Broad Street, near the end of Cambridge Street; but on examining the water, on the evening of the 3rd September, I found so little impurity in it of an organic nature, that I hesitated to come to a conclusion. Further inquiry, however, showed me that there was no other circumstance or agent common to the circumscribed locality in which this sudden increase of cholera occurred, and not extending beyond it, except the water of the above mentioned pump. I found, moreover, that the water varied, during the next two days, in the amount of organic impurity, visible to the naked eye, on close inspection, in the form of small white, flocculent particles; and I concluded that, at the commencement of the outbreak, it might possibly have been still more impure. I requested permission, therefore, to take a list, at the General Register Office, of the deaths from cholera, registered during the week ending 2nd September, in the subdistricts of Golden Square, Berwick Street, and St. Ann's, Soho, which was kindly granted. Eighty-nine deaths from cholera were registered, during the week, in the three subdistricts. Of these, only six occurred in the four first days of the week; four occurred on Thursday, the 31st August; and the remaining seventy-nine on Friday and Saturday. I considered, therefore, that the outbreak commenced on the Thursday; and I made inquiry, in detail, respecting the eighty-three deaths registered as having taken place during the last three days of the week.

On proceeding to the spot, I found that nearly all the deaths had taken place within a short distance of the pump. There were only ten deaths in houses situated decidedly nearer to another street pump. In five of these cases the families of the deceased persons informed me that they always sent to the pump in Broad Street, as they preferred the water to that of the pump which was nearer. In three other cases, the deceased were children who went to school near the pump in Broad Street. Two of them were known to drink the water; and the parents of the third think it probable that it did so. The other two deaths, beyond the district which this pump supplies, represent only the amount of mortality from cholera that was occurring before the irruption took place.

With regard to the deaths occurring in the locality belonging to the pump, there were sixty-one instances in which I was informed that the deceased persons used to drink the pump-water from Broad Street, either constantly, or occasionally. In six instances I could get no information, owing to the death or departure of everyone connected with the deceased individuals; and in six cases I was informed that the deceased persons did not drink the pump-water before their illness.

The result of the inquiry then was, that there had been no particular outbreak or increase of cholera, in this part of London, except among the persons who were in the habit of drinking the water of the above-mentioned pump-well.

I had an interview with the Board of Guardians of St. James's parish, on the evening of Thursday, 7th September, and represented the above circumstances to them. In consequence of what I said, the handle of the pump was removed on the following day.

Table 1 Grid Location of Deaths Due to Cholera in 1854 London, Plus Water Pumps and Brewery Locations

Water Pump Locations	Brewery Location	#	Day 1	Day 2	Day 3	Day 4	Day 5	Day 6	Day 7	Day 8	Day 9	Day 10
		1	L18	S4	G6	J15	G6	S14	P6	G6	Q15	M8
	X13	2	R14	P13	R11	O11	T10	W14	Q14	O11	W10	R11
T6		3	O15	O9	T14	O14	P14	K15	O16	N16	N6	R11
D7	X14	4	M13	N16	P11	O13	T10	R11	N13	R15	J11	M15
P7	X15	5	O11	L9	R14	T14	M8	Q15	J15	N9	M9	O15
G11	Y13	6	L17	Q16	M16	U17	N16	J16	O17	J19	X19	M17
P14	Y14	7	N16	S13	Q12	T18	P17	P11	M17	N17	U12	S15
Y14	Y15	8	M14	O12	L13	N11	N14	R15	O14	N13	S19	U14
I16		9	R13	S14	O12	N14	N14	M11	P16	N16	R15	S13
Z18		10	N14	Q15	P13	O12	M11	M11	L17	L17	L18	J16
J20		11	O16	O22	O9	T9	M8	G22	T9	T9	M9	L11
D21		12	N12	Q14	Q13	N17	K17	S13	L11	O15	N13	X19
L26		13	N12	N14	N14	M14	R15	Q12	N13	N15	R16	M15
		14	U20	O15	M12	P15	M14	Q15	S12	J15	S12	L17
		15	O14	O8	M17	P8	P8	M8	P6	P9	Q20	U20
		16	Q15	P17	J19	M15	N14	R11	P11	Q15	O13	L18
		17	P8	O18	L17	R16	P16	M13	N14	P15	P12	O22
		18	T9	R16	R14	M13	S15	K15	M16	Q12	R20	L21
		19	O13	T15	O14	K12	K12	P17	K15	R16	O5	O15

(Continued)

Table 1 (Continued)

Water Pump Locations	Brewery Location	#	Deaths Due to Cholera—Grid Locations									
			Day 1	Day 2	Day 3	Day 4	Day 5	Day 6	Day 7	Day 8	Day 9	Day 10
		20	O23	Q13	K15	P8	R14	R15	O12	Q16	J15	U20
		21	R15	J12	R15	M17	R14	R13	O12	U14	U14	O16
		22	N17	L13	N16	N12	N13	N17	P9	N9	L17	O16
		23	P11	K20	N14	N14	N12	R14	G19	U20	K14	L11
		24	M14	P11	M14	N17	Q15	H19	N15	N12	P23	K17
		25	P13	U20	M14	J16	W17	Q16	K14	K14	L18	R20
		26	L18	O17	L13	L17	M15	Q20	N16	N12	M15	S19
		27	M11	Q15	N14	Q15	N13	G6	R15	M17	L18	O8
		28	N13	N16	Q17	L13	M17	M11	J11	Q15	M8	M11
		29	L13	S19	N8	M13	Q16	P15	L8	P9	F17	M13
		30	R8	U6	Q15	N16	L13	R16	R14	T21	U20	
		31	P14	T21	L18	L9	M8	R15	R11	N11	L18	
		32		M13	R20	O8	P6	L8	T13	L9	T13	
		33		N13	L18	T21	N23	P9	P11	M11		
		34		N13	P6	N9	P13	P11	K9	U20		
		35		N13	S12	N13	M11	O13	N13			
		36		P14	P13	N11	M12	O13	N16			
		37			L9	L11	O13	P14	T21			
		38			O13	O21						
		39				G23						
		40				S14						
		Total	31	36	38	40	37	37	37	34	31	29

Exhibit 1 **Map Showing the Location of Deaths From Cholera in Soho District of London and Location of Water Pump Sites**

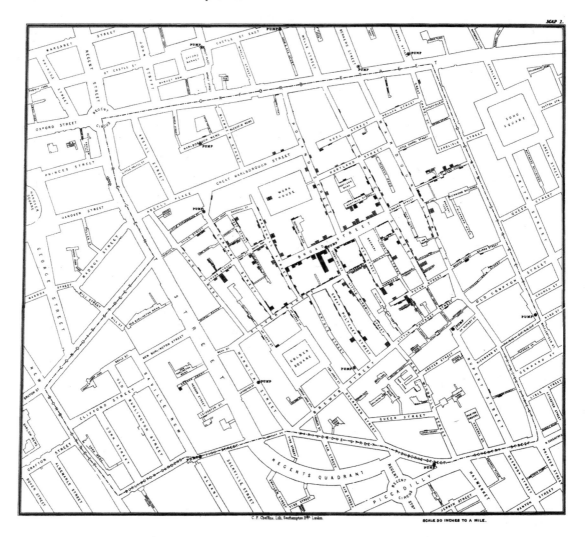

Source: Excerpt from *On the Mode of Communication of Cholera* by John Snow, M.D. London: John Churchill, New Burlington Street, England, 1855 (pp. 38–55).

Available for download from **www.corwin.com/textdependentquestions**

Videos

To read a QR code, you must have a smartphone or tablet with a camera. We recommend that you download a QR code reader app that is made specifically for your phone or tablet brand.

Videos can also be accessed at
www.corwin.com/textdependentquestions

Video 4.1 Oscar Corrigan calls attention to the word "migration," prompting his seventh grade social studies students to discuss its influence and usage in *Things Fall Apart.*

Video 4.2 After reading an article on ulcers, students in Will Mellman's seventh grade science class talk about whether the authors know what cause ulcers, using textual evidence to defend their opinions.

Video 4.3 Students in Javier Vaca's eleventh grade U.S. history class discuss Eisenhower's state of mind before the D-Day invasion, using textual evidence and a comparison of "Message to the Troops" and "In Case of Failure."

Video 4.4 A tenth grade English class, led by Heather Anderson, imagines what Maya Angelou might say to them based on their analysis of her poem "Phenomenal Woman."

Video 4.5 Marisol Thayre's eleventh grade English class discusses Susan Bordo's purpose for writing a piece on body image.

Video 4.6 Students in Kim Elliot's tenth grade biology class discuss whether scientists agree about what causes cancer to determine the author's purpose for writing "Untangling the Roots of Cancer."

5

WHAT DOES THE TEXT *INSPIRE YOU TO DO*?

In building the habit of reading closely, teachers are less like the sage on the stage and more like the guide on the side. A trail guide, if you will. Like a trail guide, teachers have specialized knowledge of the terrain, and they can point out interesting sights and warn of pitfalls. But trail guides understand that the experience any one traveler has on the journey will be a shade different from the experience of all the other travelers. A trail guide hopes that the journey itself will influence each person in some way. Like a good trail guide, a skilled teacher shows you where to look but doesn't tell you what to think.

The journey through a complex print, digital, or multimedia text requires a guide to shepherd novices through an unfamiliar landscape—someone who hones the novices' observational powers in order to deepen their understanding of what they are witnessing. This then cultivates within them the habit of reading closely, and it is something they will continue to develop and refine over their lifetimes. In classrooms, teachers show students a path for journeying through the text, pointing out the interesting details and providing space for them to coconstruct an understanding of what the text offers. This, again, is close reading—an instructional routine.

The previous chapters have been devoted to developing the habit of reading closely in order to determine

- *What the text says* through *inspection*

- *How the text works* through *investigation*

- *What the text means* through *interpretation*

The process is not strictly linear. Engaged readers roam across the landscape of a text with little regard for the teacher's lesson plan. Carefully prepared sequences of questions are discarded in situations where students find themselves naturally discussing, in advance, the very concepts that subsequent questions would have asked them to address (something that occurs more frequently as students become more skilled at reading closely). Even still, the text-dependent questions prepared for a series of discussions about a compelling text serve the important purpose of setting some trail markers for the guide and the travelers to follow. And eventually a good trail should lead somewhere.

> Like a good trail guide, a skilled teacher shows you where to look but doesn't tell you what to think.

When it comes to text, the destination is a product of some kind. Perhaps it is a debate or a Socratic seminar. Maybe it's a presentation or an essay. The destination might lie in taking action to write a letter to a politician or develop an online petition. It may come in the form of an investigation—a call for students to seek out more information about a topic or to write a formal research paper or literary critique. There are a host of possible destinations, but they have one thing in common: They change the reader in some way. The reader comes to know more about a topic, to be intrigued by a new idea, or to be troubled by an injustice he or she hadn't known existed. The text may illuminate corners of readers they hadn't noticed before, or cause them to consider another person's dilemmas differently, or built a sense of affiliation with others. In other words, it becomes a part of who they are as thinkers and as people. So our final cognitive path sets them, and us, off to explore the question, *what does the text inspire you, the reader, to do?*

An Invitation to Read Closely: *Action-Oriented* Questions and Tasks

All writers hope to transform the thinking of their readers. Texts may confirm what you, the reader, already suspected about an idea, but needed to have validated. Or they might cause you to question, critique, or take action. In every case, the text is integrated into readers' knowledge of themselves and their world. But integration doesn't come in advance of action—it happens as a result of action. How often have you caught yourself noticing what you thought while in the act of explaining your thoughts to someone else? You realize you didn't know what you thought about something until you said it. We spur students to take action precisely because it gives them the opportunity to consolidate and clarify.

In the act of creating something new, learners build a sense of autonomy.

Taking action doesn't mean being militant. It's not that every reading lends itself to social change. In fact, many of the texts we teach in school are not for that purpose at all. Taking action means applying what has been learned by creating something new. And in the act of creating something new, learners build a sense of autonomy. In this way, students learn to take responsibility for their own learning and manage their time and resources. Students figure out how to prioritize tasks and calibrate their work with others (Fisher & Frey, 2014a).

Why Students Need to Complete These Types of Tasks

Learning advances when students are able to transform information into products. The notion of the student as a blank slate has long since been disproven, and we have a far better understanding of the value of active learning (Marzano, Pickering, & Heflebower, 2011). Experiential learning and problem-based learning, to name two theoretical orientations, utilize this element of learning extensively to drive instruction. But other learning models also can be used to help students understand what the text means at a deeper level and to figure out what the text inspires them to do. For example, critical literacy theory is predicated on an assumption that students examine information with an eye toward action. They examine power structures, seek out alternative perspectives, and formulate problems (McLaughlin & DeVoogd, 2004). In each of these theoretical models, the intent is for learners to transform knowledge into something that is meaningful and integrated into their worldview. At its best, action should adequately answer the question every student has, namely, "Why do I need to learn this?"

Knowledge formation moves from initial acquisition to transfer of knowledge in novel situations. In the groundbreaking work, *How People*

Learn: Brain, Mind, Experience, and School (Bransford, Brown, & Cocking, 2000) the principles of transfer are summarized as follows:

- Knowledge that is overly contextualized can reduce transfer; abstract representations of knowledge can help promote transfer.

- Transfer is best viewed as an active, dynamic process rather than a passive end-product of a particular set of learning experiences.

- All new learning involves transfer based on previous learning, and this fact has important implications for the design of instruction that helps students learn. (p. 53)

Each of these points is worthy of further discussion, with the first sounding a cautionary bell. The evidence suggests that when students learn how to apply a skill only within a very specific context or in a single, narrowly defined space, they are less likely to apply it in a novel situation. For example, students who rely on rote memorization of an isolated list of vocabulary terms are unlikely to understand those words or phrases when encountered in texts. On the other hand, tasks that require students to utilize new information across a broader platform are more likely to activate their knowledge more effectively and accurately. That's why effective vocabulary instruction includes textual experiences ripe with opportunities for students to resolve unknown vocabulary using structural analysis, context clues, and resources (Fisher & Frey, 2008).

Transfer relies on a dynamic process "that requires learners to actively choose and evaluate strategies, consider resources, and receive feedback" (Bransford, Brown, & Cocking, 2000, p. 66). Learners need the space, opportunity, and time to interact with texts, concepts, and one another in order not only to create products that reflect their knowledge of the content presented, but also to demonstrate how they have transformed that knowledge by making it their own. Examples of these dynamic processes include continued interactions with the teacher through conferring, productive small group work with peers, investigation and research, writing, and other meaningful formative and summative assessment practices.

Previous learning plays an essential role in the transfer of knowledge, and all learners can and should apply their background knowledge and prior experiences judiciously in the creation of new knowledge. The caution about the role of personal meaning-making in close reading practices has been a point of contention among scholars and practitioners. We have heard caring educators express concern about their abilities to engage and motivate students in the absence of discussion about

> Previous learning plays an essential role in the transfer of knowledge, and all learners can and should apply their background knowledge and prior experiences judiciously in the creation of new knowledge.

WHAT DOES THE TEXT *INSPIRE YOU TO DO?*

personal connections. Likewise, we have heard equally caring educators express their concerns about privileging the personal experiences of some students at the expense of others. We believe that both camps make important points. Previous learning, both in and out of school, is an essential element in the process of transfer, as it is the means we all use to deepen new knowledge. At the same time, we must be more aware that tasks that move students too far away from the texts at hand create an unequal playing field, with some able to draw on a deeper well of personal experiences that others do not possess. Therefore, task design is essential, and should strike a balance between utilizing the information gleaned from the text and the accompanying discussions with a further opportunity to create new knowledge.

This is a point at which students can meet levels 3 and 4 of the Depth of Knowledge task demands (Webb, 2002). In this phase of learning, students analyze arguments to note what is missing or incomplete, or what warrants further investigation. They construct their own arguments using logic and reasoning, and they formulate a plan of action for next steps in their learning. The learning happens over an extended period of time, especially in terms of the preparation needed to write an essay, design a presentation, conduct an investigation, or compile research for use in a debate. Importantly, completion of these tasks does not *automatically* serve as evidence of a greater depth of knowledge. For instance, a presentation could just as easily entail the replication and recall of knowledge. For that reason, the construction of the task is vital.

> Completion of these tasks does not *automatically* serve as evidence of a greater depth of knowledge. A presentation could just as easily entail simple replication and recall. So, the construction of the task is vital.

Monique Owen's sixth grade English students read and discussed *The Circuit* (Jiménez, 1999) over two weeks. Close reading lessons were interspersed with independent reading outside of school and peer-led inquiry circles in the classroom (Daniels & Harvey, 2009). During their small group work meetings throughout the unit, students annotated text, developed their notebooks, and, at the conclusion, formulated a question for inquiry. One group decided to engage in a mini-inquiry on the status of current migrant students in their state, while another group investigated policies for supporting these students. Meanwhile, a third group of students decided they would interview two adults in their school who had been migrant workers as children and had made themselves available to Ms. Owen to serve as community resources. A fourth group wanted to follow up on the author's adult life, since the collection of short stories is autobiographical. The students spent two days compiling the research needed for their mini-inquiry and a third day developing a final product for a gallery walk.

On the fourth day, groups shared their findings and were able to explore the findings of their peers. These short informal sessions, conducted as part of the gallery walk, included a table developed by the first group showing current numbers of migrant children enrolled in public schools displayed by county and grade level. The second group wrote a one-page FAQ (frequently asked questions) document on supports for these students, including tips for accessing the district- and state-level department resources dedicated to the education of migrant children, while the third group created short audio excerpts of recorded interviews with the two school employees and played them for the class. The fourth group gathered information from the publisher's website and the author's own at Santa Clara University, where he is a professor. Ms. Owen was pleased with the outcomes.

"I want to foster a relentless need to question and wonder in my classroom, and then provide the space to do so. I want them to see that good books leave us wanting more and wondering more, and that we can and should act on these instincts," she said. "I don't need long formal presentations all the time. I want them to get comfortable standing up in front of their peers and saying, 'Here's what we wondered, and here's what we found out.' It's the basis for every meaningful intellectual interaction I've ever had," she said.

A student gives a short presentation in which she explains what her group discovered.

How Examining *What the Text Inspires You to Do* Addresses the STANDARDS

Reading Standards

The targeted standards in this group fall squarely under the cluster of integration of knowledge and ideas. As discussed in the previous chapter, **standards 7** and **9** speak to the need to contextualize readings across authors, media platforms, themes, and perspectives. **Standard 8** calls for a more specialized text that provides a springboard for examining formal argumentation and reasoning. Not all texts do so; you'll notice that this standard is not listed with literary texts, but only with informational ones. A table displaying the English language arts reading standards that focus on how texts inspire action can be found in Figure 5.1.

In the history/social studies version of **standard 8**, students examine primary and secondary sources to separate fact from opinion and to determine

Figure 5.1 ELA Reading Standards That Focus on *What the Text Inspires You to Do*

Standard (Grade)	Literary	Informational
7 (6)	Compare and contrast the experience of reading a story, drama, or poem to listening to or viewing an audio, video, or live version of the text, including contrasting what they "see" and "hear" when reading the text to what they perceive when they listen or watch.	Integrate information presented in different media or formats (e.g., visually, quantitatively) as well as in words to develop a coherent understanding of a topic or issue.
7 (7)	Compare and contrast a written story, drama, or poem to its audio, filmed, staged, or multimedia version, analyzing the effects of techniques unique to each medium (e.g., lighting, sound, color, or camera focus and angles in a film).	Compare and contrast a text to an audio, video, or multimedia version of the text, analyzing each medium's portrayal of the subject (e.g., how the delivery of a speech affects the impact of the words).
7 (8)	Analyze the extent to which a filmed or live production of a story or drama stays faithful to or departs from the text or script, evaluating the choices made by the director or actors.	Evaluate the advantages and disadvantages of using different mediums (e.g., print or digital text, video, multimedia) to present a particular topic or idea.
7 (9–10)	Analyze the representation of a subject or a key scene in two different artistic mediums, including what is emphasized or absent in each treatment (e.g., Auden's "Musée des Beaux Arts" and Breughel's Landscape with the Fall of Icarus).	Analyze various accounts of a subject told in different mediums (e.g., a person's life story in both print and multimedia), determining which details are emphasized in each account.

(Continued)

Figure 5.1 (Continued)

Standard (Grade)	Literary	Informational
7 (11–12)	Analyze multiple interpretations of a story, drama, or poem (e.g., recorded or live production of a play or recorded novel or poetry), evaluating how each version interprets the source text. (Include at least one play by Shakespeare and one play by an American dramatist.)	Integrate and evaluate multiple sources of information presented in different media or formats (e.g., visually, quantitatively) as well as in words in order to address a question or solve a problem.
8 (6)	(Not applicable to literature)	Trace and evaluate the argument and specific claims in a text, distinguishing claims that are supported by reasons and evidence from claims that are not.
8 (7)	(Not applicable to literature)	Trace and evaluate the argument and specific claims in a text, assessing whether the reasoning is sound and the evidence is relevant and sufficient to support the claims.
8 (8)	(Not applicable to literature)	Delineate and evaluate the argument and specific claims in a text, assessing whether the reasoning is sound and the evidence is relevant and sufficient; recognize when irrelevant evidence is introduced.
8 (9–10)	(Not applicable to literature)	Delineate and evaluate the argument and specific claims in a text, assessing whether the reasoning is valid and the evidence is relevant and sufficient; identify false statements and fallacious reasoning.
8 (11–12)	(Not applicable to literature)	Delineate and evaluate the reasoning in seminal U.S. texts, including the application of constitutional principles and use of legal reasoning (e.g., in U.S. Supreme Court majority opinions and dissents) and the premises, purposes, and arguments in works of public advocacy (e.g., The Federalist, presidential addresses).
9 (6)	Compare and contrast texts in different forms or genres (e.g., stories and poems; historical novels and fantasy stories) in terms of their approaches to similar themes and topics.	Compare and contrast one author's presentation of events with that of another (e.g., a memoir written by and a biography on the same person).
9 (7)	Compare and contrast a fictional portrayal of a time, place, or character and a historical account of the same period as a means of understanding how authors of fiction use or alter history.	Analyze how two or more authors writing about the same topic shape their presentations of key information by emphasizing different evidence or advancing different interpretations of facts.
9 (8)	Analyze how a modern work of fiction draws on themes, patterns of events, or character types from myths, traditional stories, or religious works such as the Bible, including describing how the material is rendered new.	Analyze a case in which two or more texts provide conflicting information on the same topic and identify where the texts disagree on matters of fact or interpretation.

Standard (Grade)	Literary	Informational
9 (9–10)	Analyze how an author draws on and transforms source material in a specific work (e.g., how Shakespeare treats a theme or topic from Ovid or the Bible or how a later author draws on a play by Shakespeare).	Analyze seminal U.S. documents of historical and literary significance (e.g., Washington's Farewell Address, the Gettysburg Address, Roosevelt's Four Freedoms speech, King's "Letter from Birmingham Jail"), including how they address related themes and concepts.
9 (11–12)	Demonstrate knowledge of eighteenth-, nineteenth- and early-twentieth-century foundational works of American literature, including how two or more texts from the same period treat similar themes or topics.	Analyze seventeenth-, eighteenth-, and nineteenth-century foundational U.S. documents of historical and literary significance (including The Declaration of Independence, the Preamble to the Constitution, the Bill of Rights, and Lincoln's Second Inaugural Address) for their themes, purposes, and rhetorical features.
10 (6)	By the end of the year, read and comprehend literature, including stories, dramas, and poems, in the grades 6–8 text complexity band proficiently, with scaffolding as needed at the high end of the range.	By the end of the year, read and comprehend literary nonfiction in the grades 6–8 text complexity band proficiently, with scaffolding as needed at the high end of the range.
10 (7)	By the end of the year, read and comprehend literature, including stories, dramas, and poems, in the grades 6–8 text complexity band proficiently, with scaffolding as needed at the high end of the range.	By the end of the year, read and comprehend literary nonfiction in the grades 6–8 text complexity band proficiently, with scaffolding as needed at the high end of the range.
10 (8)	By the end of the year, read and comprehend literature, including stories, dramas, and poems, at the high end of grades 6–8 text complexity band independently and proficiently.	By the end of the year, read and comprehend literary nonfiction at the high end of the grades 6–8 text complexity band independently and proficiently.
10 (9–10)	By the end of grade 9, read and comprehend literature, including stories, dramas, and poems, in the grades 9–10 text complexity band proficiently, with scaffolding as needed at the high end of the range. By the end of grade 10, read and comprehend literature, including stories, dramas, and poems, at the high end of the grades 9–10 text complexity band independently and proficiently.	By the end of grade 9, read and comprehend literary nonfiction in the grades 9–10 text complexity band proficiently, with scaffolding as needed at the high end of the range. By the end of grade 10, read and comprehend literary nonfiction at the high end of the grades 9–10 text complexity band independently and proficiently.
10 (11–12)	By the end of grade 11, read and comprehend literature, including stories, dramas, and poems, in the grades 11–CCR text complexity band proficiently, with scaffolding as needed at the high end of the range. By the end of grade 12, read and comprehend literature, including stories, dramas, and poems, at the high end of the grades 11–CCR text complexity band independently and proficiently.	By the end of grade 11, read and comprehend literary nonfiction in the grades 11–CCR text complexity band proficiently, with scaffolding as needed at the high end of the range. By the end of grade 12, read and comprehend literary nonfiction at the high end of the grades 11–CCR text complexity band independently and proficiently.

Figure 5.2 History, Science, and Technical Subjects Reading Standards That Focus on *What the Text Inspires You to Do*

Standard (Grade band)	History/Social Studies	Sciences and Technical Subjects
7 (6–8)	Integrate visual information (e.g., in charts, graphs, photographs, videos, or maps) with other information in print and digital texts.	Integrate quantitative or technical information expressed in words in a text with a version of that information expressed visually (e.g., in a flowchart, diagram, model, graph, or table).
7 (9–10)	Integrate quantitative or technical analysis (e.g., charts, research data) with qualitative analysis in print or digital text.	Translate quantitative or technical information expressed in words in a text into visual form (e.g., a table or chart) and translate information expressed visually or mathematically (e.g., in an equation) into words.
7 (11–12)	Integrate and evaluate multiple sources of information presented in diverse formats and media (e.g., visually, quantitatively, as well as in words) in order to address a question or solve a problem.	Integrate and evaluate multiple sources of information presented in diverse formats and media (e.g., quantitative data, video, multimedia) in order to address a question or solve a problem.
8 (6–8)	Distinguish among fact, opinion, and reasoned judgment in a text.	Distinguish among facts, reasoned judgment based on research findings, and speculation in a text.
8 (9–10)	Assess the extent to which the reasoning and evidence in a text support the author's claims.	Assess the extent to which the reasoning and evidence in a text support the author's claim or a recommendation for solving a scientific or technical problem.
8 (11–12)	Evaluate an author's premises, claims, and evidence by corroborating or challenging them with other information.	Evaluate the hypotheses, data, analysis, and conclusions in a science or technical text, verifying the data when possible and corroborating or challenging conclusions with other sources of information.
9 (6–8)	Analyze the relationship between a primary and secondary source on the same topic.	Compare and contrast the information gained from experiments, simulations, video, or multimedia sources with that gained from reading a text on the same topic.
9 (9–10)	Compare and contrast treatments of the same topic in several primary and secondary sources.	Compare and contrast findings presented in a text to those from other sources (including their own experiments), noting when the findings support or contradict previous explanations or accounts.
9 (11–12)	Integrate information from diverse sources, both primary and secondary, into a coherent understanding of an idea or event, noting discrepancies among sources.	Synthesize information from a range of sources (e.g., texts, experiments, simulations) into a coherent understanding of a process, phenomenon, or concept, resolving conflicting information when possible.
10 (6–8)	By the end of grade 8, read and comprehend history/social studies texts in the grades 6–8 text complexity band independently and proficiently.	By the end of grade 8, read and comprehend science/technical texts in the grades 6–8 text complexity band independently and proficiently.

Standard (Grade band)	History/Social Studies	Sciences and Technical Subjects
10 (9–10)	By the end of grade 10, read and comprehend history/social studies texts in the grades 9–10 text complexity band independently and proficiently.	By the end of grade 10, read and comprehend science/technical texts in the grades 9–10 text complexity band independently and proficiently.
10 (11–12)	By the end of grade 12, read and comprehend history/social studies texts in the grades 11–CCR text complexity band independently and proficiently.	By the end of grade 12, read and comprehend science/technical texts in the grades 11–CCR text complexity band independently and proficiently.

the extent to which an author has provided sufficient evidence, especially by citing source materials, contextualizing events within a historical time period, and seeking corroboration. In science and technical subjects, readers examine the use of inductive and deductive reasoning, and corroboration with data, to determine whether the conclusions are reasonable or should be challenged. Among the six texts profiled in this book, only the FDR speech in US history and the excerpt from Darwin's *Origin of the Species* possess the characteristics necessary for such analysis. In the case of the FDR speech, the text can be examined for its use of persuasive techniques and rhetorical structures, as described in Chapter 3, as well as for the way in which it identifies problems and proposes solutions that do not contain much in the way of detail. Students examining the arguments set forth by Darwin could compare his assertions with those of the Great Chain of Being philosophy of ancient times, which relied on a hierarchical structure of the universe that placed God at the top and descended through spiritual beings, humans, animals, plants, and minerals (Lovejoy, 1936). A table of standards for the disciplines on the ways a text inspires action can be located in Figure 5.2.

Language Standards

The language standards regarding conventions in speaking and writing continue in importance as students respond to tasks that ask them to create products (see Figure 5.3). **Standard 3** is worth noting in this context, because with this standard, the issues of language function and style take center stage. Each of the tasks profiled in this chapter (presentation, debate, writing, Socratic seminar, investigation, and research) demands an understanding of these issues. While some of these tasks may require students to utilize face-to-face interaction, others may use the printed word as the platform. These take on further dimension as students must consider whether the function is to explain and inform, persuade, or convey an experience. Finally, the composition of the audience must be considered. Working on extemporaneous and prepared speeches, presentations, and debates, as well as on more formal writing provides students with opportunities to consider audience as a key factor in their design. Students must ask themselves, *Is my audience my fellow classmates, or someone who doesn't know me?*

Eleventh grade English teacher Jorge Cuellar requires that students write a formal literary critique for each novel they read, and then post a parallel one on the school's learning management system for use by other students.

Figure 5.3 Language Standards That Focus on *What the Text Inspires You to Do*

	Grade 6	Grade 7	Grade 8	Grades 9–10	Grades 11–12
1	Demonstrate command of the conventions of standard English grammar and usage when writing or speaking.	Demonstrate command of the conventions of standard English grammar and usage when writing or speaking.	Demonstrate command of the conventions of standard English grammar and usage when writing or speaking.	Demonstrate command of the conventions of standard English grammar and usage when writing or speaking.	Demonstrate command of the conventions of standard English grammar and usage when writing or speaking.
	a. Ensure that pronouns are in the proper case (subjective, objective, possessive).	a. Explain the function of phrases and clauses in general and their function in specific sentences.	a. Explain the function of verbals (gerunds, participles, infinitives) in general and their function in particular sentences.	a. Use parallel structure.	a. Apply the understanding that usage is a matter of convention, can change over time, and is sometimes contested.
	b. Use intensive pronouns (e.g., myself, ourselves).	b. Choose among simple, compound, complex, and compound-complex sentences to signal differing relationships among ideas.	b. Form and use verbs in the active and passive voice.	b. Use various types of phrases (noun, verb, adjectival, adverbial, participial, prepositional, absolute) and clauses (independent, dependent; noun, relative, adverbial) to convey specific meanings and add variety and interest to writing or presentations.	b. Resolve issues of complex or contested usage, consulting references (e.g., Merriam-Webster's Dictionary of English Usage, Garner's Modern American Usage) as needed.
	c. Recognize and correct inappropriate shifts in pronoun number and person.	c. Place phrases and clauses within a sentence, recognizing and correcting misplaced and dangling modifiers.	c. Form and use verbs in the indicative, imperative, interrogative, conditional, and subjunctive mood.		
	d. Recognize and correct vague pronouns (i.e., ones with unclear or ambiguous antecedents).		d. Recognize and correct inappropriate shifts in verb voice and mood.		
	e. Recognize variations from standard English in their own and others' writing and speaking, and identify and use strategies to improve expression in conventional language.				
2	Demonstrate command of the conventions of standard English capitalization, punctuation, and spelling when writing.	Demonstrate command of the conventions of standard English capitalization, punctuation, and spelling when writing.	Demonstrate command of the conventions of standard English capitalization, punctuation, and spelling when writing.	Demonstrate command of the conventions of standard English capitalization, punctuation, and spelling when writing.	Demonstrate command of the conventions of standard English capitalization, punctuation, and spelling when writing.

	Grade 6	Grade 7	Grade 8	Grades 9–10	Grades 11–12
	a. Use punctuation (commas, parentheses, dashes) to set off nonrestrictive or parenthetical elements. b. Spell correctly.	a. Use a comma to separate coordinate adjectives (e.g., It was a fascinating, enjoyable movie but not He wore an old[,] green shirt). b. Spell correctly.	a. Use punctuation (comma, ellipsis, dash) to indicate a pause or break. b. Use an ellipsis to indicate an omission. c. Spell correctly.	a. Use a semicolon (and perhaps a conjunctive adverb) to link two or more closely related independent clauses. b. Use a colon to introduce a list or quotation. c. Spell correctly.	a. Observe hyphenation conventions. b. Spell correctly.
3	Use knowledge of language and its conventions when writing, speaking, reading, or listening. a. Vary sentence patterns for meaning, reader/listener interest, and style. b. Maintain consistency in style and tone.	Use knowledge of language and its conventions when writing, speaking, reading, or listening. a. Choose language that expresses ideas precisely and concisely, recognizing and eliminating wordiness and redundancy.	Use knowledge of language and its conventions when writing, speaking, reading, or listening. a. Use verbs in the active and passive voice and in the conditional and subjunctive mood to achieve particular effects (e.g., emphasizing the actor or the action; expressing uncertainty or describing a state contrary to fact).	Apply knowledge of language to understand how language functions in different contexts, to make effective choices for meaning or style, and to comprehend more fully when reading or listening.	Apply knowledge of language to understand how language functions in different contexts, to make effective choices for meaning or style, and to comprehend more fully when reading or listening.
6	Acquire and use accurately grade-appropriate general academic and domain specific words and phrases; gather vocabulary knowledge when considering a word or phrase important to comprehension or expression.		Acquire and use accurately general academic and domain-specific words and phrases, sufficient for reading, writing, speaking, and listening at the college and career readiness level; demonstrate independence in gathering vocabulary knowledge when considering a word or phrase important to comprehension or expression.		

"The literacy criticism papers are pretty traditional, I guess. By traditional, I mean that they follow a pattern similar to those I did in college, like a comparative literary criticism, one that uses historical criticism, another that uses critical race theory, and a fourth that relies on feminist theory," he explained. "But they also need to be able to talk about books in more friendly terms."

Mr. Cuellar has his students post "customer-friendly" reviews of books to the school's library web resources so that other students can read them.

"They can't just upload their paper," he said. "They have to condense it to 100–150 words or so but still give the book a review using one of these lenses." He adds that while they don't need to name their theoretical lens, "the voice should come though. I want them to see that these perspectives come from somewhere and don't just come out of thin air."

Speaking and Listening Standards

The speaking and listening standards, essential throughout text-based discussion, remain on center stage at this phase of instruction (see Figure 5.4). **Standard 5** in speaking and listening appears for the first time, as it addresses the need for students to make presentations that include multimedia and visual displays of information. This standard acknowledges the growing importance of visual literacy in contemporary life (e.g., Eisner, 1991). Each of the other tasks draws, to a lesser or more significant degree, on the remaining speaking and listening standards.

Writing Standards

Because this phase of instruction is action-based, writing makes its first appearance in this chapter. We know that spontaneous writing, annotation, and note taking occur through the previous phases, but we chose to spotlight these standards more formally here, because most of them speak to the qualities of finished products. **Standards 1–3** concern themselves with text types, specifically those constructed to (1) present formal argument and reasoning, (2) explain or inform, and (3) convey real and imagined experiences. These text types should not be confused with different forms of texts, which include essays, journalistic articles, research papers, lab reports, memos, and critiques. Some of these products use two or three of the text types. For example, a journalistic article may include an opening scenario (narrative text type) followed by factual information (explanatory/informational text type) and concluding with a persuasive section on the next steps a reader can take and a rationale for doing so (argumentation text type). The use of these text types varies according to the form, but all three require the use of a strong organizational structure using a cohesive technique such that ideas, concepts, events, and rationales flow in a way that readers can understand them.

Paralleling the research standards in the reading domain, **standards 7, 8, and 9** concern themselves with students' ability to formulate and complete short (middle school) and sustained (high school) research projects. The research sources should include those that represent a breadth and depth of print, digital, and multimedia texts and that rely on evidence from those sources to support claims and concepts presented in their writing. A table detailing the English writing standards is located in Figure 5.5.

Figure 5.4 Speaking and Listening Standards That Focus on *What the Text Inspires You to Do*

	Grade 6	Grade 7	Grade 8	Grades 9–10	Grades 11–12
1	Engage effectively in a range of collaborative discussions (one-on-one, in groups, and teacher-led) with diverse partners on grade 6 topics, texts, and issues, building on others' ideas and expressing their own clearly.	Engage effectively in a range of collaborative discussions (one-on-one, in groups, and teacher-led) with diverse partners on grade 7 topics, texts, and issues, building on others' ideas and expressing their own clearly.	Engage effectively in a range of collaborative discussions (one-on-one, in groups, and teacher-led) with diverse partners on grade 8 topics, texts, and issues, building on others' ideas and expressing their own clearly.	Initiate and participate effectively in a range of collaborative discussions (one-on-one, in groups, and teacher-led) with diverse partners on grades 9–10 topics, texts, and issues, building on others' ideas and expressing their own clearly and persuasively.	Initiate and participate effectively in a range of collaborative discussions (one-on-one, in groups, and teacher-led) with diverse partners on grades 11–12 topics, texts, and issues, building on others' ideas and expressing their own clearly and persuasively.
	a. Come to discussions prepared, having read or studied required material; explicitly draw on that preparation by referring to evidence on the topic, text, or issue to probe and reflect on ideas under discussion.	a. Come to discussions prepared, having read or researched material under study; explicitly draw on that preparation by referring to evidence on the topic, text, or issue to probe and reflect on ideas under discussion.	a. Come to discussions prepared, having read or researched material under study; explicitly draw on that preparation by referring to evidence on the topic, text, or issue to probe and reflect on ideas under discussion.	a. Come to discussions prepared, having read and researched material under study; explicitly draw on that preparation by referring to evidence from texts and other research on the topic or issue to stimulate a thoughtful, well-reasoned exchange of ideas.	a. Come to discussions prepared, having read and researched material under study; explicitly draw on that preparation by referring to evidence from texts and other research on the topic or issue to stimulate a thoughtful, well-reasoned exchange of ideas.
	b. Follow rules for collegial discussions, set specific goals and deadlines, and define individual roles as needed.	b. Follow rules for collegial discussions, track progress toward specific goals and deadlines, and define individual roles as needed.	b. Follow rules for collegial discussions and decision-making, track progress toward specific goals and deadlines, and define individual roles as needed.	b. Work with peers to set rules for collegial discussions and decision-making (e.g., informal consensus, taking votes on key issues, presentation of alternate views), clear goals and deadlines, and individual roles as needed.	b. Work with peers to promote civil, democratic discussions and decision-making, set clear goals and deadlines, and establish individual roles as needed.
	c. Pose and respond to specific questions with elaboration and detail by making comments that contribute to the topic, text, or issue under discussion.	c. Pose questions that elicit elaboration and respond to others' questions and comments	c. Pose questions that connect the ideas of several speakers and respond to		

(Continued)

Figure 5.4 (Continued)

	Grade 6	Grade 7	Grade 8	Grades 9–10	Grades 11–12
	d. Review the key ideas expressed and demonstrate understanding of multiple perspectives through reflection and paraphrasing.	with relevant observations and ideas that bring the discussion back on topic as needed. d. Acknowledge new information expressed by others and, when warranted, modify their own views.	others' questions and comments with relevant evidence, observations, and ideas. d. Acknowledge new information expressed by others, and, when warranted, qualify or justify their own views in light of the evidence presented.	c. Propel conversations by posing and responding to questions that relate the current discussion to broader themes or larger ideas; actively incorporate others into the discussion; and clarify, verify, or challenge ideas and conclusions. d. Respond thoughtfully to diverse perspectives, summarize points of agreement and disagreement, and, when warranted, qualify or justify their own views and understanding and make new connections in light of the evidence and reasoning presented.	c. Propel conversations by posing and responding to questions that probe reasoning and evidence; ensure a hearing for a full range of positions on a topic or issue; clarify, verify, or challenge ideas and conclusions; and promote divergent and creative perspectives. d. Respond thoughtfully to diverse perspectives; synthesize comments, claims, and evidence made on all sides of an issue; resolve contradictions when possible; and determine what additional information or research is required to deepen the investigation or complete the task.
2	Interpret information presented in diverse media and formats (e.g., visually, quantitatively, orally) and explain how it contributes to a topic, text, or issue under study.	Analyze the main ideas and supporting details presented in diverse media and formats (e.g., visually, quantitatively, orally) and explain how the ideas clarify a topic, text, or issue under study.	Analyze the purpose of information presented in diverse media and formats (e.g., visually, quantitatively, orally) and evaluate the motives (e.g., social, commercial, political) behind its presentation.	Integrate multiple sources of information presented in diverse media or formats (e.g., visually, quantitatively, orally), evaluating the credibility and accuracy of each source.	Integrate multiple sources of information presented in diverse formats and media (e.g., visually, quantitatively, orally) in order to make informed decisions and solve problems, evaluating the credibility and accuracy of each source and noting any discrepancies among the data.

	Grade 6	Grade 7	Grade 8	Grades 9–10	Grades 11–12
3	Delineate a speaker's argument and specific claims, distinguishing claims that are supported by reasons and evidence from claims that are not.	Delineate a speaker's argument and specific claims, evaluating the soundness of the reasoning and the relevance and sufficiency of the evidence.	Delineate a speaker's argument and specific claims, evaluating the soundness of the reasoning and relevance and sufficiency of the evidence and identifying when irrelevant evidence is introduced.	Evaluate a speaker's point of view, reasoning, and use of evidence and rhetoric, identifying any fallacious reasoning or exaggerated or distorted evidence.	Evaluate a speaker's point of view, reasoning, and use of evidence and rhetoric, assessing the stance, premises, links among ideas, word choice, points of emphasis, and tone used.
4	Present claims and findings, sequencing ideas logically and using pertinent descriptions, facts, and details to accentuate main ideas or themes; use appropriate eye contact, adequate volume, and clear pronunciation.	Present claims and findings, emphasizing salient points in a focused, coherent manner with pertinent descriptions, facts, details, and examples; use appropriate eye contact, adequate volume, and clear pronunciation.	Present claims and findings, emphasizing salient points in a focused, coherent manner with relevant evidence, sound valid reasoning, and well-chosen details; use appropriate eye contact, adequate volume, and clear pronunciation.	Present information, findings, and supporting evidence clearly, concisely, and logically such that listeners can follow the line of reasoning and the organization, development, substance, and style are appropriate to purpose, audience, and task.	Present information, findings, and supporting evidence, conveying a clear and distinct perspective, such that listeners can follow the line of reasoning, alternative or opposing perspectives are addressed, and the organization, development, substance, and style are appropriate to purpose, audience, and a range of formal and informal tasks.
5	Include multimedia components (e.g., graphics, images, music, sound) and visual displays in presentations to clarify information.	Include multimedia components and visual displays in presentations to clarify claims and findings and emphasize salient points.	Integrate multimedia and visual displays into presentations to clarify information, strengthen claims and evidence, and add interest.	Make strategic use of digital media (e.g., textual, graphical, audio, visual, and interactive elements) in presentations to enhance understanding of findings, reasoning, and evidence and to add interest.	Make strategic use of digital media (e.g., textual, graphical, audio, visual, and interactive elements) in presentations to enhance understanding of findings, reasoning, and evidence and to add interest.
6	Adapt speech to a variety of contexts and tasks, demonstrating command of formal English when indicated or appropriate.	Adapt speech to a variety of contexts and tasks, demonstrating command of formal English when indicated or appropriate.			

Figure 5.5 ELA Writing Standards That Focus on *What the Text Inspires You to Do*

	Grade 6	Grade 7	Grade 8	Grades 9–10	Grades 11–12
1	Write arguments to support claims with clear reasons and relevant evidence. a. Introduce claim(s) and organize the reasons and evidence clearly. b. Support claim(s) with clear reasons and relevant evidence, using credible sources and demonstrating an understanding of the topic or text. c. Use words, phrases, and clauses to clarify the relationships among claim(s) and reasons. d. Establish and maintain a formal style.	Write arguments to support claims with clear reasons and relevant evidence. a. Introduce claim(s), acknowledge alternate or opposing claims, and organize the reasons and evidence logically. b. Support claim(s) with logical reasoning and relevant evidence, using accurate, credible sources and demonstrating an understanding of the topic or text. c. Use words, phrases, and clauses to create cohesion and clarify the relationships among claim(s), reasons, and evidence.	Write arguments to support claims with clear reasons and relevant evidence. a. Introduce claim(s), acknowledge and distinguish the claim(s) from alternate or opposing claims, and organize the reasons and evidence logically. b. Support claim(s) with logical reasoning and relevant evidence, using accurate, credible sources and demonstrating an understanding of the topic or text. c. Use words, phrases, and clauses to create cohesion and clarify the relationships among claim(s), counterclaims, reasons, and evidence.	Write arguments to support claims in an analysis of substantive topics or texts, using valid reasoning and relevant and sufficient evidence. a. Introduce precise claim(s), distinguish the claim(s) from alternate or opposing claims, and create an organization that establishes clear relationships among claim(s), counterclaims, reasons, and evidence. b. Develop claim(s) and counterclaims fairly, supplying evidence for each while pointing out the strengths and limitations of both in a manner that anticipates the audience's knowledge level and concerns.	Write arguments to support claims in an analysis of substantive topics or texts, using valid reasoning and relevant and sufficient evidence. a. Introduce precise, knowledgeable claim(s), establish the significance of the claim(s), distinguish the claim(s) from alternate or opposing claims, and create an organization that logically sequences claim(s), counterclaims, reasons, and evidence. b. Develop claim(s) and counterclaims fairly and thoroughly, supplying the most relevant evidence for each while pointing out the strengths and limitations of both in a manner that anticipates the audience's knowledge level, concerns, values, and possible biases.

Grade 6	Grade 7	Grade 8	Grades 9–10	Grades 11–12
e. Provide a concluding statement or section that follows from the argument presented.	d. Establish and maintain a formal style. e. Provide a concluding statement or section that follows from and supports the argument presented.	d. Establish and maintain a formal style. e. Provide a concluding statement or section that follows from and supports the argument presented.	c. Use words, phrases, and clauses to link the major sections of the text, create cohesion, and clarify the relationships between claim(s) and reasons, between reasons and evidence, and between claim(s) and counterclaims. d. Establish and maintain a formal style and objective tone while attending to the norms and conventions of the discipline in which they are writing. e. Provide a concluding statement or section that follows from and supports the argument presented.	c. Use words, phrases, and clauses as well as varied syntax to link the major sections of the text, create cohesion, and clarify the relationships between claim(s) and reasons, between reasons and evidence, and between claim(s) and counterclaims. d. Establish and maintain a formal style and objective tone while attending to the norms and conventions of the discipline in which they are writing. e. Provide a concluding statement or section that follows from and supports the argument presented.
2 Write informative/explanatory texts to examine a topic and convey ideas, concepts, and information through the selection, organization, and analysis of relevant content.	Write informative/explanatory texts to examine a topic and convey ideas, concepts, and information through the selection, organization, and analysis of relevant content.	Write informative/explanatory texts to examine a topic and convey ideas, concepts, and information through the selection, organization, and analysis of relevant content.	Write informative/explanatory texts to examine and convey complex ideas, concepts, and information clearly and accurately through the effective selection, organization, and analysis of content.	Write informative/explanatory texts to examine and convey complex ideas, concepts, and information clearly and accurately through the effective selection, organization, and analysis of content.

(Continued)

Figure 5.5 (Continued)

Grade 6	Grade 7	Grade 8	Grades 9–10	Grades 11–12
a. Introduce a topic; organize ideas, concepts, and information, using strategies such as definition, classification, comparison/contrast, and cause/effect; include formatting (e.g., headings), graphics (e.g., charts, tables), and multimedia when useful to aiding comprehension.	a. Introduce a topic clearly, previewing what is to follow; organize ideas, concepts, and information, using strategies such as definition, classification, comparison/contrast, and cause/effect; include formatting (e.g., headings), graphics (e.g., charts, tables), and multimedia when useful to aiding comprehension.	a. Introduce a topic clearly, previewing what is to follow; organize ideas, concepts, and information into broader categories; include formatting (e.g., headings), graphics (e.g, charts, tables), and multimedia when useful to aiding comprehension.	a. Introduce a topic; organize complex ideas, concepts, and information to make important connections and distinctions; include formatting (e.g., headings), graphics (e.g., figures, tables), and multimedia when useful to aiding comprehension.	a. Introduce a topic; organize complex ideas, concepts, and information so that each new element builds on that which precedes it to create a unified whole; include formatting (e.g., headings), graphics (e.g., figures, tables), and multimedia when useful to aiding comprehension.
b. Develop the topic with relevant facts, definitions, concrete details, quotations, or other information and examples.	b. Develop the topic with relevant facts, definitions, concrete details, quotations, or other information and examples.	b. Develop the topic with relevant, well-chosen facts, definitions, concrete details, quotations, or other information and examples.	b. Develop the topic with well-chosen, relevant, and sufficient facts, extended definitions, concrete details, quotations, or other information and examples appropriate to the audience's knowledge of the topic.	b. Develop the topic thoroughly by selecting the most significant and relevant facts, extended definitions, concrete details, quotations, or other information and examples appropriate to the audience's knowledge of the topic.
c. Use appropriate transitions to clarify the relationships among ideas and concepts.	c. Use appropriate transitions to create cohesion and clarify the relationships among ideas and concepts.	c. Use appropriate and varied transitions to create cohesion and clarify the relationships among ideas and concepts.	c. Use appropriate and varied transitions to link the major sections of the text, create cohesion, and clarify the relationships among complex ideas and concepts.	c. Use appropriate and varied transitions and syntax to link the major sections of the text, create cohesion, and clarify the relationships among complex ideas and concepts.
d. Use precise language and domain-specific vocabulary to inform about or explain the topic.	d. Use precise language and domain-specific vocabulary to inform about or explain the topic.	d. Use precise language and domain-specific vocabulary to inform about or explain the topic.		
e. Establish and maintain a formal style.		e. Establish and maintain a formal style.		

	Grade 6	Grade 7	Grade 8	Grades 9–10	Grades 11–12
	f. Provide a concluding statement or section that follows from the information or explanation presented.	e. Establish and maintain a formal style. f. Provide a concluding statement or section that follows from and supports the information or explanation presented.	f. Provide a concluding statement or section that follows from and supports the information or explanation presented	d. Use precise language and domain-specific vocabulary to manage the complexity of the topic. e. Establish and maintain a formal style and objective tone while attending to the norms and conventions of the discipline in which they are writing. f. Provide a concluding statement or section that follows from and supports the information or explanation presented (e.g., articulating implications or the significance of the topic).	d. Use precise language, domain-specific vocabulary, and techniques such as metaphor, simile, and analogy to manage the complexity of the topic. e. Establish and maintain a formal style and objective tone while attending to the norms and conventions of the discipline in which they are writing. f. Provide a concluding statement or section that follows from and supports the information or explanation presented (e.g., articulating implications or the significance of the topic).
3	Write narratives to develop real or imagined experiences or events using effective technique, relevant descriptive details, and well-structured event sequences.	Write narratives to develop real or imagined experiences or events using effective technique, relevant descriptive details, and well-structured event sequences.	Write narratives to develop real or imagined experiences or events using effective technique, relevant descriptive details, and well-structured event sequences.	Write narratives to develop real or imagined experiences or events using effective technique, well-chosen details, and well-structured event sequences.	Write narratives to develop real or imagined experiences or events using effective technique, well-chosen details, and well-structured event sequences.

(Continued)

Figure 5.5 (Continued)

Grade 6	Grade 7	Grade 8	Grades 9–10	Grades 11–12
a. Engage and orient the reader by establishing a context and introducing a narrator and/or characters; organize an event sequence that unfolds naturally and logically.	a. Engage and orient the reader by establishing a context and point of view and introducing a narrator and/or characters; organize an event sequence that unfolds naturally and logically.	a. Engage and orient the reader by establishing a context and point of view and introducing a narrator and/or characters; organize an event sequence that unfolds naturally and logically.	a. Engage and orient the reader by setting out a problem, situation, or observation, establishing one or multiple point(s) of view, and introducing a narrator and/or characters; create a smooth progression of experiences or events.	a. Engage and orient the reader by setting out a problem, situation, or observation and its significance, establishing one or multiple point(s) of view, and introducing a narrator and/or characters; create a smooth progression of experiences or events.
b. Use narrative techniques, such as dialogue, pacing, and description, to develop experiences, events, and/or characters.	b. Use narrative techniques, such as dialogue, pacing, and description, to develop experiences, events, and/or characters.	b. Use narrative techniques, such as dialogue, pacing, description, and reflection, to develop experiences, events, and/or characters.	b. Use narrative techniques, such as dialogue, pacing, description, reflection, and multiple plot lines, to develop experiences, events, and/or characters.	b. Use narrative techniques, such as dialogue, pacing, description, reflection, and multiple plot lines, to develop experiences, events, and/or characters.
c. Use a variety of transition words, phrases, and clauses to convey sequence and signal shifts from one time frame or setting to another.	c. Use a variety of transition words, phrases, and clauses to convey sequence and signal shifts from one time frame or setting to another.	c. Use a variety of transition words, phrases, and clauses to convey sequence, signal shifts from one time frame or setting to another, and show the relationships among experiences and events.	c. Use a variety of techniques to sequence events so that they build on one another to create a coherent whole.	c. Use a variety of techniques to sequence events so that they build on one another to create a coherent whole and build toward a particular tone and outcome (e.g., a sense of mystery, suspense, growth, or resolution).
d. Use precise words and phrases, relevant descriptive details, and sensory language to convey experiences and events.	d. Use precise words and phrases, relevant descriptive details, and sensory language to capture the action and convey experiences and events.	d. Use precise words and phrases, relevant descriptive details, and sensory language to capture the action and convey experiences and events.	d. Use precise words and phrases, telling details, and sensory language to convey a vivid picture of the experiences, events, setting, and/or characters.	

Grade 6	Grade 7	Grade 8	Grades 9–10	Grades 11–12
e. Provide a conclusion that follows from the narrated experiences or events.	e. Provide a conclusion that follows from and reflects on the narrated experiences or events.	e. Provide a conclusion that follows from and reflects on the narrated experiences or events.	e. Provide a conclusion that follows from and reflects on what is experienced, observed, or resolved over the course of the narrative.	d. Use precise words and phrases, telling details, and sensory language to convey a vivid picture of the experiences, events, setting, and/or characters. e. Provide a conclusion that follows from and reflects on what is experienced, observed, or resolved over the course of the narrative.
7	Conduct short research projects to answer a question, drawing on several sources and refocusing the inquiry when appropriate.	Conduct short research projects to answer a question, drawing on several sources and generating additional related, focused questions for further research and investigation.	Conduct short research projects to answer a question (including a self-generated question), drawing on several sources and generating additional related, focused questions that allow for multiple avenues of exploration.	Conduct short as well as more sustained research projects to answer a question (including a self-generated question) or solve a problem; narrow or broaden the inquiry when appropriate; synthesize multiple sources on the subject, demonstrating understanding of the subject under investigation.	Conduct short as well as more sustained research projects to answer a question (including a self-generated question) or solve a problem; narrow or broaden the inquiry when appropriate; synthesize multiple sources on the subject, demonstrating understanding of the subject under investigation.

(Continued)

Figure 5.5 (Continued)

	Grade 6	Grade 7	Grade 8	Grades 9–10	Grades 11–12
8	Gather relevant information from multiple print and digital sources; assess the credibility of each source; and quote or paraphrase the data and conclusions of others while avoiding plagiarism and providing basic bibliographic information for sources.	Gather relevant information from multiple print and digital sources, using search terms effectively; assess the credibility and accuracy of each source; and quote or paraphrase the data and conclusions of others while avoiding plagiarism and following a standard format for citation.	Gather relevant information from multiple print and digital sources, using search terms effectively; assess the credibility and accuracy of each source; and quote or paraphrase the data and conclusions of others while avoiding plagiarism and following a standard format for citation.	Gather relevant information from multiple authoritative print and digital sources, using advanced searches effectively; assess the usefulness of each source in answering the research question; integrate information into the text selectively to maintain the flow of ideas, avoiding plagiarism and following a standard format for citation.	Gather relevant information from multiple authoritative print and digital sources, using advanced searches effectively; assess the strengths and limitations of each source in terms of the task, purpose, and audience; integrate information into the text selectively to maintain the flow of ideas, avoiding plagiarism and overreliance on any one source and following a standard format for citation.
9	Draw evidence from literary or informational texts to support analysis, reflection, and research. a. Apply grade 6 *Reading standards to literature* (e.g., "Compare and contrast texts in different forms or genres [e.g., stories and poems; historical novels and fantasy stories] in terms of their approaches to similar themes and topics").	Draw evidence from literary or informational texts to support analysis, reflection, and research. a. Apply grade 7 *Reading standards to literature* (e.g., "Compare and contrast a fictional portrayal of a time, place, or character and a historical account of the same period as a means of understanding how authors of fiction use or alter history").	Draw evidence from literary or informational texts to support analysis, reflection, and research. a. Apply grade 8 *Reading standards to literature* (e.g., "Analyze how a modern work of fiction draws on themes, patterns of events, or character types from myths, traditional stories, or religious works such as the Bible, including describing how the material is rendered new").	Draw evidence from literary or informational texts to support analysis, reflection, and research. a. Apply grades 9–10 *Reading standards to literature* (e.g., "Analyze how an author draws on and transforms source material in a specific work [e.g., how Shakespeare treats a theme or topic from Ovid or the Bible or how a later author draws on a play by Shakespeare]").	Draw evidence from literary or informational texts to support analysis, reflection, and research. a. Apply grades 11–12 *Reading standards to literature* (e.g., "Demonstrate knowledge of eighteenth-, nineteenth- and early-twentieth-century foundational works of American literature, including how two or more texts from the same period treat similar themes or topics").

Grade 6	Grade 7	Grade 8	Grades 9–10	Grades 11–12
b. Apply grade 6 *Reading standards* to literary nonfiction (e.g., "Trace and evaluate the argument and specific claims in a text, distinguishing claims that are supported by reasons and evidence from claims that are not").	b. Apply grade 7 *Reading standards* to literary nonfiction (e.g., "Trace and evaluate the argument and specific claims in a text, assessing whether the reasoning is sound and the evidence is relevant and sufficient to support the claims").	b. Apply grade 8 *Reading standards* to literary nonfiction (e.g., "Delineate and evaluate the argument and specific claims in a text, assessing whether the reasoning is sound and the evidence is relevant and sufficient; recognize when irrelevant evidence is introduced").	b. Apply grades 9–10 *Reading standards* to literary nonfiction (e.g., "Delineate and evaluate the argument and specific claims in a text, assessing whether the reasoning is valid and the evidence is relevant and sufficient; identify false statements and fallacious reasoning").	b. Apply grades 11–12 *Reading standards* to literary nonfiction (e.g., "Delineate and evaluate the reasoning in seminal U.S. texts, including the application of constitutional principles and use of legal reasoning [e.g., in U.S. Supreme Court Case majority opinions and dissents] and the premises, purposes, and arguments in works of public advocacy [e.g., *The Federalist*, presidential addresses]").

Unlike the discipline-specific reading standards that distinguish between history/social studies and science/technical subjects, there is a single set of writing standards for all of these subjects. A table containing these standards can be found in Figure 5.6. **Standards 1** and **2** describe writing for argumentation, as well as writing to inform and persuade, noting that these are focused on discipline-specific content. Although there is no specific standard for narrative text types, this note appears in the standards:

> Students' narrative skills continue to grow in these grades. The Standards require that students be able to incorporate narrative elements effectively into arguments and informative/explanatory texts. In history/social studies, students must be able to incorporate narrative accounts into their analyses of individuals or events of historical import. In science and technical subjects, students must be able to write precise enough descriptions of the step-by-step procedures they use in their investigations or technical work that others can replicate them and (possibly) reach the same results. (CCSSI, 2010a, p. 65)

Standards 7–9 similarly outline expectations for students to conduct short and sustained research in these subject areas, and to draw from a range of texts in both print and digital platforms.

Students in Alice Li's eighth grade science class used their knowledge of the periodic table of elements to conduct short research projects. Ms. Li was inspired by the BBC World Service Marketplace radio show's ongoing news feature on the economics of elements. Students selected one element from the table and investigated its uses, dangers, and role in the world economy.

"This is something I have students doing all throughout the year," Ms. Li said. "They write a paper addressing each of these factors, along with an infographic that reflects this information and shows the element's symbol, atomic weight, and atomic mass. Over the course of the year we replace the blocks on a standard periodic table with the infographics they have created. It brings the periodic table to life because they're the ones that create it."

Figure 5.6   History, Science, and Technical Subject Writing Standards That Focus on *What the Text Inspires You to Do*

Standard	Grade-Band Expectation
1 (6–8)	Write arguments focused on discipline-specific content. a. Introduce claim(s) about a topic or issue, acknowledge and distinguish the claim(s) from alternate or opposing claims, and organize the reasons and evidence logically. b. Support claim(s) with logical reasoning and relevant, accurate data and evidence that demonstrate an understanding of the topic or text, using credible sources. c. Use words, phrases, and clauses to create cohesion and clarify the relationships among claim(s), counterclaims, reasons, and evidence. d. Establish and maintain a formal style. e. Provide a concluding statement or section that follows from and supports the argument presented.

Standard	Grade-Band Expectation
1 **(9–10)**	Write arguments focused on discipline-specific content. a. Introduce precise claim(s), distinguish the claim(s) from alternate or opposing claims, and create an organization that establishes clear relationships among the claim(s), counterclaims, reasons, and evidence. b. Develop claim(s) and counterclaims fairly, supplying data and evidence for each while pointing out the strengths and limitations of both claim(s) and counterclaims in a discipline-appropriate form and in a manner that anticipates the audience's knowledge level and concerns. c. Use words, phrases, and clauses to link the major sections of the text, create cohesion, and clarify the relationships between claim(s) and reasons, between reasons and evidence, and between claim(s) and counterclaims. d. Establish and maintain a formal style and objective tone while attending to the norms and conventions of the discipline in which they are writing. e. Provide a concluding statement or section that follows from or supports the argument presented.
1 **(11–12)**	Write arguments focused on discipline-specific content. a. Introduce precise, knowledgeable claim(s), establish the significance of the claim(s), distinguish the claim(s) from alternate or opposing claims, and create an organization that logically sequences the claim(s), counterclaims, reasons, and evidence. b. Develop claim(s) and counterclaims fairly and thoroughly, supplying the most relevant data and evidence for each while pointing out the strengths and limitations of both claim(s) and counterclaims in a discipline-appropriate form that anticipates the audience's knowledge level, concerns, values, and possible biases. c. Use words, phrases, and clauses as well as varied syntax to link the major sections of the text, create cohesion, and clarify the relationships between claim(s) and reasons, between reasons and evidence, and between claim(s) and counterclaims. d. Establish and maintain a formal style and objective tone while attending to the norms and conventions of the discipline in which they are writing. e. Provide a concluding statement or section that follows from or supports the argument presented.
2 **(6–8)**	Write informative/explanatory texts, including the narration of historical events, scientific procedures/experiments, or technical processes. a. Introduce a topic clearly, previewing what is to follow; organize ideas, concepts, and information into broader categories as appropriate to achieving purpose; include formatting (e.g., headings), graphics (e.g., charts, tables), and multimedia when useful to aiding comprehension. b. Develop the topic with relevant, well-chosen facts, definitions, concrete details, quotations, or other information and examples. c. Use appropriate and varied transitions to create cohesion and clarify the relationships among ideas and concepts. d. Use precise language and domain-specific vocabulary to inform about or explain the topic. e. Establish and maintain a formal style and objective tone. f. Provide a concluding statement or section that follows from and supports the information or explanation presented.

(Continued)

Figure 5.6 (Continued)

Standard	Grade-Band Expectation
2 (9–10)	Write informative/explanatory texts, including the narration of historical events, scientific procedures/experiments, or technical processes. a. Introduce a topic and organize ideas, concepts, and information to make important connections and distinctions; include formatting (e.g., headings), graphics (e.g., figures, tables), and multimedia when useful to aiding comprehension. b. Develop the topic with well-chosen, relevant, and sufficient facts, extended definitions, concrete details, quotations, or other information and examples appropriate to the audience's knowledge of the topic. c. Use varied transitions and sentence structures to link the major sections of the text, create cohesion, and clarify the relationships among ideas and concepts. d. Use precise language and domain-specific vocabulary to manage the complexity of the topic and convey a style appropriate to the discipline and context as well as to the expertise of likely readers. e. Establish and maintain a formal style and objective tone while attending to the norms and conventions of the discipline in which they are writing. f. Provide a concluding statement or section that follows from and supports the information or explanation presented (e.g., articulating implications or the significance of the topic).
2 (11–12)	Write informative/explanatory texts, including the narration of historical events, scientific procedures/experiments, or technical processes. a. Introduce a topic and organize complex ideas, concepts, and information so that each new element builds on that which precedes it to create a unified whole; include formatting (e.g., headings), graphics (e.g., figures, tables), and multimedia when useful to aiding comprehension. b. Develop the topic thoroughly by selecting the most significant and relevant facts, extended definitions, concrete details, quotations, or other information and examples appropriate to the audience's knowledge of the topic. c. Use varied transitions and sentence structures to link the major sections of the text, create cohesion, and clarify the relationships among complex ideas and concepts. d. Use precise language, domain-specific vocabulary, and techniques such as metaphor, simile, and analogy to manage the complexity of the topic; convey a knowledgeable stance in a style that responds to the discipline and context as well as to the expertise of likely readers. e. Provide a concluding statement or section that follows from and supports the information or explanation provided (e.g., articulating implications or the significance of the topic).
7 (6–8)	Conduct short research projects to answer a question (including a self-generated question), drawing on several sources and generating additional related, focused questions that allow for multiple avenues of exploration.
7 (9–10) (11–12)	Conduct short as well as more sustained research projects to answer a question (including a self generated question) or solve a problem; narrow or broaden the inquiry when appropriate; synthesize multiple sources on the subject, demonstrating understanding of the subject under investigation.
8 (6–8)	Gather relevant information from multiple print and digital sources, using search terms effectively; assess the credibility and accuracy of each source; and quote or paraphrase the data and conclusions of others while avoiding plagiarism and following a standard format for citation.

Standard	Grade-Band Expectation
8 (9–10)	Gather relevant information from multiple authoritative print and digital sources, using advanced searches effectively; assess the usefulness of each source in answering the research question; integrate information into the text selectively to maintain the flow of ideas, avoiding plagiarism and following a standard format for citation.
8 (11–12)	Gather relevant information from multiple authoritative print and digital sources, using advanced searches effectively; assess the strengths and limitations of each source in terms of the specific task, purpose, and audience; integrate information into the text selectively to maintain the flow of ideas, avoiding plagiarism and overreliance on any one source and following a standard format for citation.
9 (6–8) (9–10) (11–12)	Draw evidence from informational texts to support analysis, reflection, and research.

Using Text-Dependent Tasks About *What the Text Inspires You to Do*

There are a number of different tasks that teachers can use to check for understanding. These tasks provide students an opportunity to demonstrate their thinking about the text under investigation. Importantly, these tasks often allow students to understand the text, and the ideas surrounding the text, in a much more comprehensive way. But even more importantly, these tasks all demand that students cite textual evidence in their products. In other words, students have to understand *what the text says*, *how the text works*, and *what the text means*, if they are going to be successful with these tasks.

As the adage notes, you don't always know what you think until you write it down. The same can be said for the development of a presentation; the preparation for a test, seminar, or debate; or the investigation of a claim or topic. In essence, these tasks show students that the close reading they have done is worthy of their time. Students use their annotations, ideas, and collaborative conversations in service of the task that allows them to make the text their own.

Presentations

As noted in speaking and listening **standard 5**, students are expected to develop and hone their presentation skills. The presentations they develop should be factually accurate and include a variety of multimedia components (e.g., graphics, images, music, sound) and visual displays. Of course, we know that speaking before a group remains the number one fear for the majority of people (Wallechinsky, Wallace, & Wallace, 1977). Hopefully, if students have a lot of practice with presentations while they are younger, we can overcome this social phobia. As Berkun (2010) notes, it's not as simple as picturing the audience naked!

Effective presentations are those that have good content and are delivered well. In fact, there is a science to developing and giving good presentations. For example, Bruce Woodcock from the University of Kent, in England, notes that presentations should have a structure, with appropriate notes and handouts. The presenter should be practiced. This includes the use of body language, speech, interactions with the audience, and attending to nervousness. In addition, the visuals, such as a slide presentation, should be clean and simple. A graphic representation of his ideas can be found in Figure 5.7.

Figure 5.7   Presentation Skills

Structure	Practice	Body Language
Have a logical order: introduction, middle with your main points, and a conclusion.	Practice beforehand in front of a mirror with a recorder or in front of a friend.	Smile, make eye contact , stand up straight, and move around a bit. Don't hide behind the podium!
Notes and Handouts	**PRESENTATION SKILLS**	**Speech**
Have brief notes on postcard-sized cards. Have a handout that the audience can take away afterward.	Bruce Woodcock, bw@kent.ac.uk University of Kent Careers	Speak clearly, confidently, concisely and not too fast. Use everyday language rather than jargon.
PowerPoint	**Interaction**	**Nervousness**
Keep slides clean and simple. Don't have lots of text on each slide. Use charts, diagrams, and pictures.	Build a rapport with your audience. Get them involved by asking and encouraging questions. Use humor if appropriate.	It's normal to be a bit nervous: This helps make you more energized. Preparation and practice will reduce nerves!

Source: Created by Bruce Woodcock

Available for download from **www.corwin.com/textdependentquestions**

Terry Gault (2013), public speaking expert and coach, notes on her website, speakfearlessly.net, that there are common mistakes that novices routinely make, including the following:

- Using small scale movements and gestures

- Speaking with low energy

- Playing it safe

- Not preparing enough

- Not practicing enough

- Preparing too much material

- Rushing

- Data-centric presentations

- Avoiding vulnerability

- Taking themselves way too seriously

It takes time to learn to present effectively and efficiently, and teachers need to ensure that students are provided with opportunities to engage in this type of learning.

The students in Mr. Corbrera's class were asked to develop presentations as a way of demonstrating their understanding of several aspects of the texts they had been reading. Mr. Corbrera did not want his students all developing presentations on the same content. He had noticed that students stopped listening when the presentations of their peers were similar to those that they had already heard. Instead, he divided his students into groups and assigned each group a different topic: characterization, irony and ambiguity, narration, plot structure, symbolism, and theme.

Each group had four or five students, and they were provided chart paper and markers to start. Each student was expected to contribute to each topic, in writing, on the chart paper before the laptops were opened and construction of the slide presentation began. The students talked with one another about their assigned topic and reread the text, looking for evidence that would support their topics. For example, Noah, Bradley, Cara, and Mauricio were working on narration. Noah suggested that each of them write down on their own paper what they thought about the role of the narrator.

"Let's compare ideas," Noah said. "Bradley, what do you have?"

"The narrator is the one who tells the story," Bradley said.

"It's like the storyteller," Cara added.

"But," said Mauricio, "mostly the narrator knows more than the characters in the story."

They decided that they would create a word web about the definition of *narration* as their first slide. They each contributed to the poster paper,

> It takes time to learn to present effectively and efficiently, and teachers need to ensure that students are provided with opportunities to engage in this type of learning.

adding thoughts and definitions. Then they turned their attention to the narration in *The People Could Fly* (Hamilton, 1993).

"So, the narrator is like one of the slaves," Mauricio said. "He talks like them, so I think that he is."

"I think that this narrator is omniscient, because he knows that some people can fly and others can't," Cara added. "He knows more than the characters."

Their conversation continued as they explored the role of the narrator in the text and how the narrator influenced the folktale. They also noted that the narrator could be male or female and that this was an oral tale, so people would think that the narrator was like them.

Before they started working on their laptop to create their presentation, Mr. Corbrera reminded them about the importance of visuals.

"Remember, good presentations have a lot of visual information and just a few words," he noted. *"The words should come from you when you speak. We want people to pay attention to you. The slide show is support and can help people remember information. And of course you can add sound to the presentation if it really complements the content."*

Mr. Corbrera had read and shared several books about quality visual presentations, including *Presentation Zen* (Reynolds, 2011) and *Slide:ology* (Duarte, 2008). He used a rubric to provide his students with feedback about their presentations (see Figure 5.8). Of course, he taught students the content of the rubric before using it and modeled presentations for his students such that they understood what quality would look like.

Writing From Sources

All writing should have a purpose, and these purposes fall into three categories: (1) to convey an experience, real or imagined; (2) to inform or explain an event, process, or phenomenon; and (3) to persuade. These purposes correlate to the three major text types: narrative, informational/explanatory, and arguments with evidence. The challenge is that too often writers are invited by us to turn their attention away from the text we as teachers have worked so hard to help them understand deeply. Instead, we ask them to "write about a time when someone challenged you to participate in a fight" rather than turn them back to the speech delivered by FDR. To be clear, it is not as though their personal experiences are without value to us. In fact, their ability to convey such an experience and ground it in the context of one or more readings makes the writing more powerful. But we need to be mindful of how our writing

Figure 5.8 Speech and Presentation Rubric

	Emerging (0–6 points)	Developing (7–8 points)	Advanced (9–10 points)	Score/Comments
1. Organization (10 points)	Ideas may not be focused or developed. The introduction is undeveloped. Main points are difficult to identify. Transitions may be needed. There is no conclusion, or it may not be clear the presentation has concluded. Conclusion does not tie back to the introduction. Audience cannot understand presentation, because there is no sequence of information.	Audience has difficulty understanding the presentation because the sequence of information is unclear. Ideas are evident but may not be clearly developed or always flow smoothly. The introduction may not be well developed. Transitions may be awkward. Supporting material may lack in development. The conclusion may need additional development.	Ideas are clearly organized, developed, and supported to achieve an intended outcome; the purpose is clear. The introduction gets the attention of the audience, and transitions ensure the audience anticipates content. Main points are clear and organized effectively. The conclusion is satisfying and relates back to introduction.	
2. Topic Knowledge (10 points)	Student does not have grasp of information; student cannot answer questions about the subject. Inaccurate, generalized, or inappropriate supporting material may be used. Overdependence on notes may be observed.	Student has a partial grasp of the information. Supporting material may lack in originality. Student is at ease with expected answers to all questions but fails to elaborate. Overdependence on notes may be observed.	Student has a clear grasp of information. Supporting material is original, logical, and relevant. Student demonstrates full knowledge (more than required) by answering all class questions with explanations and elaboration. Speaking outline or note cards are used for reference only.	

(Continued)

Figure 5.8 (Continued)

	Emerging (0–6 points)	Developing (7–8 points)	Advanced (9–10 points)	Score/Comments
3. Audience Adaptation (10 points)	The presenter is not able to keep the audience engaged. The verbal or nonverbal feedback from the audience may suggest a lack of interest or confusion. Topic selection does not relate to audience needs and interests.	The presenter is able to keep the audience engaged most of the time. When feedback indicates a need for idea clarification, the speaker makes an attempt to clarify or restate ideas. Generally, the speaker demonstrates audience awareness through nonverbal and verbal behaviors. Topic selection and examples are somewhat appropriate for the audience, occasion, or setting.	The presenter is able to effectively keep the audience engaged. Material is modified or clarified as needed given audience verbal and nonverbal feedback. Nonverbal behaviors are used to keep the audience engaged. Delivery style is modified as needed. Topic selection and examples are interesting and relevant for the audience and occasion.	
4. Language Use (Verbal Effectiveness) (10 points)	Language choices may be limited, peppered with slang or jargon, too complex, or too dull. Language is questionable or inappropriate for a particular audience, occasion, or setting. Some biased or unclear language may be used.	Language used is mostly respectful or inoffensive. Language is appropriate, but word choices are not particularly vivid or precise. Some grammar and pronunciation errors are noted.	Language is familiar to the audience, appropriate for the setting, and free of bias; the presenter may "code-switch" (use a different language form) when appropriate. Language choices are vivid and precise, and few errors are present in the speech.	

	Emerging (0–6 points)	Developing (7–8 points)	Advanced (9–10 points)	Score/Comments
5. Delivery (Nonverbal Effectiveness) (10 points)	The delivery detracts from the message; eye contact may be very limited; the presenter may tend to look at the floor, mumble, speak inaudibly, fidget, or read most of the speech; gestures and movements may be jerky or excessive. The delivery may appear inconsistent with the message. Nonfluencies ("ums") are used excessively. Articulation and pronunciation tend to be sloppy. Poise of composure is lost during any distractions. Audience members have difficulty hearing the presentation.	The delivery generally seems effective. However, effective use of volume, eye contact, vocal control, et cetera may not be consistent. Vocal tone, facial expressions, clothing, and other nonverbal expressions do not detract significantly from the message. The delivery style, tone of voice, and clothing choices do not seem out of place or disrespectful to the audience or occasion. Some nonfluencies are observed. Most audience members can hear the presentation.	The delivery seems extemporaneous, natural, and confident, and it enhances the message. Posture, eye contact, smooth gestures, facial expressions, volume, pace, et cetera indicate confidence, a commitment to the topic, and a willingness to communicate. The vocal tone, delivery style, and clothing are consistent with the message. Limited use of nonfluencies is observed. All audience members can hear the presentation.	

Source: Adapted from Northwest Regional Educational Laboratory (1998).

Available for download from **www.corwin.com/textdependentquestions**

prompts can lead them away from texts, thereby robbing them of the opportunity to engage in the kind of critical thinking that moves them from text interpretation (what the text means) to action (what the text inspires you to do.)

We have found the task templates developed by the Literacy Design Collaborative (LDC) (www.literacydesigncollaborative.org) to be immensely helpful for crafting writing prompts such that readers reference the text and cite evidence to support their points. The LDC task templates work for teachers in much the same way that sentence frames work for students, because they provide an academic language frame for original ideas.

The students in Nancy's ninth grade English class had spent three class periods reading and discussing "The Open Window" by Saki (the pen name of H. H. Munro) and had examined the methods of indirect and direct characterization that were used to show the protagonist and antagonist as rounded characters. They had developed annotated notes on their texts as well as completed a note-taking guide on characterization. (See Figure 2.5, also available on this book's companion website, www.corwin .com/textdependentquestions.) Much of the work on the text came in the form of text-based discussion, especially in exploring text structures, vocabulary, and the deeper meaning of the text. However, the primary teaching point in this unit was on characterization as a literary device. On the fourth day, students used their annotated texts and completed guide to respond to the following question and complete the task:

> *How do skilled writers portray characters so vividly? After reading the short story "The Open Window" by Saki, write a 250-word (minimum) character analysis essay analyzing the methods of characterization used by the author to portray Vera and Framton Nuttel. Be sure to explain each method you select to discuss (minimum of three) and include examples and quotations from the text.*

> **Tip:** *Do not analyze the film version, only the text. We don't know from the text what Vera or Mr. Nuttel looked like!*

This task was given during the second week of school, as the first major writing assignment. One of the purposes was to let students see what they were capable of doing. In an 85-minute class, they were confronted with writing an essay that drew directly from the source material. But they also had extensive notes that should have helped them scaffold their writing. To be sure, there was some tension in the air, because they weren't sure they were up to the task. But nearly every student completed the task, and in the process they all had a major boost to their confidence as writers.

Ernesto said it best: "Can you believe I did that? I'm a writer!"

Socratic Seminars

One specific type of discussion and analysis of a text is called a Socratic seminar, which is defined as a "collaborative, intellectual dialogue facilitated with open-ended questions about the text" (Roberts & Billings, 2012, p. 22). Students read and annotate the text in advance of the Socratic seminar, either in class or outside of class. In addition to reading the text, students write a short, reflective piece in advance of the Socratic seminar, addressing a question posed by the teacher or their peers. Typically, the question focuses on general understandings and key details (*what the text says*). Deeper understandings of the text emerge during the seminar, as students use their knowledge about *how the text works* and *what it means* as they interact with others.

There are four components of a Socratic seminar:

1. *The text,* which should be selected because it is worthy of investigation and discussion.

2. *The questions,* which should lead participants back to the text as they speculate, evaluate, define, and clarify the issues involved.

3. *The leader,* who is both guide and participant. The leader, who can be a student or the teacher, helps participants clarify their positions, involves reluctant participants, and restrains overactive members of the group.

4. *The participants,* who come to the discussion having read the text, ready to share their ideas and perspectives with others.

Examples of some of the questions that students might struggle with during a Socratic seminar include these:

- Could you give me an example or a metaphor to explain that?

- Can you find that in the text?

- Where does the reading support you?

- What are you assuming in that argument?

- What is the author's perspective, and how does this inform the message?

- Why is [word or phrase] pivotal to understanding this text?

- Is [concept] a good thing or a bad thing?

- What evidence in the text helps us understand whether the writer would agree or disagree with [concept]?

- What does [phrase or sentence] mean in the context of this reading?

- Where does the turning point in this piece occur, and why is it important?

- In what ways does our understanding of [character] depend on the [thoughts/actions/dialogue] of others?

- What is the theme of this text? What is your evidence?

- How does this text align or contrast with [previously read text]? (adapted from Fisher & Frey, 2014b)

In each case, the text is important, and students learn that they need to have read and understood the text to participate.

The students in Ms. Robinson's history class engaged in a Socratic seminar as a final task in their investigation of the *Narrative of the Life Frederick Douglass* (1845/1995). The opening question that began their meeting focused on the worthiness of reading. The students sat in a large circle, with the text in their hands, as Ms. Robinson posed the first question: *Was learning to read worth it for Frederick Douglass?*

Julia indicated that she wanted to talk, and Ms. Robinson reminded the class that they should engage in a conversation and that she would not be calling on specific students to talk. Rather, she would mediate the conversation and periodically pose questions. She concluded her comments, saying, *"The Socratic seminar is a forum for all of us to deepen our understanding of the text and to entertain different interpretations. It's not a debate, but an investigation."* She then prompted Julia. *"You wanted to start?"*

"Yeah," Julia said. "I don't really think it was worth it. He could have still escaped even if he didn't learn to read. I know we talked about this, but I do think it made his life worse when he learned. But then, maybe, he wouldn't have tried to escape if he didn't know how to read. I guess I really don't know what I think about that question."

"I know what I think," said Andrew. "I think he had to learn to read and that people ended up listening to him because he was educated. They didn't even believe that he was really a slave, because he could read and write, which is why he wrote the book in the first place."

As the conversation continued, Ms. Robinson and her students posed a number of different questions. They talked about how *discontent* was an important idea, and that it didn't mean that he was miserable. They noted that *master* and *mistress* were words that showed power and control. Toward the end of their discussion, Ms. Robinson posed the questions, *"What is the theme here? What messages can you find in the text?"*

"When I first read this, I wrote in the margin that 'ignorance is bliss,'" said Roland. "I hear people, like my grandma, say that, and I thought that was the message. That if he was still ignorant, like not being able to read, then he would be happier. Now I don't think that. Now I think the right words would be 'knowledge is power.' My dad says that all the time. I think that's the theme for Frederick Douglass, that his knowledge gave him power."

"I really like that," Sumaya agreed. "People used to have power over him, but he was able to get power not because he hurt people or owned them. He got his power from learning, and he could use that power to make a difference, like helping to get slavery stopped."

Debates

Similar to a Socratic seminar, debates require that students carefully analyze texts such that they can use evidence from the texts to make a case effectively. In a debate, students need to carefully examine an issue, research both sides of the issue, and be prepared to defend a position. Importantly, learning the skills of debate can improve student achievement and engagement in school (Mezuk, Bondarenko, Smith, & Tucker, 2011). In part, this is because in many cases students must read more than just the assigned texts in order to be successful. To effectively debate, students must understand a wide range of texts and be able to use those texts strategically. In addition, these achievement gains can be partially attributed to the development of oral language skills that takes place as students learn to engage in interactions with one another. And finally, these strides in achievement can be partially attributed to the depth of understanding required to engage in the debate itself. As Mezuk et al. (2011) noted, this is "particularly relevant in light of the new Common Core State Standards … [which] focus on evidence-based argument and informational text mastery as critical language arts skills" (p. 630).

Learning the skills of debate can improve student achievement and engagement in school. To effectively debate, students must understand a wide range of texts and be able to use those texts strategically.

As part of the debate process, students rely on texts for evidence. In preparing for debates, students read and reread several texts, taking notes that they can use later. During the debate, students use their resources to argue in a structured way. Of course, students have to understand the rules of a debate. Typically, a team debate has different phases, such as the following:

- Pro—Someone presents the "for" position.

- Con—Someone presents the "against" position.

- Pro—Someone presents evidence related to the "for" position.

- Con—Someone presents evidence related to the "against" position.

- Pro—Someone refutes the evidence from the "against" position.

- Con—Someone refutes the evidence from the "for" position.

- Pro—Someone salvages the most persuasive arguments left and makes a concluding statement.

- Con—Someone salvages the most persuasive arguments left and makes a concluding statement.

Typically, the judge reviews the proceedings and declares a debate winner. Figure 5.9 contains debate guidelines developed by Heather Anderson. As with other tasks that students must be taught, the rules of debate and the ways in which debates are conducted are important considerations for teachers. There are a number of resources about effective debate skills (e.g., Edwards, 2008; Marzano, Pickering, & Heflebower, 2011).

As part of their debates regarding FDR's inaugural address, the students in Mr. Vaca's class were asked to debate the merits of the plan to address the economy, as outlined by Roosevelt, and to argue about whether it was more idealistic than realistic. Mr. Vaca was specifically working with his students on refuting the arguments of other teams. He had taught them the four steps in refutation:

1. "They say. . . ." (briefly repeats the argument of the other side)

2. "But we disagree. . . . " (answers the argument of the other side)

3. "Because. . . . " (gives a reason for disagreement or counterargument)

4. "Therefore. . . . (explains what the consequence of winning this argument is) (Meany & Shuster, 2005, p. 167)

Figure 5.9   Debate Guidelines

Each team of four will have two people on the affirmative (for) side and two people on the negative (against) side.

Debate Format

1. Affirmative (for) presents case: three minutes max

2. Negative (against) presents case: three minutes max

3. Affirmative (for) and negative (against) respond to one another: four minutes max each

4. Affirmative (for) summarizes and concludes: one minute max

5. Negative (against) summarizes and concludes: one minute max

After the debate, the class will vote to see which side won. This vote will not influence your final grade.

Tips

1. **You are always right.** No matter what you really believe, if you want to win, then you have to believe that whatever you say is correct, and your opposition is always wrong.

2. **Strong central argument.** Every point you make should be linked back to this central argument.

3. **Rebut.** If the other side states an incorrect fact, rebut it. If they do not link back to their team's case, rebut it. If they give an example that has no relevance, rebut it. Remember, the opposition is always wrong.

4. **Never insult the opposition.** No matter how much you want to, don't! If you want to insult something, do it to their argument. Don't use personal attacks if you want to win.

5. **Have passion.** Believe in what you are saying, and you probably will win. Speak from the heart, but also use logic and research.

Debate Sentence Frames

I will argue that. . . .	I will show that. . . .	You can see that. . . .
The evidence shows that. . . .	My opponent believes. . . .	All the evidence points toward. . . .
That is simply not true. . . .	It is clear that. . . .	My opponent is wrong because. . . .

During the debate, one team made the claim that FDR's plan was more idealistic than realistic. As evidence they noted that the Agricultural Adjustment Act of 1933 paid farmers not to plant their land or to kill excess livestock, which was ruled unconstitutional in 1936, because it taxed the companies that processed the food, and that money went to farmers.

In their closing comments, this team said, "FDR had a plan, and he gathered the support of a lot of people. But his plan was idealistic, because implementing his plan turned out to be illegal, which is not a realistic way to solve the problems of our country."

Josiah, Melissa, and Luis had a response to this. Using the refutation guidelines, they said,

> They say that FDR's actions were more idealistic and not realistic because one component of his plan was ruled technically unconstitutional. But we disagree for several reasons. First, the Agricultural Adjustment Act of 1938 corrected the problem and allowed the government to pay the subsidies for farmers. This is important, because the price of food increased to the point that farmers could earn enough money to live off of their work. Therefore, we believe that his plans were actually realistic and provided a way for Americans to live better lives.

Investigations

Sometimes, the texts that are used for close reading generate a lot of additional questions for students. In essence, these texts inspire students to find things out. In these cases, an appropriate task is an investigation. As we have noted before, investigations can be short or long. Students are expected to "Conduct short as well as more sustained research projects based on focused questions, demonstrating understanding of the subject under investigation" (CCSSI, 2010a, p. 41). In addition, students are asked to integrate information from a range of diverse sources. This requires that they find additional resources, print or digital, that they can use to inform their research or explain the topic under investigation.

Like students over 100 years ago, our students today must identify sources, take notes, and synthesize information (Pfaffinger, 2006). The expectations of the research paper haven't changed, but the way students go about completing the task has. Students can now use technology to complete their research papers. They can Google, e-mail, highlight, cut and paste, and use all kinds of tools that make the work of the research paper easier and faster. We have organized these new strategies into four distinct categories that can be taught (Frey, Fisher, & Gonzalez, 2010):

Students can use technology to complete their research papers.

- **Finding Information.** To effectively transform knowledge to understanding, students need varied approaches, tools, and vocabulary for finding information. They need to be taught how to search for information as well as how to evaluate the credibility of the information that they find.

- **Using Information.** Once students have collected information, they need accessible ways to keep it organized. From research note cards to class notes, common tools have developed into digital versions that can save time and improve the organizational quality. In addition, students need to be taught how cite the sources they use and not plagiarize information.

- **Producing Information.** As part of the investigation process, students must synthesize the information they find and present that information in their own words with their own organizational system. This requires a great deal of practice, and students deserve feedback from their peers and teachers as they approximate success with this.

- **Sharing Information.** Producing a research paper has been the end point for many students. When students submit their papers, having found and used good information, it's fairly anticlimactic. They have worked so hard and learned so much, and there their newfound knowledge sits, in a paper in the teacher's backpack. Today's students want more. Producing is not enough for students in the 21st century. They want to share their information. This need to share may be the result of students' exposure to countless YouTube videos, blog postings, tweets, Facebook status updates, or something else, but the fact remains that our students want to share.

The students in Ms. Choi's sixth grade science class had been introduced to the general study of geology and had seen a video about the various ways that geologists work and what they find. Ms. Choi knew that there was much more to this field of study but did not feel the need to lecture about all of this to her students. Instead, she established research and investigation groups. The first task of each group was to produce research questions that interested them. The parameters of the task included an understanding that the questions had to relate to geology and that they had to be topics that were appropriate for school. To ensure that groups were investigating different topics, they were each asked to prioritize 10 questions that they could study.

Fernando's group asked a series of questions about volcanoes, from those that were fairly mundane to those that would take some significant work. On the mundane side, they asked, "How many volcanoes are there in the world?" On the more complex side, they asked, "How do volcanoes form, and why do they form in specific areas?" Ms. Choi met with each group to review their questions and helped each student decide on the question he or she would answer. Fernando focused on the more complex question noted previously.

As part of his investigation, Fernando searched the Internet for information, visited the library several times to talk with the staff there, and read a lot of texts, some of which were fairly complex and others of which were not. In the end, Fernando focused his response on the Ring of Fire, writing a fairly lengthy paper about the formation of volcanoes around the Pacific Rim. His paper included statistics (e.g., 75% of the world's volcanoes are in this area), a map of the region, and information (e.g., When rock in the mantle melts, it travels through the cracks in the earth caused by the movement of tectonic plates. At the earth's surface, we call this lava. When there are lots of layers of lava, geologists call this a volcano).

In conducting this investigation, Fernando and the other members of his class had to synthesize their knowledge and read widely to identify important information. In addition, they had to compile this information in a logical way while maintaining the focus on the topic at hand.

Tests

Summative assessments of students' understanding are another task that can be used to determine whether or not students understand a text.

The expectations of the research paper haven't changed, but the way students go about completing the task has.

Good tests allow teachers to understand students' thinking. Incorrect responses are not just random collections of answers but rather inform the teacher about students' misunderstanding. These diagnostic distractors, even on a summative assessment, can be used to guide the instruction teachers provide later in the year.

Although there are a number of formats for test questions, the ones that interest us for the purpose of close reading are those that involve the use of evidence from the text in order to determine the answer. In other words, we are less interested in recall-of-information questions when we are using tests as a task related to close reading. We are interested in questions that encourage the reader to return to the text to determine whether the evidence supports the answer. We are also interested in questions that require students to provide evidence from the text itself.

With summative assessments, we are interested in questions that encourage the reader to return to the text to determine if the evidence supports the answer.

For example, the students in Mr. Neilson's class could have had a debate about the information from *The Origin of the Species* (Darwin, 1859/2003), or they could have analyzed the arguments that Darwin made or the claims and counterclaims that have resulted from this text. But Mr. Neilson decided that his students needed to demonstrate their understanding of information from the text through some multiple-choice items that required that they produce evidence from the text. A few sample items from his assessment can be found in Figure 5.10. (Quotations within the text are taken from Darwin, 1859/2003.)

Of course, Mr. Neilson's class engaged in a number of other activities besides the test, but he wanted to be sure that his students could also demonstrate their understanding in this format. After all, tests are a genre that is not limited to school (Fisher & Frey, 2008). There are tests to be able to drive, tests to handle food, tests to get into law school, and tests for earning promotions in the police department. As Mr. Neilson noted, "My students demonstrate their understanding on tests like this several times a year. I want them to know how to do this. And I want them to learn how to debate, present, discuss, write, and think. It's about balance for me. If I only gave tests, my students would not be prepared for their futures. On the other hand, if I never gave tests, they would be similarly unprepared."

Figure 5.10   Sample Test Items

1. The following question has two parts. First, answer Part A. Then, answer Part B.

   Part A

   Which statement **best** summarizes the author's central idea in the first paragraph of the text?

      a. Selection is something that only humans can orchestrate.

      b. Organisms that have advantageous variations have the best chance of reproducing.

      c. A species that is polymorphic is subject to domestication.

      d. The physical condition of an individual is prime for injurious selection.

   Part B

   Which quote from the text **best** supports your answer in Part A?

      a. "If such do occur, can we doubt (remembering that many more individuals are born than can possibly survive) that individuals having any advantage, however slight, over others, would have the best chance of surviving and of procreating their kind?" (p. 94).

      b. "Under domestication, it may be truly said that the whole organisation becomes in some degree plastic" (p. 93).

      c. "Let it be borne in mind how infinitely complex and close-fitting are the mutual relations of all organic beings to each other and to their physical conditions of life" (p. 93).

      d. "Can the principle of selection, which we have seen is so potent in the hands of man, apply in nature?" (p. 93)

2. Read the sentence from the text reproduced below. Then, answer the question that follows.

   "Let it be <u>borne</u> in mind in what an endless number of strange peculiarities our domestic productions, and, in a lesser degree, those under nature, vary; and how strong the hereditary tendency is" (p. 93).

   What is the meaning of <u>borne</u> as it is used in the text?

      a. Having characteristics from the time of birth

      b. The method by which something is moved

      c. Brought into existence

      d. Kept or carried

3. How does the second paragraph fit in with the structure of the text as a whole?

      a. It argues the necessity of natural selection.

      b. It details the process of selecting against injurious variations.

      c. It provides examples of how the environment can affect a species.

      d. It defines two types of variation in an organism.

4. Which statement, if true, would most likely change the author's premise in the second paragraph?

      a. Climate change may result in the extinction of a species.

      b. Better adapted traits are always preserved.

    c. Climate change always positively affects a species.

    d. Immigration can lead to competition amongst different species.

5. Read the sentence from the text reproduced below. Then, answer the question that follows.

"In such case, every slight modification, which in the course of ages chanced to arise, and which in any way favoured the individuals of any of the species, by better adapting them to their altered conditions, would tend to be preserved; and natural selection would thus have free <u>scope</u> for the work of improvement" (p. 95).

What does the word <u>scope</u> mean as it is used in this excerpt?

    a. opportunity

    b. length

    c. aim

    d. effectiveness

6. Which **two** sentences from the text support the idea that natural selection favors beneficial traits?

    a. "This preservation of favourable variations and the rejection of injurious variations, I call Natural Selection" (p. 94).

    b. "The proportional numbers of its inhabitants would almost immediately undergo a change, and some species might become extinct" (p. 95).

    c. "Let it be remembered how powerful the influence of a single introduced tree or mammal has been shown to be" (p. 95).

    d. "In such case, every slight modification, which in the course of ages chanced to arise, and which in any way favoured the individuals of any of the species, by better adapting them to their altered conditions, would tend to be preserved; and natural selection would thus have free scope for the work of improvement" (p. 95).

    e. "Under domestication, it may be truly said that the whole organisation becomes in some degree plastic" (p. 93).

Answer Key

1. Part A. b
   Part B. a

2. d

3. c

4. c

5. a

6. a, d

•YOURSELF

QUESTION

This chapter has focused on tasks that require students to use the texts they have read to demonstrate their understanding. More specifically, these tasks allow students to respond to the question, *"What does the text mean to me, and what does it inspire me to do?"* The level of thinking required in these tasks assumes students know *what the text says, how the text works,* and *what the text means.* The range of tasks includes presentations, writing from sources, Socratic seminars, debates, research and investigation, and tests.

Now we invite you to test yourself. We have included a summary of the Bill of Rights (Figure 5.11) as well as "The Bill of Rights: A Transcription" (Figure 5.12) both from the National Archives and Records Administration. Take a few minutes to read the texts. Then turn your attention to the tasks you could use to determine students' understanding of the texts and their ability to apply that knowledge in a variety of ways. Remember that this phase is focused on *deep understanding* and *application.* What is it that students should understand about this text? There is any number of things that students could do with these texts, including investigations, presentations, discussions, and writing in response to prompts. We encourage you to create your own, so that students are inspired to take action after reading.

Figure 5.11   Excerpt From Introduction to *A More Perfect Union: The Creation of the United States Constitution* by Roger A. Bruns

The call for a bill of rights had been the anti-Federalists' most powerful weapon. Attacking the proposed Constitution for its vagueness and lack of specific protection against tyranny, Patrick Henry asked the Virginia convention, "What can avail your specious, imaginary balances, your rope-dancing, chain-rattling, ridiculous ideal checks and contrivances." The anti-Federalists, demanding a more concise, unequivocal Constitution, one that laid out for all to see the right of the people and limitations of the power of government, claimed that the brevity of the document only revealed its inferior nature. Richard Henry Lee despaired at the lack of provisions to protect "those essential rights of mankind without which liberty cannot exist." Trading the old government for the new without such a bill of rights, Lee argued, would be trading Scylla for Charybdis.

A bill of rights had been barely mentioned in the Philadelphia convention, most delegates holding that the fundamental rights of individuals had been secured in the state constitutions. James Wilson maintained that a bill of rights was superfluous because all power not expressly delegated to the new government was reserved to the people. It was clear, however, that in this argument the anti-Federalists held the upper hand. Even Thomas Jefferson, generally in favor of the new government, wrote to Madison that a bill of rights was "what the people are entitled to against every government on earth."

By the fall of 1788 Madison had been convinced that not only was a bill of rights necessary to ensure acceptance of the Constitution but that it would have positive effects. He wrote, on October 17, that such "fundamental maxims of free Government" would be "a good ground for an appeal to the sense of community" against potential oppression and would "counteract the impulses of interest and passion."

Madison's support of the bill of rights was of critical significance. One of the new representatives from Virginia to the First Federal Congress, as established by the new Constitution, he worked tirelessly to persuade the House to enact amendments. Defusing the anti-Federalists' objections to the Constitution, Madison was able to shepherd through 17 amendments in the early months of the Congress, a list that was later trimmed to 12 in the Senate. On October 2, 1789, President Washington sent to each of the states a copy of the 12 amendments adopted by the Congress in September. By December 15, 1791, three-fourths of the states had ratified the 10 amendments now so familiar to Americans as the "Bill of Rights."

Benjamin Franklin told a French correspondent in 1788 that the formation of the new government had been like a game of dice, with many players of diverse prejudices and interests unable to make any uncontested moves. Madison wrote to Jefferson that the welding of these clashing interests was "a task more difficult than can be well conceived by those who were not concerned in the execution of it." When the delegates left Philadelphia after the convention, few, if any, were convinced that the Constitution they had approved outlined the ideal form of government for the country. But late in his life James Madison scrawled out another letter, one never addressed. In it he declared that no government can be perfect, and "that which is the least imperfect is therefore the best government."

Source: Introduction by Roger A. Bruns to *A More Perfect Union: The Creation of the United States Constitution.* Washington, DC: Published for the National Archives and Records Administration by the National Archives Trust Fund Board, 1986.

Available for download from **www.corwin.com/textdependentquestions**

Figure 5.12   The Bill of Rights: A Transcription

The Preamble to the Bill of Rights

Congress of the United States begun and held at the City of New-York, on Wednesday the fourth of March, one thousand seven hundred and eighty nine.

THE Conventions of a number of the States, having at the time of their adopting the Constitution, expressed a desire, in order to prevent misconstruction or abuse of its powers, that further declaratory and restrictive clauses should be added: And as extending the ground of public confidence in the Government, will best ensure the beneficent ends of its institution.

RESOLVED by the Senate and House of Representatives of the United States of America, in Congress assembled, two thirds of both Houses concurring, that the following Articles be proposed to the Legislatures of the several States, as amendments to the Constitution of the United States, all, or any of which Articles, when ratified by three fourths of the said Legislatures, to be valid to all intents and purposes, as part of the said Constitution; viz.

ARTICLES in addition to, and Amendment of the Constitution of the United States of America, proposed by Congress, and ratified by the Legislatures of the several States, pursuant to the fifth Article of the original Constitution.

Note: The following text is a transcription of the first ten amendments to the Constitution in their original form. These amendments were ratified December 15, 1791, and form what is known as the "Bill of Rights."

Amendment I

Congress shall make no law respecting an establishment of religion, or prohibiting the free exercise thereof; or abridging the freedom of speech, or of the press; or the right of the people peaceably to assemble, and to petition the Government for a redress of grievances.

Amendment II

A well regulated Militia, being necessary to the security of a free State, the right of the people to keep and bear Arms, shall not be infringed.

Amendment III

No Soldier shall, in time of peace be quartered in any house, without the consent of the Owner, nor in time of war, but in a manner to be prescribed by law.

Amendment IV

The right of the people to be secure in their persons, houses, papers, and effects, against unreasonable searches and seizures, shall not be violated, and no Warrants shall issue, but upon probable cause, supported by Oath or affirmation, and particularly describing the place to be searched, and the persons or things to be seized.

Amendment V

No person shall be held to answer for a capital, or otherwise infamous crime, unless on a presentment or indictment of a Grand Jury, except in cases arising in the land or naval forces, or in the Militia, when in actual service in time of War or public danger; nor shall any person be subject for the same offence to be twice put in jeopardy of life or limb; nor shall be compelled in any criminal case to be a witness against himself, nor be deprived of life, liberty, or property, without due process of law; nor shall private property be taken for public use, without just compensation.

Amendment VI

In all criminal prosecutions, the accused shall enjoy the right to a speedy and public trial, by an impartial jury of the State and district wherein the crime shall have been committed, which district shall have been previously ascertained by law, and to be informed of the nature and cause of the accusation; to be confronted with the witnesses against him; to have compulsory process for obtaining witnesses in his favor, and to have the Assistance of Counsel for his defence.

Amendment VII

In Suits at common law, where the value in controversy shall exceed twenty dollars, the right of trial by jury shall be preserved, and no fact tried by a jury, shall be otherwise re-examined in any Court of the United States, than according to the rules of the common law.

Amendment VIII

Excessive bail shall not be required, nor excessive fines imposed, nor cruel and unusual punishments inflicted.

Amendment IX

The enumeration in the Constitution, of certain rights, shall not be construed to deny or disparage others retained by the people.

Amendment X

The powers not delegated to the United States by the Constitution, nor prohibited by it to the States, are reserved to the States respectively, or to the people.

Videos

To read a QR code, you must have a smartphone or tablet with a camera. We recommend that you download a QR code reader app that is made specifically for your phone or tablet brand.

Videos can also be accessed at
www.corwin.com/textdependentquestions

Video 5.1 Students in Oscar Corrigan's seventh grade social studies class write a summary of a passage from *Things Fall Apart,* using textual examples to support their main points.

Video 5.2 Will Mellman prompts his seventh grade science class to write a letter to someone they care about describing the causes and symptoms of an ulcer, based on what they learned in an article on peptic ulcers.

Video 5.3 After reading two texts written by Eisenhower, Javier Vaca prompts his eleventh grade U.S history students to write about the qualities of military leadership, using textual evidence to support their claims.

Video 5.4 Heather Anderson reminds her tenth grade English students of the essential question "Do looks matter?" in order to compare two poems—Maya Angelou's "Phenomenal Woman" and Virginia Satir's "I Am Me."

Video 5.5 Students in Marisol Thayre's eleventh grade English class work on a Literacy Letter, using Susan Bordo's article on body image and their personal experience with advertisements.

Video 5.6 Kim Elliot asks her tenth grade biology class to list two causes of cancer in a graphic organizer before performing Internet research to determine the effects of each cause.

CODA

We have spent a great deal of time discussing the role of text-dependent questions in helping students understand complex texts. We think that these questions are a critical scaffold for students to develop their understanding of the texts they read. We also think it's important that students learn to ask questions themselves. In fact, when students learn to ask these types of questions of their own reading, we know that they're prepared for their futures. In essence, the text-dependent questions that we ask should build students' habits, habits for inquiry and investigation that students can use across their academic careers. In fact, it's learning to ask and answer these types of questions, and to complete these types of tasks, that ensure that students are college- and career-ready.

APPENDICES

Developed by Heather Anderson and Marisol Thayre

Texts and Questions for . . .

	High School	Middle School
English	**Appendix I** *Letters to a Young Poet* by Rainer Maria Rilke (letters) 192 "St. Lucy's Home for Girls Raised by Wolves" by Karen Russell (short story) 207 "A Very Short Story" by Ernest Hemingway (short story) 210 "Melting Pot" by Anna Quindlen (essay) 212 "Conjecture" by Mark Twain (essay) 215	**Appendix II** "The Tell-Tale Heart" by Edgar Allan Poe (short story) 220 *Anne Frank: The Diary of a Young Girl* (diary) 222 *The Metamorphosis* by Franz Kafka (novella) 236 "Oranges," by Gary Soto (poem) 250 "Paul Revere's Midnight Ride" by Henry Wadsworth Longfellow (poem) 255
Social Studies/ History	**Appendix III** "Speech to the Troops at Tilbury" by Queen Elizabeth (speech) 263 The Nobel Acceptance Speech Delivered by Elie Wiesel in Oslo on December 10, 1986 (speech) 266	**Appendix IV** "Blood, Toil, Tears, and Sweat" by Winston Churchill (speech) 270 "On Women's Right to Vote" by Susan B. Anthony, 1873 (speech) 274
Science	**Appendix V** The United Nations World Water Development Report 2014: Water and Energy (technical document) 279 Excerpt From *The Log From the Sea of Cortez* (nonfiction) 283	**Appendix VI** "Why Leaves Turn Colors in the Fall" by Diane Ackerman (article) 286 "Animal Craftsmen" by Bruce Brooks (article) 291

APPENDIX I
HIGH SCHOOL ENGLISH

A·I

LETTERS TO A YOUNG POET BY RAINER MARIA RILKE
(LETTERS)

Letter 1 of *Letters to a Young Poet* by Rainer Maria Rilke

Paris
February 17, 1903

Dear Sir,

Your letter arrived just a few days ago. I want to thank you for the great confidence you have placed in me. That is all I can do. I cannot discuss your verses; for any attempt at criticism would be foreign to me. Nothing touches a work of art so little as words of criticism: they always result in more or less fortunate misunderstandings. Things aren't all so tangible and sayable as people would usually have us believe; most experiences are unsayable, they happen in a space that no word has ever entered, and more unsayable than all other things are works of art, those mysterious existences, whose life endures beside our own small, transitory life.

With this note as a preface, may I just tell you that your verses have no style of their own, although they do have silent and hidden beginnings of something personal. I feel this most clearly in the last poem, "My Soul." There, some thing of your own is trying to become word and melody. And in the lovely poem "To Leopardi" a kind of kinship with that great, solitary figure does perhaps appear. Nevertheless, the poems are not yet anything in themselves, not yet anything independent, even the last one and the one to Leopardi. Your kind letter, which accompanied them managed to make clear to me various faults that I felt in reading your verses, though I am not able to name them specifically.

You ask whether your verses are any good. You ask me. You have asked others before this. You send them to magazines. You compare them with other poems, and you are upset when certain editors reject your work. Now (since you have said you want my advice) I beg you to stop doing that sort of thing. You are looking outside, and that is what you should most avoid right now. No one can advise or help you—no one. There is only one thing you should do. Go into yourself. Find out the reason that commands you to write; see whether it has spread its roots into the very depths of your heart; confess to yourself whether you would have to die if you were forbidden to write. This most of all: ask yourself in the most silent hour of your night: must I write? Dig into yourself for a deep answer. And if this answer rings out in assent, if you meet this solemn question with a strong, simple "I must," then build your life in accordance with this necessity; your whole life, even into its humblest and most indifferent hour, must become a sign and witness to this impulse. Then come close to Nature. Then, as if no one had ever tried before, try to say what you see and feel and love and lose. Don't write love poems; avoid those forms that are too facile and ordinary: they are the hardest to work with, and it takes a great, fully ripened power to create something individual where good, even glorious, traditions exist in abundance. So rescue yourself from these general themes and write about what your everyday life offers you; describe your sorrows and desires, the thoughts that pass through your mind and your belief in some kind of beauty. Describe all these with heartfelt, silent, humble sincerity and, when you express yourself, use the Things around you, the images from your dreams, and the objects that you remember. If your everyday life seems poor, don't blame it; blame yourself; admit to yourself that you are not enough of a poet to call forth its riches; because for the creator there is no poverty and no poor, indifferent place. And even if you found yourself in some prison, whose walls let in none of the world's sound—wouldn't you still have your childhood, that jewel beyond all price, that treasure house of memories? Turn your attention to it. Try to raise up the sunken feelings of this enormous past; your personality will grow stronger, your solitude will expand and become a place where you can live in the twilight, where the noise of other people passes by, far in the distance. And if out of this turning within, out of this immersion in your own world, poems come, then you will not think of asking anyone whether they are good or not. Nor will you try to interest magazines in these works: for you will see them as your dear natural possession, a piece of your life, a voice from it. A work of art is good if it has arisen out of necessity. That is the only way one can judge it. So, dear Sir, I can't give you any advice but this: to go into yourself and see how deep the place is from which your life flows; at its source you will find the answer to the question of whether you must create. Accept that answer, just as it is given to you, without trying to interpret it. Perhaps you will discover that you are called to be an artist. Then take that destiny upon yourself, and bear it, its burden and its greatness, without ever asking what reward might come from outside. For the creator must be a world for himself and must find everything in himself and in Nature, to whom his whole life is devoted.

But after this descent into yourself and into your solitude, perhaps you will have to renounce becoming a poet (if, as I have said, one feels one could live without writing, then one shouldn't write at all). Nevertheless, even then, this self searching that I ask of you will not have been for nothing. Your life will still find its own paths from there, and that they may be good, rich, and wide is what I wish for you, more than I can say.

What else can I tell you? It seems to me that everything has its proper emphasis; and finally I want to add just one more bit of advice: to keep growing, silently and earnestly, through your whole development; you couldn't disturb it any more violently than by looking outside and waiting for outside answers to questions that only your innermost feeling, in your quietest hour, can perhaps answer.

It was a pleasure for me to find in your letter the name of Professor Horacek; I have great reverence for that kind, learned man, and a gratitude that has lasted through the years. Will you please tell him how I feel; it is very good of him to still think of me, and I appreciate it.

The poem that you entrusted me with, I am sending back to you. And I thank you once more for your questions and sincere trust, of which, by answering as honestly as I can, I have tried to make myself a little worthier than I, as a stranger, really am.

Yours very truly,

Rainer Maria Rilke

Source: From *Letters to a Young Poet* by Rainer Maria Rilke, translated by M.D Herter Norton. Copyright 1934, 1954 by W.W. Norton & Company, Inc., renewed © 1962, 1982 by Herter Norton. Used by permission of W.W. Norton & Company Inc.

Questions for Letter 1 of
Letters to a Young Poet by Rainer Maria Rilke

LEVEL 1

General Understandings

- Who is the narrator (writer) of the letter?
- Why is Rilke writing to Mr. Kappus?
  - o What are the concerns that Rilke has for Mr. Kappus?

Key Details

- What can you infer about the concerns Mr. Kappus wrote to Rilke about?
- What criticism does Rilke have for Mr. Kappus's poems?
- What reasons does Rilke cite for not being able to give criticism?
- According to Rilke, who is the only person who can counsel someone?
- What makes a work of art "good"?
- What kinds of poems should Mr. Kappus write? Why?
- How does Rilke attempt to make Mr. Kappus feel better? Be sure to point to specific phrases that inform your thinking. Why does he do this?

LEVEL 2

Vocabulary

- How does Rilke define "good" in terms of art?
- How does Rilke define "nature"?

Structure

- Briefly summarize the subject of each paragraph. Why does Rilke address such varied topics in this letter?
- Find areas were Rilke uses questions. What effect does it have on how the letter is read?

Author's Craft

- What tone does Rilke close the letter with? Why?
- How does Rilke describe Mr. Kappus's poetry? Why?
- Examine the words Rilke uses to describe himself to Mr. Kappus. Why does he do this?

LEVEL 3

Author's Purpose

- Why does Rilke hesitate to give Mr. Kappus criticism?
- How should Mr. Kappus measure the value of his art?
- Where should Mr. Kappus find his inspiration?
- What question does Mr. Kappus need to answer in order to discover whether he is an artist or not?
- What does Rilke NOT want Mr. Kappus to do, regarding his poetry?

Intertextual Connections

- How does the opening paragraph conflict with the body paragraphs of this letter? Use specific evidence to defend your answer.

Available for download from **www.corwin.com/textdependentquestions**

Letter 6 of *Letters to a Young Poet* by Rainer Maria Rilke

My dear Mr. Kappus,

I don't want you to be without a greeting from me when Christmas comes and when you, in the midst of the holiday, are bearing your solitude more heavily than usual. But when you notice that it is vast, you should be happy; for what (you should ask yourself) would a solitude be that was not vast; there is only one solitude, and it is vast, heavy, difficult to bear, and almost everyone has hours when he would gladly exchange it for any kind of sociability, however trivial or cheap, for the tiniest outward agreement with the first person who comes along, the most unworthy. But perhaps these are the very hours during which solitude grows; for its growing is painful as the growing of boys and sad as the beginning of spring. But that must not confuse you. What is necessary, after all, is only this: solitude, vast inner solitude. To walk inside yourself and meet no one for hours—that is what you must be able to attain. To be solitary as you were when you were a child, when the grownups walked around involved with matters that seemed large and important because they looked so busy and because you didn't understand a thing about what they were doing.

And when you realize that their activities are shabby, that their vocations are petrified and no longer connected with life, why not then continue to look upon it all as a child would, as if you were looking at something unfamiliar, out of the depths of your own world, from the vastness of your own solitude, which is itself work and status and vocation? Why should you want to give up a child's wise not-understanding in exchange for defensiveness and scorn, since not understanding is, after all, a way of being alone, whereas defensiveness and scorn are a participation in precisely what, by these means, you want to separate yourself from.

Think, dear Sir, of the world that you carry inside you, and call this thinking whatever you want to: a remembering of your own childhood or a yearning toward a future of your own—only be attentive to what is arising within you, and place that above everything you perceive around you. What is happening in your innermost self is worthy of your entire love; somehow you must find a way to work at it, and not lose too much time or too much courage in clarifying your attitude toward people. Who says that you have any attitude at all? I know, your profession is hard and full of things that contradict you, and I foresaw your lament and knew that it would come. Now that it has come, there is nothing I can say to reassure you, I can only suggest that perhaps all professions are like that, filled with demands, filled with hostility toward the individual, saturated as it were with the hatred of those who find themselves mute and sullen in an insipid duty. The situation you must live in now is not more heavily burdened with conventions, prejudices, and false ideas than all the other situations, and if there are some that pretend to offer a greater freedom, there is nevertheless none that is, in itself, vast and spacious and connected to the important Things that the truest kind of life consists of. Only the individual who is solitary is placed under the deepest laws like a Thing, and when he walks out into the rising dawn or looks out into the event-filled evening and when he feels what is happening there, all situations drop from him as if from a dead man, though he stands in the midst of pure life. What you, dear Mr. Kappus, now have to experience as an officer, you would have felt in just the same way in any of the established professions; yes, even if, outside any position, you had simply tried to find some easy and independent contact with society, this feeling of being hemmed in would not have been spared you. It is like this everywhere; but that is no cause for anxiety or sadness; if there is nothing you can share with other people, try to be close to Things; they will not abandon you; and the nights are still there, and the winds that move through the trees and across many lands; everything in the world of Things and animals is still filled with happening, which you can take part in; and children are still the way you were as a child, sad and happy in just the same way and if you think of your childhood, you once again live among them, among the solitary children, and the grownups are nothing, and their dignity has no value.

And if it frightens and torments you to think of childhood and of the simplicity and silence that accompanies it, because you can no longer believe in God, who appears in it everywhere, then ask yourself, dear Mr. Kappus, whether you have really lost God. Isn't it much truer to say that you have never yet possessed him? For when could that have been? Do you think that a child can hold him, him whom grown men bear only with great effort and whose weight crushes the old? Do you suppose that someone who really has him could lose him like a little stone? Or don't you think that someone who once had him could only be lost by him? But if you realize that he did not exist in your childhood, and did not exist previously, if you suspect that Christ was deluded by his yearning and Muhammad deceived by his pride—and if you are terrified to feel that even now he does not exist, even at this moment when we are talking about him— what justifies you then, if he never existed, in missing him like someone who has passed away and in searching for him as though he were lost?

Why don't you think of him as the one who is coming, who has been approaching from all eternity, the one who will someday arrive, the ultimate fruit of a tree whose leaves we are? What keeps you from projecting his birth into the ages that are coming into existence, and living your life as a painful and lovely day in the history of a great pregnancy? Don't you see how everything that happens is again and again a beginning, and couldn't it be His beginning, since, in itself, starting is always so beautiful? If he is the most perfect one, must not what is less perfect precede him, so that he can choose himself out of fullness and superabundance? Must he not be the last one, so that he can include everything in himself, and what meaning would we have if he whom we are longing for has already existed?

As bees gather honey, so we collect what is sweetest out of all things and build Him. Even with the trivial, with the insignificant (as long as it is done out of love) we begin, with work and with the repose that comes afterward, with a silence or with a small solitary joy, with everything that we do alone, without anyone to join or help us, we start Him whom we will not live to see, just as our ancestors could not live to see us. And yet they, who passed away long ago, still exist in us, as predisposition, as burden upon our fate, as murmuring blood, and as gesture that rises up from the depths of time.

Is there anything that can deprive you of the hope that in this way you will someday exist in Him, who is the farthest, the outermost limit?

Dear Mr. Kappus, celebrate Christmas in this devout feeling, that perhaps He needs this very anguish of yours in order to begin; these very days of your transition are perhaps the time when everything in you is working at Him, as you once worked at Him in your childhood, breathlessly. Be patient and without bitterness, and realize that the least we can do is to make coming into existence no more difficult for Him than the earth does for spring when it wants to come.

And be glad and confident.

Yours,

Rainer Maria Rilke

Source: From *Letters to a Young Poet* by Rainer Maria Rilke, translated by M.D Herter Norton. Copyright 1934, 1954 by W.W. Norton & Company, Inc., renewed © 1962, 1982 by Herter Norton. Used by permission of W.W. Norton & Company Inc.

Questions for Letter 6 of
Letters to a Young Poet by Rainer Maria Rilke

LEVEL 1

General Understandings

- Who is the narrator (writer) of the letter?
- Why is Rilke writing to Mr. Kappus?
  - What are the concerns that Rilke has for Mr. Kappus?
  - What can you infer about the concerns Mr. Kappus wrote to Rilke about?

Key Details

- What job does Mr. Kappus hold? What emotions does it cause him?
- What major relationship is Mr. Kappus struggling with?

LEVEL 2

Vocabulary

- How does Rilke define solitude?
- What does *petrified* mean in the way Rilke uses it? Could it have more than one meaning?
- How does Rilke define "having" God? Does it mean the same as possession?
- Consider Rilke's use of the word *solitary*. Does it have a positive or negative connotation?

Structure

- Briefly summarize the subject of each paragraph. Why does Rilke address such varied topics in this letter?

Author's Craft

- What tone does the letter begin with? What tone does the letter close with? Point out specific words and phrases that led you to this conclusion.
- How does Rilke use questioning to lead Mr. Kappus to the type of thinking he wants? Be sure to provide examples to support your answer.
- What do the capitalizations in the text, particularly Paragraph 3, represent? Why do you think Rilke chose to capitalize these words?

LEVEL 3

Author's Purpose

- How does the author want the reader(s) of the letter to think about solitude?
- How does Rilke attempt to comfort Mr. Kappus and address his concerns about losing God?

- Are all jobs fulfilling, according to Rilke?
- What is Rilke's reason for Mr. Kappus feeling as if he has "lost God"?
- What is Rilke's suggestion to Mr. Kappus in terms of thinking about God?

Intertextual Connections

- At the beginning of the letter, Rilke tells Mr. Kappus to "rejoice because" his solitude is great. Using the rest of the letter to support your answer, consider the reasons why Rilke thinks this loneliness is not a negative thing.

LEVEL 4

Opinion With Evidence or Argument

- What other characters have you read about that suffer from feelings of isolation? Which parts of Letter 6 describe their situation?

Letter 8 of *Letters to a Young Poet* by Rainer Maria Rilke

I want to talk to you again for a little while, dear Mr. Kappus, although there is almost nothing I can say that will help you, and I can hardly find one useful word. You have had many sadnesses, large ones, which passed. And you say that even this passing was difficult and upsetting for you. But please, ask yourself whether these large sadnesses haven't rather gone right through you. Perhaps many things inside you have been transformed; perhaps somewhere, someplace deep inside your being, you have undergone important changes while you were sad. The only sadnesses that are dangerous and unhealthy are the ones that we carry around in public in order to drown them out with the noise; like diseases that are treated superficially and foolishly, they just withdraw and after a short interval break out again all the more terribly; and gather inside us and are life, are life that is unlived, rejected, lost, life that we can die of. If only it were possible for us to see farther than our knowledge reaches, and even a little beyond the outworks of our presentiment, perhaps we would bear our sadnesses with greater trust than we have in our joys. For they are the moments when something new has entered us, something unknown; our feelings grow mute in shy embarrassment, everything in us withdraws, a silence arises, and the new experience, which no one knows, stands in the midst of it all and says nothing.

It seems to me that almost all our sadnesses are moments of tension, which we feel as paralysis because we no longer hear our astonished emotions living. Because we are alone with the unfamiliar presence that has entered us; because everything we trust and are used to is for a moment taken away from us; because we stand in the midst of a transition where we cannot remain standing. That is why the sadness passes: the new presence inside us, the presence that has been added, has entered our heart, has gone into its innermost chamber and is no longer even there, is already in our bloodstream. And we don't know what it was. We could easily be made to believe that nothing happened, and yet we have changed, as a house that a guest has entered changes. We can't say who has come, perhaps we will never know, but many signs indicate that the future enters us in this way in order to be transformed in us, long before it happens. And that is why it is so important to be solitary and attentive when one is sad: because the seemingly uneventful and motionless moment when our future steps into us is so much closer to life than that other loud and accidental point of time when it happens to us as if from outside. The quieter we are, the more patient and open we are in our sadnesses, the more deeply and serenely the new presence can enter us, and the more we can make it our own, the more it becomes our fate; and later on, when it "happens" (that is, steps forth out of us to other people), we will feel related and close to it in our innermost being. And that is necessary. It is necessary—and toward this point our development will move, little by little—that nothing alien happen to us, but only what has long been our own. People have already had to rethink so many concepts of motion; and they will also gradually come to realize that what we call fate does not come into us from the outside, but emerges from us. It is only because so many people have not absorbed and transformed their fates while they were living in them that they have not realized what was emerging from them; it was so alien to them that, in their confusion and fear, they thought it must have entered them at the very moment they became aware of it, for they swore they had never before found anything like that inside them. Just as people for a long time had a wrong idea about the sun's motion, they are even now wrong about the motion of what is to come. The future stands still, dear Mr. Kappus, but we move in infinite space.

How could it not be difficult for us?

And to speak of solitude again, it becomes clearer and clearer that fundamentally this is nothing that one can choose or refrain from. We are solitary. We can delude ourselves about this and act as if it were not true. That is all. But how much better it is to recognize that we are alone; yes, even to begin from this realization. It will, of course, make us dizzy; for all points that our eyes used to rest on are taken away from us, there is no longer anything near us, and everything far away is infinitely far. A man taken out of his room and, almost without preparation or transition, placed on the heights of a great mountain range, would feel something like that: an unequalled insecurity, an abandonment to the nameless, would almost annihilate him. He would feel he was falling or think he was being catapulted out into space or exploded into a thousand pieces: what a colossal lie his brain would have to invent in order to catch up with and explain the situation of his senses. That is how all distances, all measures, change for the person who becomes solitary; many of these changes occur suddenly and then, as with the man on the mountaintop, unusual fantasies and strange feelings arise, which seem to grow out beyond all that is bearable. But it is necessary for us to experience that too. We must accept our reality as vastly as we possibly can; everything, even the unprecedented, must be possible within it. This is in the end the only kind of courage that is required of us: the courage to face the strangest, most unusual, most inexplicable experiences that can meet us. The fact that people have in this sense been cowardly has done infinite harm to life; the experiences that are called apparitions, the whole so-called "spirit world," death, all these Things that are so closely related to us, have through our daily defensiveness been so entirely pushed out of life that the senses with which we might have been able to grasp them have atrophied. To say nothing of God. But the fear of the inexplicable has not only impoverished the reality of the individual; it has also narrowed the relationship between one human being and another, which has as it were been lifted out of the riverbed of infinite possibilities and set down in a fallow place on the bank, where nothing happens. For it is not only indolence that causes human relationships to be repeated from case to case with such unspeakable monotony and boredom; it is timidity before any new, inconceivable experience, which we don't think we can deal with. But only someone who is ready for everything, who doesn't exclude any experience, even the most incomprehensible, will live the relationship with another person as something alive and will himself sound the depths of his own being. For if we imagine this being of the individual as a larger or smaller room, it is obvious that most people come to know only one corner of their room, one spot near the window, one narrow strip on which they keep walking back and forth. In this way they have a certain security. And yet how much more human is the dangerous insecurity that drives those prisoners in Poe's stories to feel out the shapes of their horrible dungeons and not be strangers to the unspeakable terror of their cells. We, however, are not prisoners. No traps or snares have been set around us, and there is nothing that should frighten or upset us. We have been put into life as into the element we most accord with, and we have, moreover, through thousands of years of adaptation, come to resemble this life so greatly that when we hold still, through a fortunate mimicry we can hardly be differentiated from everything around us. We have no reason to harbor any mistrust against our world, for it is not against us. If it has terrors, they are our terrors; if it has abysses, these abysses belong to us; if there are dangers, we must try to love them. And if only we arrange our life in accordance with the principle which tells us that we must always trust in the difficult, then what now appears to us as the most alien will become our most intimate and trusted experience. How could we forget those ancient myths that stand at the beginning of all races, the myths about dragons that at the last moment are transformed into princesses? Perhaps all the dragons in our lives are princesses who are only waiting to see us act, just once, with beauty and courage. Perhaps everything that frightens us is, in its deepest essence, something helpless that wants our love.

So you mustn't be frightened, dear Mr. Kappus, if a sadness rises in front of you, larger than any you have ever seen; if an anxiety, like light and cloud-shadows, moves over your hands and over everything you do. You must realize that something is happening to you, that life has not forgotten you, that it holds you in its hand and will not let you fall. Why do you want to shut out of your life any uneasiness, any misery, any depression, since after all you don't know what work these conditions are doing inside you? Why do you want to persecute yourself with the question of where all this is coming from and where it is going? Since you know, after all, that you are in the midst of transitions and you wished for nothing so much as to change. If there is anything unhealthy in your reactions, just bear in mind that sickness is the means by which an organism frees itself from what is alien; so one must simply help it to be sick, to have its whole sickness and to break out with it, since that is the way it gets better. In you, dear Mr. Kappus, so much is happening now; you must be patient like someone who is sick, and confident like some one who is recovering; for perhaps you are both. And more: you are also the doctor, who has to watch over himself. But in every sickness there are many days when the doctor can do nothing but wait. And that is what you, insofar as you are your own doctor, must now do, more than anything else.

Don't observe yourself too closely. Don't be too quick to draw conclusions from what happens to you; simply let it happen. Otherwise it will be too easy for you to look with blame (that is: morally) at your past, which naturally has a share in everything that now meets you. But whatever errors, wishes, and yearnings of your boyhood are operating in you now are not what you remember and condemn. The extraordinary circumstances of a solitary and helpless childhood are so difficult, so complicated, surrendered to so many influences and at the same time so cut off from all real connection with life that, where a vice enters it, one may not simply call it a vice. One must be so careful with names anyway; it is so often the name of an offense that a life shatters upon, not the nameless and personal action itself, which was perhaps a quite definite necessity of that life and could have been absorbed by it without any trouble. And the expenditure of energy seems to you so great only because you overvalue victory; it is not the "great thing" that you think you have achieved, although you are right about your feeling; the great thing is that there was already something there which you could replace that deception with, something true and real. Without this even your victory would have been just a moral reaction of no great significance; but in fact it has become a part of your life. Your life, dear Mr. Kappus, which I think of with so many good wishes. Do you remember how that life yearned out of childhood toward the "great thing"? I see that it is now yearning forth beyond the great thing toward the greater one. That is why it does not cease to be difficult, but that is also why it will not cease to grow.

And if there is one more thing that I must say to you, it is this: Don't think that the person who is trying to comfort you now lives untroubled among the simple and quiet words that sometimes give you pleasure. His life has much trouble and sadness, and remains far behind yours. If it were otherwise, he would never have been able to find those words.

Yours,

Rainer Maria Rilke

Questions for Letter 8 of
Letters to a Young Poet by Rainer Maria Rilke

LEVEL 1

General Understandings

- Who is the narrator (writer) of the letter?
- Why is Rilke writing to Mr. Kappus?
  - What are the concerns that Rilke has for Mr. Kappus?

Key Details

- What struggles is Mr. Kappus having in his life, prompting him to write to Rilke?
- What is the role of solitude and pain in the human experience?
- How do humans avoid feeling loneliness and suffering?
- Is Rilke free from the sufferings that Mr. Kappus writes to him about?

LEVEL 2

Vocabulary

- How does Rilke define "dangerous" sadnesses?
- What are "visions"?
- How does Rilke use the word *alien*? Does this have a negative or positive connotation?
- What does Rilke mean when he says in Paragraph 5, "One must be careful with names anyway"? What is his definition of "names"?
- How does Rilke define "sickness" in Paragraph 4?

Structure

- What is the purpose of using questions in this letter?
- Why does Rilke use "we" throughout the letter when addressing Mr. Kappus's troubles?

Author's Craft

- What is the tone of this letter? Point out specific words and phrases that led you to this conclusion.
- What archetype does Rilke use in Paragraph 3? How does this illustrate his main point?
- Which famous author does Rilke mention in this letter? What connection are we meant to make between the characters in this author's works and Mr. Kappus's situation?

LEVEL 3

Author's Purpose

- How does the author want the reader(s) of the letter to think about sadness? Should it be avoided?

- Can one avoid loneliness?

- What would Rilke say is a helpful way to deal with the sad and troubling experiences in our lives?

- Why is it important to be "lonely and attentive when one is sad"?

- How should we deal with fear of the unknown and sadness, according to Rilke?

Intertextual Connections

- In the Paragraph 4, Rilke says, "Perhaps all the dragons of our lives are princesses who are only waiting to see us once beautiful and brave." What are examples of "dragons" in this letter? How can we make them "princesses"?

LEVEL 4

Opinion With Evidence or Argument

- What advice would Rilke give the characters in "St. Lucy's Home for Girls Raised by Wolves" about dealing with their troubles? Are they taking action he would approve of?

- Do you think fate comes from inside of us or outside of us? What would Rilke say in response to this question? Be sure to use evidence from the letter to support your claims.

'ST. LUCY'S HOME FOR GIRLS RAISED BY WOLVES' BY KAREN RUSSELL

(SHORT STORY)

Questions for "St. Lucy's Home for Girls Raised by Wolves" by Karen Russell

LEVEL 1

General Understanding

- What is happening in this story?
- Why are the girl-wolves at St. Lucy's?
- How do the girl-wolves feel being at St. Lucy's?
- Why were the girl-wolves sent to St. Lucy's?
- How do each of the girl-wolves adapt to being at St. Lucy's?
- How do the characters develop over the course of the story?
- What is the role of the pack?
- How does the narrator view her parents?

Key Details

- Who is the narrator, and how did you figure that out? [You do not find out who the narrator is until you have read more than half the story.]
- What is the role of the pack?
- What is the setting of the story? Can you identify a specific location?
- Where do you think the nuns came from?
- What challenges do the girl-wolves face adapting to their new environment?
- How is the pack dynamic continuing to change?
- Why does the pack hate Jeanette and Mirabella?
- How is the narrator's view of herself altering?
- How is the narrator's memory impacted throughout the story?
- Why does Claudette react so strongly at the dance?
- What is the significance behind Claudette's physical journey to visit her parents?

- Why do you think that Claudette's parents are waiting for a "display" of what she has learned?
- What is Claudette's identity at the end of the story?

LEVEL 2

Vocabulary

- What is the significance of the lines, "We would go to St. Lucy's to study a better culture. We didn't know at the time that our parents were sending us away for good. Neither did they."
- Why does the narrator make the connection of erasing their scent with erasing them? "Someone was coming in and erasing us."
- What is the significance behind the narrator referring to herself and the other students as dogs and not wolves?
- What does Sister Maria de la Guardia mean when she says, "You see? What are you holding on to? Nothing, little one. Nothing"?
- Why does the author refer to a "shadow question"?
- Why do the narrator and author use the word *rehabilitated* to describe the process the wolf-girls are going through?
- What is the significance behind, "We graduated from St. Lucy's shortly thereafter. As far as I can recollect, that was our last communal howl"?
- Why does the author finish the story with, "'So,' I said, telling my first human lie. 'I'm home'"?

Structure

- How does Russell's analogy between domesticating wolves and humans draw attention to societal issues? Find specific examples that support your thinking.
- Find examples of the author's use of discordant language in this selection. Why does she use this writing technique?

Author's Craft

- How does the author's use of dialogue create a better sense of character for each of the girl wolves?
- How does the passage of time in the story influence your thoughts about the characters and events?

LEVEL 3

Author's Purpose

- Why does the author have wolf-girls as characters?
- What is the author's attitude toward social norms? What is your evidence of this from the text?

- How is this text a reflection of modern society?
- How do the characters in this text reflect society?
- What happens when one does not adapt?

Intertextual Connections

- Why would parents send their children to an alternative school?
- How does one decide whether one culture is better than another?
- What happens when one does not conform, both in the text and modern-day society?
- How does language define Claudette? How does language define each individual in a society?
- Can you relate the challenges that the girl-wolves face at St. Lucy's to issues you have personally witnessed or experienced in modern-day society?

LEVEL 4

Opinion With Evidence or Argument

- What is the significance of the names in this text? [Mirabella, St. Lucy's]
- Why is the narrator reluctant to say goodbye to Mirabella?
- Are the wolf-girls better off at St. Lucy's or after attending St. Lucy's?
- Define success and failure in the context of this story.
- Was Claudette successfully rehabilitated?
- Are humans dependent upon a pack for survival?
- How would the author define success and failure based upon the events in the story?
- What is the author's message about social conformity?
- How do the characters develop over the course of the story?
- Which character can you relate to and why?
- What is the significance of the "pack" throughout the story? How is it similar to or different from a traditional family?
- How has your thinking changed over the course of your readings? Why?

'A VERY SHORT STORY' BY ERNEST HEMINGWAY

(SHORT STORY)

Please note this text is widely available online to print and distribute in class.

Questions for "A Very Short Story" by Ernest Hemingway

LEVEL 1

General Understanding

- Where does the story take place?
- What event is taking place while the story unfolds?
- What do we know about the soldier? What do we know about Luz?
- How do Luz and the soldier meet?

Key Details

- What is the relationship between Luz and the soldier like in the beginning?
- What is the soldier supposed to do when he goes back to America, and what does this tell us about his relationship with Luz?
- What insight does this give us into his relationship with Luz?
- What does Luz say about her relationship with the soldier in Paragraph 6? Who is she comparing him to?
- Who does Luz have an affair with? Why is this important?
- Why did Luz and the soldier want to get married?

LEVEL 2

Vocabulary

- What does the author mean when he says Luz "expected, absolutely and unexpectedly, to be married in the spring." What does this reveal about the author's feelings toward her?
- What is an armistice?
- What is a "boy and girl affair?"
- What is the tone of this story?
- What does "Luz" mean? How is this significant to her role in the story?

Structure

- How does the text use foreshadowing to alert us to the end of the relationship? Where do we first see this?

Author's Craft

- None of the characters, except for Luz, has a name. Why do you think the author chose to do this? Use evidence from the story to support your answer.

- Why do you think this is titled "A Very Short Story"?

- Examine Hemingway's use of direct, uncomplicated sentences. How does this affect the tone of the story?

- How does the story end? Why did Hemingway choose to leave his main character in the state that he did? Be sure to use evidence from the story to support your ideas.

LEVEL 3

Author's Purpose

- What does war do to the people, according to the text?

- Is Luz liked by her patients? What does this tell us about her?

- What does war do to love according to the story?

- How does the narrator react to Luz's affair? Why?

- What is the rank of the soldier? Why is this important to the meaning of the story?

- Who does the soldier think is to blame for this affair gone wrong? How do you know?

- How do you think the author feels about love? Why?

Intertextual Connections

- How is the relationship between Luz and the soldier similar to that of Romeo and Juliet? How is it different? Is age a factor in this comparison?

LEVEL 4

Opinion With Evidence or Argument

- This text was written and published in 1924 by Hemingway, a World War I veteran. He was injured in Italy and fell in love with an Italian nurse—this story is based on their relationship. With this in mind, answer the following questions:

  o Who does the author think is to blame for this affair gone wrong? Why?

  o Use evidence from the text to support your answer.

'MELTING POT' BY ANNA QUINDLEN
(ESSAY)

Questions for "Melting Pot" by Anna Quindlen

LEVEL 1

General Understanding
- Who is speaking, and what setting is she describing?
- What types of people live in the narrator/speaker's neighborhood?
- Is this fiction or nonfiction?

Key Details
- What is the narrator/speaker's ethnic background?
- Do the neighbors in this text like one another? Support your answer with textual evidence.
- Does the narrator like her neighbors?

LEVEL 2

Vocabulary
- What is the tone of the first five paragraphs? Point to specific words to support your thinking.
- Where does the tone of the text shift? How does that reflect the author's mood?
- What role does food play in this essay? How does it represent people?
- What is the significance of the line, "You're not one of them"?
- Explain the lack of names. How does this hint at the author's opinions on individuality?
- Explain in your own words to a partner/small group what the author is saying in Paragraph 5.
- What does the saying "Sometimes the baby slips out with the bathwater" mean? Is the author commenting on herself or her neighbors?
- What role do the words *me* and *them* play in the text?

Structure
- How does the author use irony to point out the flaws in her neighbor's thinking?
- Why does the author use dialogue in the middle of the text but nowhere else?

Author's Craft

- Does the author contradict herself? If so, where and how?
- What conflict does the author present when the "rough types" start to move out of her neighborhood?
- How much time passes during the course of the text?

LEVEL 3

Author's Purpose

- Does the author favor neighborhoods changing as time passes? Use evidence to support your thinking.
- What kinds of situations unite Quindlen's neighbors? What does this say about human nature?
- What role does money play in the text?
- Does the title reflect the author's true feelings about her neighborhood? Why or why not?
- How does the text reflect your school, neighborhood, city, or nation, or the world?

Intertextual Connections

Interviewee: Gertrude (Gudrun) Hildebrandt Moller

Date of Birth: June 15, 1920

Date of Interview: October 5, 1992

Interviewer: Janet Levine, PhD

Immigrated from Germany in 1929 at age 9

Ellis Island Collection: EI-222

Moller (Name Change in School):

I was born Gudrun Hildebrandt and married Moller, Mr. Moller, who was from Denmark. He immigrated here many years later and we met in New York. However when I started school in Chicago, where I grew up, needless to say, first of all, I couldn't speak a word of English, and I was the only child in the school that couldn't speak English. And (she laughs) it wasn't too happy the first couple of years but my mama said "Take heart because some day you're going to be able to speak two languages and all the ones that were teasing you will speak only one." And it was true. She was always right. So, my teacher suggested, since none of the children could pronounce *Gudrun*, which is an old Germanic-Scandinavian name, and a very

(Continued)

(Continued)

beautiful name (I hear), she gave me a list of girls' names to choose from. So that all the kids could converse, you know, know what to call me. So I picked the name starting with a g, as with my name, and it was Gertrude. I'm not very happy with it, but it has stuck with me all of these years.

Source: Ellis Island Oral History Collection.

- Review the interview from an Ellis Island immigrant above. How does her experience reflect the America that Quindlen describes in her essay? Compare the two texts using evidence from each.

LEVEL 4

Opinion With Evidence or Argument

> We become not a melting pot but a beautiful mosaic.
> Different people, different beliefs, different yearnings,
> different hopes, different dreams.

—Jimmy Carter

- Consider this quotation by Jimmy Carter. Would Anna Quindlen agree with this statement? Using evidence from the text, write a speech explaining why she would or wouldn't agree that America is a mosaic rather than a melting pot.

'CONJECTURE' BY MARK TWAIN
(ESSAY)

The historians "suppose" that Shakespeare attended the Free School in Stratford from the time he was seven years old till he was thirteen. There is no *evidence* in existence that he ever went to school at all.

The historians "infer" that he got his Latin in that school—the school which they "suppose" he attended.

They "suppose" his father's declining fortunes made it necessary for him to leave the school they supposed he attended, and get to work and help support his parents and their ten children. But there is no evidence that he ever entered or retired from the school they suppose he attended.

They "suppose" he assisted his father in the butchering business; and that, being only a boy, he didn't have to do full-grown butchering, but only slaughtered calves. Also, that whenever he killed a calf he made a high-flown speech over it. This supposition rests upon the testimony of a man who wasn't there at the time; a man who got it from a man who could have been there, but did not say whether he was or not; and neither of them thought to mention it for decades, and decades, and decades, and two more decades after Shakespeare's death (until old age and mental decay had refreshed and vivified their memories). They hadn't two facts in stock about the long-dead distinguished citizen, but only just the one: he slaughtered calves and broke into oratory while he was at it. Curious. They had only one fact, yet the distinguished citizen had spent twenty-six years in that little town—just half his lifetime. However, rightly viewed, it was the most important fact, indeed almost the only important fact, of Shakespeare's life in Stratford. Rightly viewed. For experience is an author's most valuable asset; experience is the thing that puts the muscle and the breath and the warm blood into the book he writes. Rightly viewed, calf-butchering accounts for *Titus Andronicus*, the only play—ain't it?—that the Stratford Shakespeare ever wrote; and yet it is the only one everybody tries to chouse him out of, the Baconians included.

The historians find themselves "justified in believing" that the young Shakespeare poached upon Sir Thomas Lucy's deer preserves and got haled before that magistrate for it. But there is no shred of respectworthy evidence that anything of the kind happened.

The historians, having argued the thing that *might* have happened into the thing that *did* happen, found no trouble in turning Sir Thomas Lucy into Mr. Justice Shallow. They have long ago convinced the world—on surmise and without trustworthy evidence—that Shallow *is* Sir Thomas.

The next addition to the young Shakespeare's Stratford history comes easy. The historian builds it out of the surmised deer-stealing, and the surmised trial before the magistrate, and the surmised vengeance-prompted satire upon the magistrate in the play: result, the young Shakespeare was a wild, wild, wild, oh *such* a wild young scamp, and that gratuitous slander is established for all time! It is the very way Professor Osborn and I built the colossal skeleton brontosaur that stands fifty-seven feet long and sixteen feet high in the Natural History Museum, the awe and admiration of all the world, the stateliest skeleton that exists on the planet. We had nine bones, and we built the rest of him out of plaster of paris. We ran short of plaster of paris, or we'd have built a brontosaur that could sit down beside the Stratford Shakespeare and none but an expert could tell which was biggest or contained the most plaster.

Shakespeare pronounced *Venus and Adonis* "the first heir of his invention," apparently implying that it was his first effort at literary composition. He should not have said it. It has been an embarrassment to his historians these many, many years. They have to make him write that graceful and polished and flawless and beautiful poem before he escaped from Stratford and his family—1586 or '87—age, twenty-two, or along there; because within the next five years he wrote five great plays, and could not have found time to write another line.

It is sorely embarrassing. If he began to slaughter calves, and poach deer, and rollick around, and learn English, at the earliest likely moment—say at thirteen, when he was supposably wrenched from that school where he was supposably storing up Latin for future literary use—he had his youthful hands full, and much more than full. He must have had to put aside his Warwickshire dialect, which wouldn't be understood in London, and study English very hard. Very hard indeed; incredibly hard, almost, if the result of that labor was to be the smooth and rounded and flexible and letter-perfect English of the *Venus and Adonis* in the space of ten years; and at the same time learn great and fine and unsurpassable literary form.

Source: Mark Twain, Is Shakespeare Dead? From My Autobiography © 1909

Questions for "Conjecture" by Mark Twain

General Understanding

- What topic is being discussed?
- What type of text (fiction, nonfiction) do you think this is? Support your opinion with evidence from the text.
- Who is the audience for this text? How do you know?

Key Details

- What are the reasons given by historians that Shakespeare left school?
- Why does Twain call *Venus and Adonis* "sorely embarrassing"?
- How are historians described?
- According to the article, did Shakespeare attend school?

Vocabulary

- What is the tone of the piece? How do we know? Point out specific words or phrases.
- Why are quotation marks used around the words *infer* and *suppose*?
- What is the tone when Twain says, "The next addition to the young Shakespeare's Stratford history comes easy"? What is he implying about how historians document history?
- How is history defined in this piece? Is it reliable?

Structure

- Why do you think this is titled, "Conjecture"?
- How does Twain use personal and popular anecdotes to illustrate his position on Shakespeare's identity?

Author's Craft

- How does Twain use humor to prove his view of Shakespeare and his origins?
- What purpose does the reference to the skeleton brontosaur in the Natural History Museum serve?
- What role does the calf butchering anecdote in Paragraph 3 serve in proving Twain's point that Shakespeare is not who we think he is?

LEVEL 3

Author's Purpose

- What does Twain think of historians who posit that Shakespeare is indeed the man from Stratford-Upon-Avon? Use evidence that supports your opinion.
- How does Twain present historians? What are his views of them?
- Is Twain reliable himself? Why or why not? Use evidence from the text to support your answer.
- How is history made, according to Twain?

Intertextual Connections

- Does it matter whether or not we know who the author of famous works is? Using "Conjecture" and other texts you have read this year, write an editorial piece arguing for or against the importance of the author's identity when evaluating a text.

LEVEL 4

Opinion With Evidence or Argument

- What do you think of Twain's opinion on Shakespeare? Do you agree or disagree? Conduct your own research on Shakespeare's identity; compose an argumentative speech using your research and "Conjecture" to help prove your point.

APPENDIX II
MIDDLE SCHOOL ENGLISH

A·II

'THE TELL-TALE HEART' BY EDGAR ALLAN POE
(SHORT STORY)

*Please note this text is widely available online to print and distribute in class.

Questions for "The Tell-Tale Heart" by Edgar Allan Poe

LEVEL 1

General Understanding

- What is the time period of the story?
- How does the narrator's state of mind develop over the course of the story?
- What is the relationship between the narrator and the old man?
- What are the reasons the narrator gives for killing the old man?

Key Details

- Who is the narrator? What evidence did you use to deduce that?
- What is the role of the eye?
- What is the role of the watch?
- How is the old man described?
- Which emotion attacks both the narrator and the old man?
- Explain whose heart is beating, using evidence from the passage.
- Why do the police arrive at the narrator's residence?
- How does the narrator interact with and react to the police visiting his residence?
- Using evidence, describe whether or not the officers suspect the narrator of murder.

LEVEL 2

Vocabulary

- What is the "disease" that the narrator references?
- What does Poe/narrator mean by the word "mad"?
- What words or phrases does the narrator repeat, and how does this affect the tone of this passage?
- Using context clues, define Poe's definition of "damned."

Structure

- How does the author's use of symbolism impact the story?
- Discuss Poe's analogy when he writes, "It increased my fury, as the beating of a drum stimulates the soldier into courage."

Author's Craft

- How does Poe's craft (specifically punctuation and repetition) assist in demonstrating the narrator's state of mind?
- How does Poe's use of craft change, increase, or decrease over the course of the story? What is the impact of this style on the reader?

LEVEL 3

Author's Purpose

- Why does the author not name the narrator?
- What is the author's attitude toward mental health? What is your evidence of this from the text?
- How does the narrator's retelling of the events lead the reader into understanding his state of mind?
- How does the narrator in this text reflect society and society's views toward mental health?

Intertextual Connections

- Compare "The Tell-Tale Heart" to "The Raven." How and why does Poe use imagery, symbolism, and metaphors in these texts?
- Examine Poe's use of suspense and tension in "The Tell-Tale Heart" and "The Black Cat." Discuss their effectiveness given the content of the texts.
- Discuss the narrators' motives for committing crimes in both "The Black Cat" and "The Tell-Tale Heart."

LEVEL 4

Opinion With Evidence or Argument

- How does one decide whether or not the narrator is mentally stable?
- What is the symbolism of the eye and watch in this story?
- Why does the narrator declare his guilt at the end?
- Is the narrator mentally stable or not? How do you know?
- Determine guilt or innocence in the story using evidence to support your theory.
- How does Poe address the topic/theme of good versus evil?

ANNE FRANK: THE DIARY OF A YOUNG GIRL

(DIARY)

Questions for *The Diary of Anne Frank*

Diary Entry: Saturday, 20 June, 1942

LEVEL 1

General Understanding

- Where is Holland in relationship to Germany?
- Why does Anne have a diary in the first place?
- What kind of "early life" did Anne have?

Key Details

- Describe Anne's family and social circle.
- Would you consider Anne vain? Why or why not, using evidence from the text?
- Why is Anne compelled to write her diary to Kitty?
- What restrictions were placed on Jews?
- Explain Anne's feelings about school. What evidence supports your opinion?

LEVEL 2

Vocabulary

- What does the saying "paper is more patient than man" mean? How is this relevant to Anne beginning her diary?

Structure

- How does Anne's style in writing about the restrictions placed on Jews affect the tone of this entry?
- Describe the passage of time in this entry.

Author's Craft

- Describe the tone of this entry.
- How does Anne share that the situation in Holland is progressively getting worse?

LEVEL 3

Author's Purpose

- What is the purpose of this entry from Anne? What is she attempting to get across to her diary, Kitty?

Intertextual Connections

- Describe whether or not Anne is able to connect with other people she knows. What leads you to think this?

LEVEL 4

Opinion With Evidence or Argument

- Explain what was happening in Germany during 1933 that would motivate the Frank family to flee to Holland.

Questions for *The Diary of Anne Frank*

Diary Entry: Friday, 9 October, 1942

LEVEL 1

General Understanding

- What do you know about concentration camps in World War II?
- Who is involved in World War II in the year 1942?

Key Details

- Who is the Gestapo? Why are they taking Anne's Jewish friends away?
- How does Anne describe Westerbork?
- Why does Miep not take in the Jewess?
- Who are the greatest enemies in the world according to Anne?

LEVEL 2

Vocabulary

- What does "frightful immorality" mean according to Anne's entry?
- What is Anne insinuating when she writes, "a lot of the women, and even the girls, who stay there any length of time are expecting babies"? Why would this upset Anne?
- Who are the hostages and saboteurs?

Structure

- Find evidence of humor being used to allude to a stronger emotion. What does Anne *really* want to say?

Author's Craft

- Describe the tone of this entry.
- Find examples of hopelessness in this entry.
- How is Anne continuing to create a "relationship" with Kitty? How does writing to Kitty change the feeling of the entries for you as the reader?

LEVEL 3

Author's Purpose

- What emotions and/or information is Anne conveying in this entry?
- Who is the *real* enemy? How does this impact Anne?

Intertextual Connections

- Does Anne consider herself to be a German in any previous entries? How does she feel about being German in this entry?

LEVEL 4

Opinion With Evidence or Argument

- What emotions is Anne feeling while writing this entry? Use evidence to support your claim.

- Anne writes of jokes that people are using such as, "He's not likely to get a million" or "It only takes one bomb." How is humor used by Anne and people in general during times of crisis?

Questions for *The Diary of Anne Frank*

Diary Entry: Friday, 20 November, 1942

LEVEL 1

General Understanding
- How much time have they been in the "Secret Annexe"?
- What stories are being conveyed to the Secret Annexe?

Key Details
- Why is the Secret Annexe upset by the stories that are being conveyed to them?
- Why haven't they been informed about what is happening outside of the Secret Annexe?
- What are the effects of hearing stories about the treatment of Jews?
- What role does Anne's father fill in her world?

LEVEL 2

Vocabulary
- Examine how often Anne describes emotions in this entry. Why is there an emphasis on emotion?

Structure
- What is the tone of this entry?
- Describe the author's voice.

Author's Craft
- Anne's writing connects with people of all ages and time periods. Why? What in this entry specifically demonstrates her universal appeal?

LEVEL 3

Author's Purpose
- Anne writes, "In time this gloom will wear off." What is the *gloom* that she is referring to?
- It could be argued that Anne is attempting to justify her feelings. Find examples of this in this passage. What is she attempting to justify?

Intertextual Connections
- How would you describe Anne at this stage of the book? What are her characteristics?

LEVEL 4

Opinion With Evidence or Argument

- Anne poses the question: "And what would be the object of making our Secret Annexe into a Secret Annexe of Gloom?" Argue the significance of this statement.

- Anne herself writes that she is ungrateful. Is she? Find evidence to support your opinion.

Questions for *The Diary of Anne Frank*

Diary Entry: Monday, 26 July, 1943

LEVEL 1

General Understanding

- How long has Anne been living in the "Secret Annexe"?
- How has the war progressed up to this time?
- What is happening in this entry?
- How does Anne feel about what she hears and sees?

Key Details

- What is happening around the Secret Annexe?
- How does Anne describe what she sees and hears in this entry?
- How does the family react to warning sirens? Why?
- Why do Anne and Margot hide in the passage?
- How are they receiving their information?
- Who does Anne go to for comfort? Why?
- Who is Mussolini?
- Why are they excited that he has resigned?

LEVEL 2

Vocabulary

- Anne refers to this entry as "excitement." What does this convey?
- She writes, "But now the suspense over Italy will awaken the hope that it will soon end, perhaps even this year." What is *it*?

Structure

- Anne, although young, has a sophisticated usage of punctuation. Find examples of this in this entry.

Author's Craft

- How does Anne's description of the outside world contrast or compare with the activity inside the Secret Annexe?
- Describe her emotional journey within the passage. What does this reflect?

LEVEL 3

Author's Purpose

- What is "safe" in Anne's world right now? Explain your thinking using evidence from the entry.

Intertextual Connections

- What is Anne's emotional state like in this entry versus prior entries?

LEVEL 4

Opinion With Evidence or Argument

- What does Anne's "escape bag" represent both literally and figuratively?
- Anne believes in hope. What hope is she referring to? How does the belief in hope sustain her? How does hope sustain you in your life?

Questions for *The Diary of Anne Frank*

Diary Entry: Monday Evening, 8 November, 1943

LEVEL 1

General Understanding

- How long have Anne and her family been in the "Secret Annexe"?
- What happens in this entry?
- What is Anne's frame of mind?

Key Details

- How do books influence Anne?
- What effect does fear have on Anne?
- Why do Anne's nightmares scare her so deeply?

LEVEL 2

Vocabulary

- Anne repeatedly uses the word *queer* in her entries. What does this mean?
- What is the "castle in the air"?
- How does Anne's description of the Secret Annexe reflect or mirror her emotional state?
- What is the "black circle" that Anne writes of?

Structure

- How would you define the tone of this entry? Why?

Author's Craft

- Find examples of metaphors in this entry. What do they mean?
- What is Anne's relationship with Kitty?
- Anne begins to talk about the Anne before the Secret Annexe and the Anne during the Secret Annexe. What is the significance behind this? How does this explain her emotional state?

LEVEL 3

Author's Purpose

- Anne is talking about how the outsiders perceive the Secret Annexe to be. What is the irony behind the sentence, "Miep often says she envies us for possessing such tranquility here"? What is the irony for Miep along with the Secret Annexe residents?

Intertextual Connections

- How do Anne's nightmares mimic what is happening in the war? Refer to her past entries for evidence.

LEVEL 4

Opinion With Evidence or Argument

- Anne writes, "I'm going through a spell of being depressed. I really couldn't tell you why it is, but I believe it's just because I'm a coward, and that's what I keep bumping up against."

- Why does she describe herself as depressed? Use evidence to support your claim.

Questions for *The Diary of Anne Frank*

Diary Entry: Wednesday, 23 February, 1944

LEVEL 1

General Understanding

- How long has Anne been in hiding?
- What is Anne describing in this entry?

Key Details

- What is the significance of nature to Anne?
- Where is Anne's favorite place? Why is this her favorite place?
- Describe her relationship with Peter in this entry.
- What is Anne's definition of happiness?
- How does one overcome sorrow and sadness?

LEVEL 2

Vocabulary

- Find examples of descriptive language in this entry. Why do authors use descriptive language? Discuss Anne's attempt at descriptive language.

Structure

- For the first time, Anne breaks her writing structure. Why does she add on to her entry?

Author's Craft

- What is the symbolism behind nature?
- What is nature a metaphor for?

LEVEL 3

Author's Purpose

- What is happiness to Anne?
- What does one need in order to remain happy?

Intertextual Connections

- Anne very rarely mentions religion in her entries. What role does religion play in this entry and in previous entries? Why does she mention God more in this entry?
- How is Anne continuing to grow and change throughout the entries? How would you define/describe her at this moment in time?

LEVEL 4

Opinion With Evidence or Argument

- What is the "spell" that shall not be broken? Why is this important to Anne?

- Anne has expressed her feelings to Kitty about Peter, yet she writes, "Perhaps it won't be long before I can share this overwhelming feeling of bliss with someone who feels the way I do about it." Although she is in the same space with Peter, she does not feel that Peter shares her beliefs. What does this show about Anne and her feelings for Peter?

- Who is Anne speaking to in her additional mini entry? Use evidence to support your thinking.

Questions for *The Diary of Anne Frank*

Diary Entry: Wednesday, 29 March, 1944

LEVEL 1

General Understanding

- How long has Anne been secluded?
- What is happening in Amsterdam in this entry?

Key Details

- Give specific examples of the turmoil in Amsterdam.
- Why is there such a high volume of theft in the city?
- What is happening to the people of Amsterdam? Who is being impacted? Why?

LEVEL 2

Vocabulary

- Why would Anne consider her potential publication to be a "romance"?

Structure

- Define irony. Find examples of irony in this entry.
- Where does Anne show her naiveté in this entry?

Author's Craft

- Describe Anne's writing style thus far in the book.
- What is the tone of this entry?

LEVEL 3

Author's Purpose

- Who is in control of Amsterdam right now? How are the people living their lives outside of the "Secret Annexe"?
- Describe the positive and the negative things that Anne writes about.

Intertextual Connections

- How does Anne feel about the Dutch?
- Does she consider herself to be one of them? Why or why not? Refer to past entries for evidence.

LEVEL 4

Opinion With Evidence or Argument

- What is the role of the nonsoldier in this entry? What responsibility does the average citizen have during times of war? Research how average citizens made a difference during World War II.

THE METAMORPHOSIS
BY FRANZ KAFKA
(NOVELLA)

This novella is broken into three parts. In the following section of the Appendix you will find level 1–4 questions for each part of Kafka's work. You will also find four short text excerpts with Quick-Write questions to support students' practice with writing using textual evidence. The entire text of The Metamorphosis *is widely available online to print and distribute in class.*

Questions for Part I From *The Metamorphosis* by Franz Kafka

LEVEL 1

General Understanding

- What is happening at the beginning of the story?
- What is Gregor's profession?
- Why is Gregor working as a salesman?
- How does Gregor react to his metamorphosis in the beginning of the story?
- Describe Gregor's relationship and feelings toward each of his family members at the beginning of the story.
- Describe Gregor's turmoil in getting out of bed in the morning.

Key Details

- Use evidence from the text to describe Gregor's new body and functions.
- How does Gregor feel about his coworkers?
- Describe what Gregor's morning and work routine were before his metamorphosis.
- What are Gregor's feelings toward his boss?
- What is happening to Gregor's voice? How are others reacting to it? What does Gregor think about his voice?
- Kafka writes, "But I can't stay in bed doing nothing." Why is Gregor obsessed with getting out of bed?
- How does Gregor react to the chief clerk himself arriving at their residence? How does this reaction enforce his feelings about his job?
- How does each of his family members react to Gregor not going to work?

- Why does the chief clerk insinuate that Gregor is not at work?
- Describe the father's, mother's, and chief clerk's reactions to seeing Gregor for the first time.
- Gregor used to be a soldier. Why did Gregor leave the military?
- Why is Gregor concerned about the chief clerk leaving? Who does he wish were there to help reconcile and pacify the situation? Why?

LEVEL 2

Vocabulary

- Why does Kafka write, "The calmest possible reflection is far preferable to desperate decisions"?
- Kafka is intentional in his use of words. How does his writing style influence the author's message and tone of this short story?

Structure

- What is the significance of Kafka dividing the text into three distinct parts?
- How does each section of the text support elements of story?
- The theme of metamorphosis is evident throughout the text. How does Kafka demonstrate both physical and emotional metamorphosis?
- How does Kafka's use of the third person omniscient narrator influence the reader?

Author's Craft

- How does Kafka's description of the weather outside influence the tone/mood of the text?
- What do Gregor's thoughts about how his family and the chief clerk *should have* responded to his opening the door of his bedroom tell the reader about his feelings and their overall relationship?

LEVEL 3

Author's Purpose

- Why does Kafka select a cockroach for Gregor's metamorphosis?
- Kafka writes, "Despite all his tribulations, he was unable to suppress a smile at that thought." Why is it inconceivable for Gregor to think of asking for help?

Intertextual Connections

- Describe the family dynamics in Part I. Use evidence to support your claims.

LEVEL 4

Opinion With Evidence or Argument

- Find evidence to describe Gregor's father's habits and routines. What do these show about the father's character?

- How does Gregor's having been a lieutenant in the military influence your feelings about and opinion of him?

- What were Gregor's intentions after everyone saw his cockroach form?

- What are your feelings toward Gregor's father at the end of Part I? Why?

Excerpt A From *The Metamorphosis* by Franz Kafka

He slid back into his former position. "Getting up early like this," he thought, "makes you totally idiotic. People must have their sleep. Other traveling salesmen live like harem women. For instance, when during the course of the morning I go back to the hotel to copy out the orders I've received, those fine gentlemen are just having their breakfast. I should try that with my boss; I'd be fired on the spot. Anyway, who knows whether that wouldn't be a good thing for me after all. If I didn't hold myself back because of my parents, I would have quit long ago; I would have walked right up to the boss and let my heart out to him. He would surely have fallen off his desk! That's a peculiar habit of his, too, sitting on his desk and talking down to his employees from up above; and, besides, they have to step way up close because the boss is so hard of hearing. Now, I haven't given up all hope yet; once I have the money together to pay off my parents' debt to him—that should still take five or six years—I'll definitely go through with it. Then I'll make the big break. At the moment, of course, I've got to get up, because my train leaves at five."

Source: Franz Kafka, *The Metamorphosis and Other Stories.* Trans. Stanley Appelbaum. Dover Thrift Editions © 1915/1996.

Quick-Write Questions for Excerpt A From *The Metamorphosis* by Franz Kafka

Find evidence and write a couple of sentences that answer these questions:

- Why is Gregor in the position, or job, he's in?
- How does he feel about it?
- Why does he remain in this position and or job?

Questions for Part II From *The Metamorphosis* by Franz Kafka

LEVEL 1

General Understanding

- Why hasn't Gregor experienced his father reading the afternoon paper? How does he know about this family ritual?
- What happens to Gregor's mother when she finally sees Gregor in his room?
- Describe the relationship between Gregor and Grete after the furniture removal. How is it altering?

Key Details

- How is Gregor fed?
- How does Grete handle the food? What does this show?
- How does Gregor describe his family regarding work?
- How is Gregor and Grete's relationship changing? Why?
- What happens when the mother enters Gregor's room for the first time?
- Why is the furniture placement an issue?
- What does Gregor's mother think about his metamorphosis?
- How does Gregor feel about the removal of the furniture in his room?

LEVEL 2

Vocabulary

- Later in the story, Kafka writes, "While he stared ahead into the darkness, he felt very proud of himself for having been able to provide his parents and sister with a life like that, in such a beautiful apartment. But what if now all the peace, all the prosperity, all the contentment were to come to a fearful end?"
  o What does this show about Gregor's character?
- Gregor takes possession of one item in his room. Why? How does Kafka describe Gregor in this scene?
- Why does the father attack Gregor? How does Kafka describe Gregor's thinking regarding his father's acceptance or denial of the metamorphosis?

Structure

- How much time has passed since Gregor's transformation?

Author's Craft

- What does Gregor's room symbolize? How does he feel about his room?
- Why does Kafka go into so much detail describing the feeding of Gregor?
- What does the window represent in Part II?

LEVEL 3

Author's Purpose

- Gregor assumes that his sister, Grete, left him the milk and bread. What does this show about their relationship?
- What are you learning about Grete and Gregor's relationship?
- How would you have reacted to your brother being a human-sized cockroach?
- What emotions do you think Gregor feels while locked in his room? What does Kafka write that reinforces your opinions?
- Why does Gregor feel shame and sorrow about the idea of his family having to work?
- How do Gregor's physical actions and decisions reflect his emotional state? Does this in any way reflect upon the role of family?

Intertextual Connections

- Compare the role of happiness and acceptance in Kafka's "The Metamorphosis" and "A Hunger Artist."
- How does Kafka introduce social issues of the time in "The Metamorphosis" and "A Hunger Artist"?

LEVEL 4

Opinion With Evidence or Argument

- How is Gregor physically and emotionally affected by his father's actions?
- Is Gregor more human-like or insect-like? What evidence supports your claim?
- Kafka writes, "Gregor couldn't find out what excuses had been used on that first morning to get the doctor and the locksmith out of the apartment again, because the others, even his sister, not understanding him, had no idea that *he* could understand *them*; and so, when his sister was in his room, he had to content himself with hearing her occasional sighs and invocations of the saints." Outside of the literal implications, does Gregor's family understand him? Why or why not?
- How has Gregor's father managed the finances? How does Gregor feel about this? How do you feel about this?

- How is Gregor caught between being a cockroach and a human? Is he more one than the other? How?

- Who saves Gregor? What does this show the reader?

Excerpt B From *The Metamorphosis* by Franz Kafka

Even in the course of the first day the father already laid their entire financial situation and prospects before both the mother and the sister. From time to time he got up from the table and took some document or some memorandum book out of his small Wertheim safe, which he had held onto even after the collapse of his business five years earlier. He could be heard opening the complicated lock and closing it again after removing what he had been looking for. In part, these declarations by his father were the first heartening things Gregor had heard since his captivity. He had believed that his father had nothing at all left from that business— at least, his father had never told him anything to the contrary—and naturally Gregor hadn't asked him about it. Gregor's concern at the time had been to do everything in his power to make his family forget as quickly as possible the commercial disaster that had reduced them all to complete hopelessness. And so, at that time he had begun to work with extreme enthusiasm and almost overnight had changed from a junior clerk into a traveling salesman; as such, he naturally had many more possibilities of earning money, and his successful efforts were immediately transformed into cash in the form of commissions, cash that could be plunked down on the table at home before the eyes of his amazed and delighted family. Those had been good times and had never been repeated later, at least not so gloriously, even though Gregor subsequently earned so much money that he was enabled to shoulder the expenses of the entire family, and did so. They had grown used to it, the family as well as Gregor; they accepted the money gratefully, he handed it over gladly, but no particularly warm feelings were generated any longer. Only his sister had still remained close to Gregor all the same, and it was his secret plan—because, unlike Gregor, she dearly loved music and could play the violin soulfully—to send her to the conservatory the following year, regardless of the great expenses which that had to entail, and which would have to be made up for in some other way. Often during Gregor's brief sojourns in the city the conservatory was referred to in his conversations with his sister, but always merely as a lovely dream, which couldn't possibly come true, and their parents disliked hearing even those innocent references; but Gregor was planning it most resolutely and intended to make a formal announcement at Christmas Eve.

Source: Franz Kafka, *The Metamorphosis and Other Stories*. Trans. Stanley Appelbaum. Dover Thrift Editions © 1915/1996.

Quick-Write Questions for Excerpt B From *The Metamorphosis* by Franz Kafka

- What are we learning about Gregor's father? Use evidence to support your thinking.
- Why does Kafka use the word *captivity*?
- What role does money play in this passage?
- What does the line, "Those had been good times and had never been repeated later" mean?

- Kafka informs us more about the relationship between Gregor and Grete. Find evidence in this passage that discusses their relationship. What does this evidence show you?

- Why does Gregor have the position that he has for work? How does he feel about it?

- Kafka said, "It is often safer to be in chains than to be free." How does this quote relate to Gregor and the situation that he is in both physically and emotionally?

Excerpt C From *The Metamorphosis* by Franz Kafka

Although Gregor told himself over and over that nothing unusual was going on, just a few pieces of furniture being moved around, he soon had to admit to himself that this walking to and fro by the women, their brief calls to each other and the scraping of the furniture on the floor affected him like a tremendous uproar, sustained on all sides; and, no matter how tightly he pulled his head and legs and pressed his body all the way to the floor, he was irresistibly compelled to tell himself that he wouldn't be able to endure all of this very long. They were emptying out his room, taking away from him everything he was fond of; they had already carried out the wardrobe, which contained his fretsaw and other tools; now they were prying loose the desk, which had long been firmly entrenched in the floor, and at which he had done his homework when he was in business college, in secondary school and even back in primary school. At this point, he really had no more time for testing the good intentions of the two women, whose existence he had almost forgotten, anyway, because in their state of exhaustion they were now working in silence, and only their heavy footfalls could be heard.

And so he broke out—at the moment, the women were leaning on the desk in the adjoining room, to catch their breath a little—he changed direction four times, not really knowing what he should rescue first; and then he saw hanging conspicuously on the now otherwise bare wall the picture of the lady dressed in nothing but furs. He crawled up to it in haste and pressed against the glass, which held him fast and felt good on his hot belly. That picture, at least, which Gregor was now completely covering, surely no one would now take away. He twisted his head around toward the door of the parlor in order to observe the women when they returned.

Source: Franz Kafka, The Metamorphosis and Other Stories. Trans. Stanley Appelbaum. Dover Thrift Editions © 1915/1996.

Quick-Write Questions for Excerpt C From *The Metamorphosis* by Franz Kafka

- How does Gregor react to his room changes? Why is this significant? What does this show us about his state of mind?

Questions for Part III From *The Metamorphosis* by Franz Kafka

LEVEL 1

General Understanding

- What are the professions of each family member? How do they feel about their jobs?
- Why won't the family move?
- Describe Gregor's physical state.
- How is Gregor's room being used once the lodgers arrive?
- Why is Gregor so weak?

Key Details

- Since Gregor's severe injury, how is the family treating him now? What is his privilege?
- How has the family dynamic changed? Who is responsible for what?
- How is being a cockroach affecting Gregor's memory?
- How is Gregor's care now?
- What is the family attempting to do to save money?
- What is happening to Gregor physically in Part III?
- What are Grete and the father deciding to do with Gregor?
- How does the family react to seeing his body?

LEVEL 2

Vocabulary

- How does Kafka describe Gregor's feelings about how his family is caring for him? Is Gregor justified?
- What is the symbolism behind the world becoming brighter?
- How is Gregor's body described after his death?

Structure

- How much time has passed?

Author's Craft

- How is Gregor's death verbally relayed to his family? What do you think of Kafka's word choice?
- What do you think of how Kafka ends the story? What is Grete's role in the family now?

LEVEL 3

Author's Purpose

- Is Gregor a part of the family? Why or why not?
- Why does Gregor get angered when the family is arguing about cleaning his room?
- Gregor lies in the "darkest corner of the room." Why does he do this?
- What do you think Grete's intentions are for saying, "We have to try to get rid of it."
- Kafka writes, "His last look was at his mother, who had fallen asleep completely." Why is it significant that Gregor's last look was at his mother?
- What reasoning do you think the father had for kicking the lodgers out of the house?
- What does the family do after the lodgers are kicked out? Why is this important? What does it show about their individual characters?
- The cleaning woman says, "You don't have to worry your heads about how to clear out that trash next door. It's all taken care of." How do you feel about Gregor being referred to as trash and that a family member did not assist?
- Did the family ever love Gregor? Why or why not?

LEVEL 4

Opinion With Evidence or Argument

- Why do you think that the mother and Grete close Gregor's door every night?
- Grete refers to her brother as a "monstrous creature," "monster," and "it." How does her refusal to use Gregor's name model her emotional state?
- Who locks Gregor into his room? What is the significance of this person locking him in?
- When Gregor is dying, Kafka writes, "His opinion about the necessity for him to disappear was, if possible, even firmer than his sister's." What does this show about Gregor's character? Is this a strength or a weakness? Why?
- How is Gregor's metamorphosis similar to Grete's, and how are they different? You must use evidence from the text to support your claims.
- Describe how love, or lack of it, influences actions, feelings, and character development throughout the novel. You must use evidence from the text to support your claims.
- Describe how the fear of alienation motivated Gregor's life decisions and the results of those choices.
- What is a family? Describe the role of family in this story.

Excerpt D From *The Metamorphosis* by Franz Kafka

To be sure, no one was paying attention to him. The family was completely engrossed in the violin performance; on the other hand, the lodgers, who had placed themselves much too close behind the sister's music stand, so that they could all have looked at the sheet music, which assuredly had to disturb the sister, soon withdrew, with semiaudible remarks and lowered heads, to the window, where they stayed put, watched by the father with concern. It was now abundantly evident that they were disappointed in their assumption that they were going to hear some pretty or entertaining violin music; they were clearly tired of the whole performance and were permitting their peace and quiet to be disturbed merely out of courtesy. It was especially the way they all blew their cigar smoke up into the air through their noses and mouths that indicated a terrific strain on their nerves. And yet the sister was playing beautifully. Her face was inclined to one side, her eyes followed the lines of music searchingly and sorrowfully. Gregor crawled a little bit further forward, keeping his head close to the floor in hopes of making eye contact with her. Was he an animal if music stirred him that way? He felt as if he were being shown the way to the unknown nourishment he longed for. He was resolved to push his way right up to his sister and tug at her skirt, as an indication to her to come into his room again, at least as long as he lived; his horrifying shape was to be beneficial to him for the first time; he would be on guard at all the doors to his room at once, and spit at his assailants like a cat; but his sister would remain with him not under compulsion but voluntarily; she was to sit next to him on the couch and incline her ear toward him, and he would then confide to her that he had had the firm intention of sending her to the conservatory, and that, if the misfortune hadn't intervened, he would have told everyone so last Christmas—Christmas *was* over by now, wasn't it?—without listening to any objections. After this declaration his sister would burst into tears of deep emotion, and Gregor would raise himself to the level of her shoulder and kiss her neck, which, since she had begun her job, she had left bare, without any ribbon or collar.

Source: Franz Kafka, The Metamorphosis and Other Stories. Trans. Stanley Appelbaum. Dover Thrift Editions © 1915/1996.

Quick-Write Questions for Excerpt D
From *The Metamorphosis* by Franz Kafka

- What do you think of the lodgers' behavior?
- Do you think Gregor's opinion of the lodgers influences his description of them? Find evidence to support your opinion.
- Respond to the question, "Was he an animal if music stirred him that way?" Why do you believe Kafka poses this question?
- What makes someone/something human or animal?
- What do you believe is the "unknown nourishment he [Gregor] longed for"?

- What could it represent? Annotate the text, record your thoughts, and make connections.

- Are you surprised by Gregor's thoughts of locking his sister in his room? Why or why not? Refer to your previous readings to support your opinion.

- What do you think might happen next? Make a prediction and write it on the back of your close reading handout.

'ORANGES' BY GARY SOTO
(POEM)

The first time I walked

With a girl, I was twelve,

Cold, and weighted down

With two oranges in my jacket.

December. Frost cracking

Beneath my steps, my breath

Before me, then gone,

As I walked toward

Her house, the one whose

Porch light burned yellow

Night and day, in any weather.

A dog barked at me, until

She came out pulling

At her gloves, face bright

With rouge. I smiled,

Touched her shoulder, and led

Her down the street, across

A used car lot and a line

Of newly planted trees,

Until we were breathing

Before a drugstore. We

Entered, the tiny bell

Bringing a saleslady

Down a narrow aisle of goods.

I turned to the candies

Tiered like bleachers,

And asked what she wanted—

Light in her eyes, a smile

Starting at the corners

Of her mouth. I fingered

A nickle in my pocket,

And when she lifted a chocolate

That cost a dime,

I didn't say anything.

I took the nickle from

My pocket, then an orange,

And set them quietly on

The counter. When I looked up,

The lady's eyes met mine,

And held them, knowing

Very well what it was all

About.

Outside,

A few cars hissing past,

Fog hanging like old

Coats between the trees.

I took my girl's hand

In mine for two blocks,

Then released it to let

Her unwrap the chocolate.

I peeled my orange

That was so bright against

The gray of December

That, from some distance,

Someone might have thought

I was making a fire in my hands.

Source: From *New and Selected Poems* © 1995 by Gary Soto. Used with permission of Chronicle Books LLC, San Francisco. Visit ChronicleBooks.com.

Questions for "Oranges" by Gary Soto

LEVEL 1

General Understanding

- Is this poem taking place in the past or present?
- How old is the narrator?
- How many oranges does the narrator have, and what does this indicate?
- What "event" is taking place?

Key Details

- Describe the neighborhood the narrator and his companion live in.
- How much money does the narrator have to spend?
- How much does the candy the girl picks out cost?

LEVEL 2

Vocabulary

- What is the tone of the poem? Point to specific words or phrases that give you clues.
- What is the significance of the word *walked* in the first line? What does walking mean in the context of this poem?
- The narrator describes the girl's house as "the one whose/ Porch light burned yellow/ Night and day, in any weather." What can we infer about the narrator's relationship to the girl? What does this tell us about her home life?

Structure

- Based on the subject matter in the poem, why do you think the author chose to set this poem in past tense?
- The poem is written in free verse, which is characterized by a lack of pattern or rhyme scheme. How does this choice of structure reflect the subject matter of the poem?
- Examine the stanza breaks in the poem. What change has occurred between the two sections of the poem? How do you know?
- Circle instances in the poem when oranges are mentioned. Does their meaning change from the beginning of the poem to the end?

Author's Craft

- How does the author use figurative language to describe the setting to his readers?
- The title of the poem is "Oranges." What is the importance of oranges in this piece? What do they symbolize?
- What details does the author include to indicate the socioeconomic status of the narrator and the girl?

LEVEL 3

Author's Purpose

- What is the significance of the narrator's two oranges? How does he describe them in the first stanza? Why is he "weighted down" by them?

- How does the saleslady react when the narrator pays for the chocolate with money and an orange? Why?

- Does the saleslady let the narrator take the chocolate? How do you know? Why?

- What does the author compare the orange to in the last line? How does this indicate how his feelings have evolved over the course of the poem?

Intertextual Connections

- Soto has said, when asked what drives his poetry, "I'm also a listener. I hear lines of poetry issue from the mouths of seemingly ordinary people. And, as a writer, my duty is not to make people perfect, particularly Mexican Americans. I'm not a cheerleader. I'm one who provides portraits of people in the rush of life." Where can you find evidence of his source of inspiration in the poem "Oranges"? Does this poem match what he says are his sources of ideas?

- Read John Clare's poem "First Love" on the following page. What elements does it have in common with Gary Soto's "Oranges"? What is different? Think of structure, tone, and details when making your comparison.

LEVEL 4

Opinion With Evidence or Argument

- "Oranges" and "First Love" both describe young love using very different methods. Which is more effective in portraying the experience of first love? Using evidence from both poems, write a persuasive essay in which you compare and contrast the two poems, proving which one is more successful.

"First Love" by John Clare

I ne'er was struck before that hour

    With love so sudden and so sweet,

Her face it bloomed like a sweet flower

    And stole my heart away complete.

My face turned pale as deadly pale,

    My legs refused to walk away,

And when she looked, what could I ail?

    My life and all seemed turned to clay.

And then my blood rushed to my face

    And took my eyesight quite away,

The trees and bushes round the place

    Seemed midnight at noonday.

I could not see a single thing,

    Words from my eyes did start—

They spoke as chords do from the string,

    And blood burnt round my heart.

Are flowers the winter's choice?

    Is love's bed always snow?

She seemed to hear my silent voice,

    Not love's appeals to know.

I never saw so sweet a face

    As that I stood before.

My heart has left its dwelling-place

    And can return no more.

'PAUL REVERE'S MIDNIGHT RIDE'
BY HENRY WADSWORTH LONGFELLOW
(POEM)

Listen my children and you shall hear

Of the midnight ride of Paul Revere,

On the eighteenth of April, in Seventy-five;

Hardly a man is now alive

Who remembers that famous day and year.

He said to his friend, "If the British march

By land or sea from the town to-night,

Hang a lantern aloft in the belfry arch

Of the North Church tower as a signal light,—

One if by land, and two if by sea;

And I on the opposite shore will be,

Ready to ride and spread the alarm

Through every Middlesex village and farm,

For the country folk to be up and to arm."

Then he said "Good-night!" and with muffled oar

Silently rowed to the Charlestown shore,

Just as the moon rose over the bay,

Where swinging wide at her moorings lay

The Somerset, British man-of-war;

A phantom ship, with each mast and spar

Across the moon like a prison bar,

And a huge black hulk, that was magnified

By its own reflection in the tide.

Meanwhile, his friend through alley and street

Wanders and watches, with eager ears,

Till in the silence around him he hears

The muster of men at the barrack door,

The sound of arms, and the tramp of feet,

And the measured tread of the grenadiers,

Marching down to their boats on the shore.

Then he climbed the tower of the Old North Church,

By the wooden stairs, with stealthy tread,

To the belfry chamber overhead,

And startled the pigeons from their perch

On the sombre rafters, that round him made

Masses and moving shapes of shade,—

By the trembling ladder, steep and tall,

To the highest window in the wall,

Where he paused to listen and look down

A moment on the roofs of the town

And the moonlight flowing over all.

Beneath, in the churchyard, lay the dead,

In their night encampment on the hill,

Wrapped in silence so deep and still

That he could hear, like a sentinel's tread,

The watchful night-wind, as it went

Creeping along from tent to tent,

And seeming to whisper, "All is well!"

A moment only he feels the spell

Of the place and the hour, and the secret dread

Of the lonely belfry and the dead;

For suddenly all his thoughts are bent

On a shadowy something far away,

Where the river widens to meet the bay,—

A line of black that bends and floats

On the rising tide like a bridge of boats.

Meanwhile, impatient to mount and ride,

Booted and spurred, with a heavy stride

On the opposite shore walked Paul Revere.

Now he patted his horse's side,

Now he gazed at the landscape far and near,

Then, impetuous, stamped the earth,

And turned and tightened his saddle girth;

But mostly he watched with eager search

The belfry tower of the Old North Church,

As it rose above the graves on the hill,

Lonely and spectral and sombre and still.

And lo! as he looks, on the belfry's height

A glimmer, and then a gleam of light!

He springs to the saddle, the bridle he turns,

But lingers and gazes, till full on his sight

A second lamp in the belfry burns.

A hurry of hoofs in a village street,

A shape in the moonlight, a bulk in the dark,

And beneath, from the pebbles, in passing, a spark

Struck out by a steed flying fearless and fleet;

That was all! And yet, through the gloom and the light,

The fate of a nation was riding that night;

And the spark struck out by that steed, in his flight,

Kindled the land into flame with its heat.

He has left the village and mounted the steep,

And beneath him, tranquil and broad and deep,

Is the Mystic, meeting the ocean tides;

And under the alders that skirt its edge,

Now soft on the sand, now loud on the ledge,

Is heard the tramp of his steed as he rides.

It was twelve by the village clock

When he crossed the bridge into Medford town.

He heard the crowing of the cock,

And the barking of the farmer's dog,

And felt the damp of the river fog,

That rises after the sun goes down.

It was one by the village clock,

When he galloped into Lexington.

He saw the gilded weathercock

Swim in the moonlight as he passed,

And the meeting-house windows, black and bare,

Gaze at him with a spectral glare,

As if they already stood aghast

At the bloody work they would look upon.

It was two by the village clock,

When he came to the bridge in Concord town.

He heard the bleating of the flock,

And the twitter of birds among the trees,

And felt the breath of the morning breeze

Blowing over the meadow brown.

And one was safe and asleep in his bed

Who at the bridge would be first to fall,

Who that day would be lying dead,

Pierced by a British musket ball.

You know the rest. In the books you have read

How the British Regulars fired and fled,—

How the farmers gave them ball for ball,

From behind each fence and farmyard wall,

Chasing the redcoats down the lane,

Then crossing the fields to emerge again

Under the trees at the turn of the road,

And only pausing to fire and load.

So through the night rode Paul Revere;

And so through the night went his cry of alarm

To every Middlesex village and farm,—

A cry of defiance, and not of fear,

A voice in the darkness, a knock at the door,

And a word that shall echo for evermore!

For, borne on the night-wind of the Past,

Through all our history, to the last,

In the hour of darkness and peril and need,

The people will waken and listen to hear

The hurrying hoof-beats of that steed,

And the midnight message of Paul Revere.

Source: Henry Wadsworth Longfellow © 1861

Questions for "Paul Revere's Midnight Ride" by Henry Wadsworth Longfellow

LEVEL 1

General Understanding

- What was the purpose of Paul Revere's ride?
- Who are the people involved in this poem?
- Was Paul Revere successful given his purpose? How do you know?
- What time period is Longfellow referring to?
- What was life like back in 1775?

Key Details

- What were the modes of transportation used by people of this time?
- How was war fought in 1775?
- Who was America at battle with in 1775? Why?
- How did Paul Revere and his friend communicate given the distance between them?
- What was the friend's mission?
- How is the cemetery described? What imagery is Longfellow creating by describing it this way?
- Using evidence from the text, describe Paul Revere and his friend's actions and emotions although they are across the river from one another.
- Describe Paul Revere's friend's response when he goes to the belfry. How does Longfellow describe his actions and ultimately, his emotions?

LEVEL 2

Vocabulary

- Where does the author refer to death? Why is this repeated throughout the poem?
- Who is the "spark" that Longfellow writes of?
- What is the Mystic?
- Some could say the moon is its own character in the poem. What role does the moon have in this event? How is the moon described?

Structure

- How does Longfellow's use of foreshadowing influence the tone of the poem?
- How does foreshadowing affect your understanding of the events of the poem?
- How does the use of rhyme influence you as a reader?

- Describe the passage of time in the poem. How much time has passed from the beginning of the poem to the end?
- How would you describe the tone of the poem?

Author's Craft

- Which poetic devices does Longfellow use in this poem? Explain their effectiveness.
- What roles do light and darkness have in this poem?
- Where in the poem does Longfellow speak directly to the reader? How does this influence you as the reader?

LEVEL 3

Author's Purpose

- Who is the intended audience of this poem? Why do you think that?
- Longfellow writes, "The fate of a nation was riding that night." What does this mean? What might have happened had the Americans not been notified of the British coming?

Intertextual Connections

- What was Paul Revere's message in the text? What was Longfellow's message to the reader in writing this poem?
- Longfellow writes, "And a word that shall echo for evermore!" What word is he referring to?
- Compare this poem to the actual events of Paul Revere's ride. A short comparison text for this purpose can be found at *The Paul Revere House* website: http://www.paulreverehouse.org/ride/real.html.

LEVEL 4

Opinion With Evidence or Argument

- How does Longfellow's poem compare to the actual events of the night of April 18, 1775?
- Does Longfellow accurately portray Paul Revere and his actions? Why or why not?
- Why did Longfellow intentionally choose to write an inaccurate poem?
- Longfellow writes, "A cry of defiance, and not of fear." How is this reflected in modern-day rebellion and or war?

APPENDIX III

HIGH SCHOOL
SOCIAL STUDIES/HISTORY

A·III

'SPEECH TO THE TROOPS AT TILBURY' BY QUEEN ELIZABETH[1]

(SPEECH)

My loving people,

We have been persuaded by some that are careful of our safety, to take heed how we commit our selves to armed multitudes, for fear of treachery; but I assure you I do not desire to live to distrust my faithful and loving people. Let tyrants fear, I have always so behaved myself that, under God, I have placed my chiefest strength and safeguard in the loyal hearts and good-will of my subjects; and therefore I am come amongst you, as you see, at this time, not for my recreation and disport, but being resolved, in the midst and heat of the battle, to live and die amongst you all; to lay down for my God, and for my kingdom, and my people, my honour and my blood, even in the dust. I know I have the body but of a weak and feeble woman; but I have the heart and stomach of a king, and of a king of England too, and think foul scorn that Parma or Spain, or any prince of Europe, should dare to invade the borders of my realm; to which rather than any dishonour shall grow by me, I myself will take up arms, I myself will be your general, judge, and rewarder of every one of your virtues in the field. I know already, for your forwardness you have deserved rewards and crowns; and We do assure you in the word of a prince, they shall be duly paid you. In the mean time, my lieutenant general[2] shall be in my stead, than whom never prince commanded a more noble or worthy subject; not doubting but by your obedience to my general, by your concord in the camp, and your valour in the field, we shall shortly have a famous victory over those enemies of my God, of my kingdom, and of my people.

Notes:

1. Delivered by Elizabeth to the land forces assembled at Tilbury (Essex) to repel the anticipated invasion of the Spanish Armada, 1588.

2. Robert Dudley, Earl of Leicester; he was the queen's favorite, once rumored to be her lover.

Questions for "Speech to the Troops at Tilbury" by Queen Elizabeth

LEVEL 1

General Understanding

- What is the rhetorical situation of this speech? How do we know?
- What event is about to take place? How do you know?

Key Details

- What can you infer about the social status of the queen's audience?
- What concerns might her subjects have about her? Which parts of the speech reveal this?
- What is the audience's attitude toward women as leaders? Be sure to use evidence from the text to support your thinking.
- What might some of her subjects be expecting in exchange for their service?

LEVEL 2

Vocabulary

- What is the tone of the passage? Point to specific words or phrases that support your thinking.
- Why does the queen say, "Let tyrants fear"? What purpose does this serve?
- Where does the queen say she places her "chiefest strength and safeguard"? What purpose does this statement serve?

Structure

- This is a very short speech, fewer than 400 words. Why would the queen choose to spend so few words on such an important topic?
- Where does Queen Elizabeth consider the opposition's viewpoint on her suitability as a leader? Why does she do this?

Author's Craft

- How does Elizabeth use emotion, or pathos, to appeal to her audience? Where do you see it?
- How does Queen Elizabeth create credibility or ethos in her speech?
- How does Queen Elizabeth create "common ground" with her people? Use specific lines from the text.
- Why does she address her audience as "my loving people"?
- At one point in the speech, Queen Elizabeth says, "I myself will take up arms, I myself will be your general." Does she contradict this statement later on in the text? Why would she do this?

LEVEL 3

Author's Purpose

- Why does the queen mention that she has been warned against meeting with her own people?
- Though she places herself on the same level as her subjects, where in the speech does Queen Elizabeth reveal the inequalities of power in the text?

Intertextual Connections

- Think of other successful speeches you have read, such as Martin Luther King Jr.'s "I Have a Dream" or the Gettysburg Address.
  - Consider the rhetorical situation of each speech, and compare the use of rhetorical strategies to Queen Elizabeth's.
  - How do the audience and purpose change the use of techniques?
  - Which remain the same?

LEVEL 4

Opinion With Evidence or Argument

- This speech is considered one of the most successful pieces of rhetoric delivered up until its time, especially given the social context in which it was delivered.
  - On a separate piece of paper, evaluate the effectiveness of Queen Elizabeth's speech. Was it convincing or not? Provide specific evidence (at least two quotations) to support your thinking.

THE NOBEL ACCEPTANCE SPEECH DELIVERED BY ELIE WIESEL IN OSLO ON DECEMBER 10, 1986

(SPEECH)

Questions for the Nobel Acceptance Speech Delivered by Elie Wiesel

LEVEL 1

General Understanding

- What is the Nobel Peace Prize?
- Who is Elie Wiesel?
- Why did Wiesel receive the Nobel Peace Prize?

Key Details

- How does Wiesel feel about receiving the award?
- Who is the Creator?
- Find examples in the speech of Wiesel's religious beliefs.
- Who is the boy that Wiesel refers to?
- Why does Wiesel order the people in the beginning of his speech this way?
- What is his plea in regard to Israel?
- Wiesel says, "Thank you, people of Norway, for declaring on this singular occasion that our survival has meaning for mankind." Who is he referring to when he says "our survival"? Why?

LEVEL 2

Vocabulary

- Wiesel is intentional with his use of vocabulary. He says, "Should Israel lose but one war, it would mean her end and ours as well." What is the symbolism behind the use of the pronoun *her* in that sentence?
- Wiesel mentions many different countries and individuals throughout his speech. Work with a partner or small group to identify the locations and people he discusses.
- What is the Kingdom of Night?

- What does Wiesel mean when he says, "Thank you for building bridges between people and generations"?

Structure

- How does Wiesel's use of the past and present help connect the listener to his purpose?
- There is a theme that people are interconnected and we must work together. Find evidence of this in the text.
- Wiesel says, "I know your choice transcends my person." What does he mean? How does this connect to his concept of time in the speech?

Author's Craft

- The theme of the hero, victim, bystander, and perpetrator runs throughout this speech. Find examples of each within the speech.
- What metaphor does the bridge represent?

LEVEL 3

Author's Purpose

- What is Wiesel's message to the audience? To the world?
- How does his past (the young Jewish boy) influence the man he is today?
- Wiesel's inner child is asking what he's done with his life after surviving the Holocaust. What has Wiesel done? What is his response?
- What is Wiesel's message about injustice? What is our responsibility?

Intertextual Connections

- The issue of forgiveness is addressed in Simon Wiesenthal's book *The Sunflower.* Compare Wiesenthal's experience with forgiveness to your belief about whether or not Elie Wiesel is forgiving in this speech. Would the two men agree or disagree about forgiveness? Why?
- Analyze how Wiesel and his views may have been altered or strengthened since he wrote *Night.*

LEVEL 4

Opinion With Evidence or Argument

- Is history repeating itself?
- Wiesel writes, "How could the world remain silent?" Do we remain silent today?
- Wiesel says that "More people are oppressed than free." Do you agree or disagree? Find evidence of this in our world.

- Compare Wiesel Wiesel's Nobel Peace Prize speech to Martin Niemöller's poem, *First They Came.*
  - How would Wiesel change the groups represented in this famous poem, given his speech?
  - Rewrite it as if Wiesel were the poet, and then write your own version.
- What is Elie Wiesel's message to all who listen to his speech or read his work?

'BLOOD, TOIL, TEARS, AND SWEAT' BY WINSTON CHURCHILL

(SPEECH)

May 13, 1940, First Speech as Prime Minister to House of Commons

On May 10, 1940, Winston Churchill became prime minister. When he met his cabinet on May 13, he told them that "I have nothing to offer but blood, toil, tears, and sweat." He repeated that phrase later in the day when he asked the House of Commons for a vote of confidence in his new all-party government. The response of the Labour Party was heart-warming; the Conservative Party's reaction was lukewarm. They still really wanted Neville Chamberlain. For the first time, the people had hope, but Churchill commented to General Ismay: "Poor people, poor people. They trust me, and I can give them nothing but disaster for quite a long time."

I beg to move,

That this House welcomes the formation of a Government representing the united and inflexible resolve of the nation to prosecute the war with Germany to a victorious conclusion.

On Friday evening last I received His Majesty's commission to form a new Administration. It is the evident wish and will of Parliament and the nation that this should be conceived on the broadest possible basis and that it should include all parties, both those who supported the late Government and also the parties of the Opposition. I have completed the most important part of this task. A War Cabinet has been formed of five Members, representing, with the Opposition Liberals, the unity of the nation. The three party Leaders have agreed to serve, either in the War Cabinet or in high executive office. The three Fighting Services have been filled. It was necessary that this should be done in one single day, on account of the extreme urgency and rigour of events. A number of other positions, key positions, were filled yesterday, and I am submitting a further list to His Majesty to-night. I hope to complete the appointment of the principal Ministers during to-morrow. The appointment of the other Ministers usually takes a little longer, but I trust that, when Parliament meets again, this part of my task will be completed, and that the administration will be complete in all respects.

I considered it in the public interest to suggest that the House should be summoned to meet today. Mr. Speaker agreed, and took the necessary steps, in accordance with the powers conferred upon him by the Resolution of the House. At the end of the proceedings today, the Adjournment of the House will be proposed until Tuesday, 21st May, with, of course, provision for earlier meeting, if need be. The business to be considered during that week will be notified to Members at the earliest opportunity. I now invite the House, by the Motion which stands in my name, to record its approval of the steps taken and to declare its confidence in the new Government.

To form an Administration of this scale and complexity is a serious undertaking in itself, but it must be remembered that we are in the preliminary stage of one of the greatest battles in history, that we are in action at many other points in Norway and in Holland, that we have to be prepared in the Mediterranean, that the air battle is continuous and that many preparations, such as have been indicated by my hon. Friend below the Gangway, have to be made here at home. In this crisis I hope I may be pardoned if I do not address the House at any length today. I hope that any of my friends and colleagues, or former colleagues, who are affected by the political reconstruction, will make allowance, all allowance, for any lack of ceremony with which it has been necessary to act. I would say to the House, as I said to those who have joined this government: "I have nothing to offer but blood, toil, tears and sweat."

We have before us an ordeal of the most grievous kind. We have before us many, many long months of struggle and of suffering. You ask, what is our policy? I can say: It is to wage war, by sea, land and air, with all our might and with all the strength that God can give us; to wage war against a monstrous tyranny, never surpassed in the dark, lamentable catalogue of human crime. That is our policy. You ask, what is our aim? I can answer in one word: It is victory, victory at all costs, victory in spite of all terror, victory, however long and hard the road may be; for without victory, there is no survival. Let that be realised; no survival for the British Empire, no survival for all that the British Empire has stood for, no survival for the urge and impulse of the ages, that mankind will move forward towards its goal. But I take up my task with buoyancy and hope. I feel sure that our cause will not be suffered to fail among men. At this time I feel entitled to claim the aid of all, and I say, "come then, let us go forward together with our united strength."

Questions for "Blood, Toil, Tears, and Sweat" by Winston Churchill

LEVEL 1

General Understanding

- Who is Winston Churchill?
- Who is Churchill's audience?
- What is the danger that he speaks of?
- What is the time period in which he is delivering this speech? What was happening at that time in history?
- Describe the monarchy system of England.

Key Details

- What is the "new all-party government" that Churchill speaks of?
- Whom do you think Churchill is attempting to go to war against?
- What is the War Cabinet?
- Why is he breaking tradition (for a country that is steeped in tradition) and moving so quickly?
- Who is His Majesty?
- Who is Churchill reporting directly to?
- What is the role of Parliament? What is their time line for making a decision?
- What is the time frame that Churchill proposes to his audience that the impending war will take? Why is this significant?
- How does he describe Hitler and his actions?

LEVEL 2

Vocabulary

- Churchill is very meticulous in his word choice. Find examples of power words in his speech that evoke emotional appeal.
- Find examples of urgency in this speech. What words or phrases does Churchill use to convey this sense?
- Churchill repeats the word *victory* five times in his closing paragraph. Why?

Structure

- How do you envision the pacing of this speech? Read it out loud, and practice the cadence of his words.
- How does he use repetition to capture the attention of his audience? Find examples of repetition in the text.

- Find examples of emotional appeal in this speech, and discuss their effectiveness.
- How does Churchill's speech differ from the beginning to the end? Why do you think he designed it this way?

Author's Craft

- Toward the end of the speech, Churchill adapts a question-and-response delivery style. Discuss the effectiveness of this technique and why you think he chose it.
- Discuss the theme of unity in this speech. Find examples of unity and togetherness in the speech. Why does Churchill focus on this theme?

LEVEL 3

Author's Purpose

- What is Winston Churchill's goal in delivering this speech?
- How does Churchill create buy in from his audience? Does his knowledge that he does (or doesn't) have support from the audience influence his choice of words or delivery?
- What does Churchill mean when he says, "I have nothing to offer but blood, toil, tears, and sweat"? What does this say about his character as a leader?

Intertextual Connections

- Benjamin Franklin said at the signing of the Declaration of Independence, "We must all hang together, or assuredly we shall all hang separately."
  o How does Churchill's speech connect to this statement?
  o What message are the two men trying to make to the people?

LEVEL 4

Opinion With Evidence or Argument

- Research the British Empire's involvement in World War II. What was its role and, ultimately, the outcome?
- Define leadership. Using examples from the text, determine whether Churchill would be an effective leader during a time of crisis.
- Churchill himself states that they are in a time of crisis. What other evidence from the text supports that they are, in fact, facing a crisis?

'ON WOMEN'S RIGHT TO VOTE' BY SUSAN B. ANTHONY, 1873

(SPEECH)

Friends and fellow citizens: I stand before you tonight under indictment for the alleged crime of having voted at the last presidential election, without having a lawful right to vote. It shall be my work this evening to prove to you that in thus voting, I not only committed no crime, but, instead, simply exercised my citizen's rights, guaranteed to me and all United States citizens by the National Constitution, beyond the power of any state to deny.

The preamble of the Federal Constitution says:

"We, the people of the United States, in order to form a more perfect union, establish justice, insure domestic tranquility, provide for the common defense, promote the general welfare, and secure the blessings of liberty to ourselves and our posterity, do ordain and establish this Constitution for the United States of America."

It was we, the people; not we, the white male citizens; nor yet we, the male citizens; but we, the whole people, who formed the Union. And we formed it, not to give the blessings of liberty, but to secure them; not to the half of ourselves and the half of our posterity, but to the whole people—women as well as men. And it is a downright mockery to talk to women of their enjoyment of the blessings of liberty while they are denied the use of the only means of securing them provided by this democratic-republican government—the ballot.

For any state to make sex a qualification that must ever result in the disfranchisement of one entire half of the people, is to pass a bill of attainder, or, an ex post facto law, and is therefore a violation of the supreme law of the land. By it the blessings of liberty are forever withheld from women and their female posterity.

To them this government has no just powers derived from the consent of the governed. To them this government is not a democracy. It is not a republic. It is an odious aristocracy; a hateful oligarchy of sex; the most hateful aristocracy ever established on the face of the globe; an oligarchy of wealth, where the rich govern the poor. An oligarchy of learning, where the educated govern the ignorant, or even an oligarchy of race, where the Saxon rules the African, might be endured; but this oligarchy of sex, which makes father, brothers, husband, sons, the oligarchs over the mother and sisters, the wife and daughters, of every household—which ordains all men sovereigns, all women subjects, carries dissension, discord, and rebellion into every home of the nation.

Webster, Worcester, and Bouvier all define a citizen to be a person in the United States, entitled to vote and hold office.

The only question left to be settled now is: Are women persons? And I hardly believe any of our opponents will have the hardihood to say they are not. Being persons, then, women are citizens; and no state has a right to make any law, or to enforce any old law, that shall abridge their privileges or immunities. Hence, every discrimination against women in the constitutions and laws of the several states is today null and void, precisely as is every one against Negroes.

Questions for "On Women's Right to Vote" by Susan B. Anthony, 1873

LEVEL 1

General Understanding

- What happened?
- Why is Susan B. Anthony delivering this speech?
- Who is she speaking to?

Key Details

- Why was she arrested?
- Which historical documents does Susan B. Anthony refer to?
- Where is she?
- Who are Webster, Worcester, and Bouvier?
- How does Susan B. Anthony connect the plight of the African American to that of women? Why does she relate the two?
- What election did she vote in?

LEVEL 2

Vocabulary

- What does "sex" represent in this text?
- She repeats "to them" several times throughout her speech (specifically in Paragraph 6). Who is she speaking of?
- Define all unknown words and terms in Paragraph 6. Discuss your findings with your partner/ table. Reread the paragraph again. What is she saying?

Structure

- Discuss the effectiveness of the use of evidence throughout her speech.
- Read the speech out loud to a partner or table. Discuss the length of the speech. Is it sufficient?

Author's Craft

- Discuss the persuasive techniques used and their effectiveness.
- What is the tone of this speech? Why do you think this?
- How does Susan B. Anthony justify her actions?

LEVEL 3

Author's Purpose

- What does the right to vote represent to Susan B. Anthony? Where specifically does she insinuate the importance of voting for women?

- How does Susan B. Anthony discuss class?

Intertextual Connections

- Research Susan B. Anthony's life in other texts and examine where her motivation for the women's suffrage movement began.

LEVEL 4

Opinion With Evidence or Argument

- Susan B. Anthony asks the question, "Are women persons?" Discuss the rights of women in 1873 versus their rights today.

- What type of person is Susan B. Anthony, as evidenced solely in this speech?

- Women were finally granted the right to vote in 1920 with the passing of the 19th Amendment to the US Constitution, which reads, "The right of citizens of the United States to vote shall not be denied or abridged by the United States or by any State on account of sex." This was passed 48 years after Susan B. Anthony's death. Research what happened between the time she delivered this speech and the time women were finally granted the right to vote.

- Even though women were granted the right to vote in 1920, numbers of women voting did not match numbers of men voting until 1980. Currently, a higher percentage of women are voters than men. President Obama had 55% of his votes come from females. What is changing in society? Why are more women voting now?

APPENDIX V
HIGH SCHOOL SCIENCE

THE UNITED NATIONS WORLD WATER DEVELOPMENT REPORT 2014: WATER AND ENERGY

(TECHNICAL DOCUMENT)

The Challenge to Come: Meeting Growing Demands

Demands for freshwater and energy will continue to increase significantly over the coming decades to meet the needs of growing populations and economies, changing lifestyles and evolving consumption patterns, greatly amplifying existing pressures on limited natural resources and on ecosystems. The resulting challenges will be most acute in countries undergoing accelerated transformation and rapid economic growth, or those in which a large segment of the population lacks access to modern services.

Global water demand (in terms of water withdrawals) is projected to increase by some 55% by 2050, mainly because of growing demands from manufacturing (400%), thermal electricity generation (140%) and domestic use (130%). As a result, freshwater availability will be increasingly strained over this time period, and more than 40% of the global population is projected to be living in areas of severe water stress through 2050.

There is clear evidence that groundwater supplies are diminishing, with an estimated 20% of the world's aquifers being over-exploited, some critically so. Deterioration of wetlands worldwide is reducing the capacity of ecosystems to purify water.

Global energy demand is expected to grow by more than one-third over the period to 2035, with China, India and the Middle Eastern countries accounting for about 60% of the increase. Electricity demand is expected to grow by approximately 70% by 2035. This growth will be almost entirely in non-Organisation for Economic Co-operation and Development countries, with India and China accounting for more than half that growth.

What Rising Energy Demand Means for Water

Energy comes in different forms and can be produced in several ways, each having a distinct requirement for—and impact on—water resources. Thus, as a country's or region's energy mix evolves, from fossil fuels to renewables for example, so too do the implications on water and its supporting ecosystem services evolve. Approximately 90% of global power generation is water intensive.

The International Energy Agency estimated global water withdrawals for energy production in 2010 at 583 billion m³ (representing some 15% of the world's total withdrawals), of which

66 billion m^3 was consumed. By 2035, withdrawals could increase by 20% and consumption by 85%, driven via a shift towards higher efficiency power plants with more advanced cooling systems (that reduce water withdrawals but increase consumption) and increased production of biofuel. Local and regional impacts of biofuels could be substantial, as their production is among the most water intensive types of fuel production.

The incentives to increase efficiency facing the two domains are asymmetrical: energy users have little or no incentive to conserve water due to zero or low prices, but water users normally do pay for energy, even though prices may be subsidized. Water and energy prices are strongly affected by political decisions and subsidies that support major sectors such as agriculture and industry, and these subsidies often distort the true economic relationship between water and energy. Particularly for water, price is rarely a true reflection of cost—it is often even less than the cost of supply. A coherent policy—which is to say an adequate public response to the interconnectedness of the water, energy and related domains—requires a hierarchy of actions. These include:

- Developing coherent national policies affecting the different domains
- Creating legal and institutional frameworks to promote this coherence
- Ensuring reliable data and statistics to make and monitor decisions
- Encouraging awareness through education, training and public information media
- Supporting innovation and research into technological development
- Ensuring availability of finance for sustainable and mutually compatible development of water and energy.
- Allowing markets and businesses to develop

Together these actions make up the *enabling environment* necessary to bring about the changes needed for the sustainable and mutually compatible development of water and energy. The international community can bring actors together and catalyse support for national, subnational and local governments as well as utility providers, who have a major role in how the water–energy nexus plays out at the national and local levels.

Source: Excerpt from WWAP (United Nations World Water Assessment Programme), *The United Nations World Water Development Report 2014: Water and Energy.* Paris, UNESCO. http://unesdoc.unesco.org/images/0022/002257/225741e.pdf

Questions for The United Nations World Water Development Report 2014: Water and Energy

LEVEL 1

General Understanding

- What issue is being presented? How do you know?
- Who are the authors of this piece? What does this tell us about the audience?

Key Details

- What is happening in regard to global water demand?
- Who will be most impacted by the growing demands for freshwater and energy?
- Which countries are expected to grow the most in terms of water usage?
- What are the main causes of increased water demand?
- The excerpt talks about two domains in Section 2. What are they?

LEVEL 2

Vocabulary

- What is the tone of this text? Point to specific words or phrases that reveal this.
- Why do the authors say the world's water sources are "over-exploited"? What does *exploit* mean in this context?
- Explain the difference between withdrawals and consumption.
- What is a subsidy? Why is this significant to the meaning of the text, in particular Section 2?
- According to the text, what does *coherent* mean?

Structure

- Skim the headers of each section. What purpose do they serve? How do they help the reader understand the text better?
- What do you notice about the format of Section 2? What is the effect of including a bulleted list amongst paragraphs?

Author's Craft

- How do the authors of the text use statistics to support their claims? Why do you think they use percentages to illustrate their point?
- Describe the cause-and-effect relationship between water and energy. How does this help to illustrate the report's purpose?

LEVEL 3

Author's Purpose

- What is the authors' attitude toward subsidies? How do you know?

- What reason does the report give for consumers not knowing how much water really costs? What can you infer about why the extent to which certain industries use water remains unclear to consumers?

- What do the authors mean by an *enabling environment*? What would this look like? Use evidence from the text to support your thinking.

Intertextual Connections

- Compare and contrast the "UNESCO Water Report" to Al Gore's blog in The Huffington Post (www.huffingtonpost.com/al-gore/antarctic-glaciers-and-th_b_1254304.html). Are these two articles similar or different? How?

LEVEL 4

Opinion With Evidence or Argument

- Research why China and India account for more than half of the estimated growth in water use. What is, or is not, happening in these countries that supports this claim?

- Evaluate the water situation in your town, city, and or state. What is the current water and energy status? How does the article support or disclaim your town's, city's, or state's situation?

- Research and evaluate different options available to conserve water and energy. Which options are the most efficient? Why?

EXCERPT FROM *THE LOG FROM THE SEA OF CORTEZ* BY JOHN STEINBECK

(NONFICTION)

*Reference the passage "This strange identification of man with boat is so complete . . . " ending "So far the murder trait of our species . . ."

Questions for Excerpt From *The Log From the Sea of Cortez* by John Steinbeck

LEVEL 1

General Understanding

- What species of animal is the narrator discussing, and what physical behaviors does he observe?
- Do you think the narrator is a scientist? Why or why not?

Key Details

- Are men, according to Steinbeck, closely connected to the things they make?
- What do the narrator and his companions do in the tide pools he mentions?
- What do scientists base their conclusions on?
- What motivates men to destroy human-made things?
- When crayfish first encounter one another, what do they do? Why is this significant?
- How are traits bred out of a species?

LEVEL 2

Vocabulary

- What is the tone of the passage? Point to specific words or phrases that give you clues.
- Steinbeck uses the word *species* in multiple ways throughout the passage. Identify where he mentions species and what it means in the context of the sentence.
- What is Steinbeck's attitude toward human nature? How do you know?

Structure

- In the first paragraph of the passage, Steinbeck mentions the human tendency to "murder the things we love best." How does he extend and illustrate this argument throughout the rest of the excerpt? What effect does this have on the purpose of the piece?
- How does Steinbeck use comparisons to crayfish to demonstrate his point that humans also follow socially or genetically ingrained traits? Is he equating humans to animals? Why?
- As the narrative progresses, what alternate reason does Steinbeck give for crayfish fighting? Do you agree? How does this reasoning serve to reveal the purpose of the passage?

Author's Craft

- What is the tone of the following lines: "It is not known whether this [human tendency to destroy] is caused by a virus, some airborne spore, or whether it be a species reaction to some meteorological stimulus as yet undetermined"? Why does Steinbeck choose to use scientific language to make his point? Who is speaking in this portion of the text?

- Based on his word choice, who is Steinbeck's audience? Which words or phrases led you to this conclusion?

LEVEL 3

Author's Purpose

- Steinbeck mentions three traits when describing human behavior. What are they, and do they appear in other animals as well?

- Do humans learn from their mistakes, according to Steinbeck?

- Do humans "objectively observe [their] species as a species"? Why is this a problem, according to Steinbeck?

- What would humans have to accomplish in order to establish their lack of a "murder trait"? Based on what he says, do you think Steinbeck believes this is possible?

Intertextual Connections

- Steinbeck's discussion of human traits in comparison to those of other species in the animal kingdom calls to mind Charles Darwin's ideas on natural selection and how a species evolves. Where else do you see connections between Steinbeck's thinking and the scientific findings of Charles Darwin?

LEVEL 4

Opinion With Evidence or Argument

- Aside from documenting a specimen-collecting expedition, *The Log from the Sea of Cortez* examines the impact of humans on themselves and the environment. Using evidence from the text, write an essay in which you determine Steinbeck's view on humankind and humans' effect on ecosystems. Does he believe we can change for the better? What is your position? Are humans evolving in a way that betters the world, or are we simply reinforcing our "murder traits" over and over again?

APPENDIX VI
MIDDLE SCHOOL SCIENCE

A·VI

'WHY LEAVES TURN COLORS IN THE FALL' BY DIANE ACKERMAN
(ARTICLE)

The stealth of autumn catches one unaware. Was that a goldfinch perching in the early September woods, or just the first turning leaf? A red-winged blackbird or a sugar maple closing up shop for the winter? Keen-eyed as leopards, we stand still and squint hard, looking for signs of movement. Early-morning frost sits heavily on the grass, and turns barbed wire into a string of stars. On a distant hill, a small square of yellow appears to be a lighted stage. At last the truth dawns on us: Fall is staggering in, right on schedule, with its baggage of chilly nights, macabre holidays, and spectacular, heart-stoppingly beautiful leaves. Soon the leaves will start cringing on the trees, and roll up in clenched fists before they actually fall off. Dry seedpods will rattle like tiny gourds. But first there will be weeks of gushing color so bright, so pastel, so confetti-like, that people will travel up and down the East Coast just to stare at it—a whole season of leaves.

Where do the colors come from? Sunlight rules most living things with its golden edicts. When the days begin to shorten, soon after the summer solstice on June 21, a tree reconsiders its leaves. All summer it feeds them so they can process sunlight, but in the dog days of summer the tree begins pulling nutrients back into its trunk and roots, pares down, and gradually chokes off its leaves. A corky layer of cells forms at the leaves' slender petioles, then scars over.

Undernourished, the leaves stop producing the pigment chlorophyll, and photosynthesis ceases. Animals can migrate, hibernate, or store food to prepare for winter. But where can a tree go? It survives by dropping its leaves, and by the end of autumn only a few fragile threads of fluid-carrying xylem hold leaves to their stems.

A turning leaf stays partly green at first, then reveals splotches of yellow and red as the chlorophyll gradually breaks down. Dark green seems to stay longest in the veins, outlining and defining them. During the summer, chlorophyll dissolves in the heat and light, but it is also being steadily replaced. In the fall, on the other hand, no new pigment is produced, and so we notice the other colors that were always there, right in the leaf, although chlorophyll's shocking green hid them from view. With their camouflage gone, we see these colors for the first time all year, and marvel, but they were always there, hidden like a vivid secret beneath the hot glowing greens of summer.

The most spectacular range of fall foliage occurs in the northeastern United States and in eastern China, where the leaves are robustly colored, thanks in part to a rich climate. European maples don't achieve the same flaming reds as their American relatives, which thrive on cold nights and sunny days. In Europe, the warm, humid weather turns the leaves brown or mildly yellow. Anthocyanin, the pigment that gives apples their red and turns leaves red or red-violet, is produced by sugars that remain in the leaf after the supply of nutrients dwindles. Unlike the carotenoids, which color carrots, squash, and corn, and turn leaves orange and yellow, anthocyanin varies from year to year, depending on the temperature and amount of sunlight. The fiercest colors occur in years when the fall sunlight is strongest and the nights are cool and dry (a state of grace scientists find vexing to forecast). This is also why leaves appear dizzyingly bright and clear on a sunny fall day: The anthocyanin flashes like a marquee.

Not all leaves turn the same colors. Elms, weeping willows, and the ancient ginkgo all grow radiant yellow, along with hickories, aspens, bottle brush buckeyes, cottonweeds, and tall, keening poplars. Basswood turns bronze, birches bright gold. Water-loving maples put on a symphonic display of scarlets. Sumacs turn red, too, as do flowering dogwoods, black gums, and sweet gums. Though some oaks yellow, most turn a pinkish brown. The farmlands also change color, as tepees of cornstalks and bales of shredded-wheat-textured hay stand drying in the fields. In some spots, one slope of a hill may be green and the other already in bright color, because the hillside facing south gets more sun and heat than the northern one.

An odd feature of the colors is that they don't seem to have any special purpose. We are predisposed to respond to their beauty, of course. They shimmer with the colors of sunset, spring flowers, the tawny buff of a colt's pretty rump, the shuddering pink of a blush. Animals and flowers color for a reason—adaptation to their environment—but there is no adaptive reason for leaves to color so beautifully in the fall any more than there is for the sky or ocean to be blue. It's just one of the haphazard marvels the planet bestows every year. We find the sizzling colors thrilling, and in a sense they dupe us. Colored like living things, they signal death and disintegration. In time, they will become fragile and, like the body, return to dust. They are as we hope our own fate will be when we die: Not to vanish, just to sublime from one beautiful state into another. Though leaves lose their green life, they bloom with urgent colors, as the woods grow mummified day by day, and Nature becomes more carnal, mute, and radiant.

We call the season "fall," from the Old English *feallan*, to fall, which leads back through time to the Indo-European *phol*, which also means to fall. So the word and the idea are both extremely ancient, and haven't really changed since the first of our kind needed a name for fall's leafy abundance. As we say the word, we're reminded of that other Fall, in the garden of Eden, when fig leaves never withered and scales fell from our eyes. Fall is the time when leaves fall from the trees, just as spring is when flowers spring up, summer is when we simmer, and winter is when we whine from the cold.

Children love to play in piles of leaves, hurling them into the air like confetti, leaping into soft unruly mattresses of them. For children, leaf fall is just one of the odder figments of Nature, like hailstones or snowflakes. Walk down a lane overhung with trees in the never-never land of autumn, and you will forget about time and death, lost in the sheer delicious spill of color. Adam and Eve concealed their nakedness with leaves, remember? Leaves have always hidden our awkward secrets.

But how do the colored leaves fall? As a leaf ages, the growth hormone, auxin, fades, and cells at the base of the petiole divide. Two or three rows of small cells, lying at right angles to the axis of the petiole, react with water, then come apart, leaving the petioles hanging on by only a few threads of xylem. A light breeze, and the leaves are airborne. They glide and swoop, rocking in invisible cradles. They are all wing and may flutter from yard to yard on small whirlwinds or updrafts, swiveling as they go. Firmly tethered to earth, we love to see things rise up and fly—soap bubbles, balloons, birds, fall leaves. They remind us that the end of a season is capricious, as is the end of life. We especially like the way leaves rock, careen, and swoop as they fall. Everyone knows the motion. Pilots sometimes do a maneuver called a "falling leaf," in which the plane loses altitude quickly and on purpose, by slipping first to the right, then to the left. The machine weighs a ton or more, but in one pilot's mind it is a weightless thing, a falling leaf. She has seen the motion before, in the Vermont woods where she played as a child. Below her the trees radiate gold, copper, and red. Leaves are falling, although she can't see them fall, as she falls, swooping down for a closer view.

At last the leaves leave. But first they turn color and thrill us for weeks on end. Then they crunch and crackle underfoot. They shush, as children drag their small feet through leaves heaped along the curb. Dark, slimy mats of leaves cling to one's heels after a rain. A damp, stucco-like mortar of semi-decayed leaves protects the tender shoots with a roof until spring, and makes a rich humus. An occasional bulge or ripple in the leafy mounds signals a shrew or a field mouse tunneling out of sight. Sometimes one finds in fossil stones the imprint of a leaf, long since disintegrated, whose outlines remind us how detailed, vibrant, and alive are the things of this earth that perish.

Questions for "Why Leaves Turn Colors in the Fall" by Diane Ackerman

LEVEL 1

General Understanding

- What phenomenon is being described in this text?
- Which natural element directly affects the leaves on trees?
- What begins the process of trees losing their leaves?
- What point is the author trying to make when she says, "Animals can migrate, hibernate, or store food to prepare for winter. But where can a tree go?"
- Describe the progression of a "turning leaf."
- Do leaves actually "change" color in fall? Why or why not?

Key Details

- What does it mean when leaves turn yellow and red?
- How does the chlorophyll supply change between summer and fall? Why is this important to the process being described?
- Do all leaves turn the same color? Why or why not?
- How does anthocyanin differ from carotenoids?
- What process causes leaves to physically fall off of trees?

LEVEL 2

Vocabulary

- How does the use of simile help paint a vivid picture for the reader?
- Where does the author use personification? Why?
- What is the meaning of the word *sublime* in Paragraph 7?

Structure

- Identify where the tone shifts in the text. How is this related to the type of information being conveyed?
- Identify areas where the author uses vivid imagery—how does this affect the tone of the text?
- What physical phenomenon in humans does the falling of the leaves represent? Where does Ackerman mention this comparison?
- In Paragraph 10, Ackerman explains that pilots often mimic falling leaves in their maneuvers. What reasons does she give for this? Does this idea appear in any other paragraphs?

Author's Craft

- In Paragraph 8, the author reviews the multiple meanings of the word *fall*. What are these meanings?
- What is ironic about the vivid colors of fall leaves?

- Ackerman uses irony in multiple points throughout the text, specifically in the line, "Walk down a lane overhung with trees in the never-never land of autumn, and you will forget about time and death, lost in the sheer delicious spill of color." How does this statement oppose the scientific reason for trees losing their leaves?
- According to Ackerman, what do leaves symbolize to humans? How do you know?

LEVEL 3

Author's Purpose

- Is the purpose of this text merely to inform readers about the falling of leaves? Why or why not?
- What argument does the author make about the significance of leaves to humans?
- Is Ackerman a scientist or merely an observer? How do you know?
- Why does the author use the word *we* in this text?
- Do fall leaves simply indicate a change in season? What would the author like us to believe is significant about leaves?
- Why do we "love to see things rise up and fly"?

Intertextual Connections

- In Paragraph 8, Ackerman refers to another text. What is this text, and how does the example she gives support her idea that leaves symbolize more than just a changing of seasons?
- Read about the changing of leaves on the US Forest Service website at www.na.fs.fed.us/fhp/pubs/leaves/leaves.shtm.
    - Is the information the same? With a partner, examine areas in both texts with similar information, and compare how the use of figurative language changes the way we receive knowledge.
    - Which text do you prefer? Why? Be sure to use evidence from both texts to support your thinking.

LEVEL 4

Opinion With Evidence or Argument

- Ackerman claims that leaves intrigue us because they "remind us how detailed, vibrant, and alive are the things of this earth that perish." Do you agree or disagree? Using evidence from Ackerman's argument, support or refute the idea that leaves are symbolic of the life and death cycle.

'ANIMAL CRAFTSMEN'
BY BRUCE BROOKS
(ARTICLE)

One evening, when I was about five, I climbed up a ladder on the outside of a rickety old tobacco barn at sunset. The barn was part of a small farm near the home of a country relative my mother and I visited periodically; though we did not really know the farm's family, I was allowed to roam, poke around, and conduct sudden studies of anything small and harmless. On this evening, as on most of my jaunts, I was not looking for anything; I was simply climbing with an open mind. But as I balanced on the next-to-the-top rung and inhaled the spicy stink of the tobacco drying inside, I did find something under the eaves—something very strange.

It appeared to be a kind of gray paper sphere, suspended from the dark planks by a thin stalk, like an apple made of ashes hanging on its stem. I studied it closely in the clear light. I saw that the bottom was a little ragged, and open. I could not tell if it had been torn, or if it had been made that way on purpose—for it was clear to me, as I studied it, that this thing had been made. This was no fruit or fungus. Its shape, rough but trim; its intricately colored surface with subtle swirls of gray and tan; and most of all the uncanny adhesiveness with which the perfectly tapered stem stuck against the rotten old pine boards—all of these features gave evidence of some intentional design. The troubling thing was figuring out who had designed it, and why.

I assumed the designer was a human being: someone from the farm, someone wise and skilled in a craft that had so far escaped my curiosity. Even when I saw wasps entering and leaving the thing (during a vigil I kept every evening for two weeks), it did not occur to me that the wasps might have fashioned it for themselves. I assumed it was a man-made "wasp house" placed there expressly for the purpose of attracting a family of wasps, much as the "martin hotel," a giant birdhouse on a pole near the farmhouse, was maintained to shelter migrant purple martins who returned every spring. I didn't ask myself why anyone would want to give wasps a bivouac; it seemed no more odd than attracting birds.

As I grew less wary of the wasps (and they grew less wary of me), and as my confidence on the ladder improved, I moved to the upper rung and peered through the sphere's bottom. I could see that the paper swirled in layers around some secret center the wasps inhabited, and I marveled at the delicate hands of the craftsman who had devised such tiny apertures for their protection.

I left the area in the late summer, and in my imagination I took the strange structure with me. I envisioned unwrapping it, and in the middle finding—what? A tiny room full of bits of wool for sleeping, and countless manufactured pellets of scientifically determined wasp food? A glowing blue jewel that drew the wasps at twilight, and gave them a cool infusion of energy as they clung to it overnight? My most definite idea was that the wasps lived in a small block of fine cedar the craftsman had drilled full of holes, into which they slipped snugly, rather like the bunks aboard submarines in World War II movies.

291

As it turned out, I got the chance to discover that my idea of the cedar block had not been wrong by much. We visited our relative again in the winter. We arrived at night, but first thing in the morning I made straight for the farm and its barn. The shadows under the eaves were too dense to let me spot the sphere from far off. I stepped on the bottom rung of the ladder—slick with frost—and climbed carefully up. My hands and feet kept slipping, so my eyes stayed on the rung ahead, and it was not until I was secure at the top that I could look up. The sphere was gone.

I was crushed. That object had fascinated me like nothing I had come across in my life; I had even grown to love wasps because of it. I sagged on the ladder and watched my breath eddy around the blank eaves. I'm afraid I pitied myself more than the apparently homeless wasps.

But then something snapped me out of my sense of loss: I recalled that I had watched the farmer taking in the purple martin hotel every November, after the birds left. From its spruce appearance when he brought it out in March, it was clear he had cleaned it and repainted it and kept it out of the weather. Of course he would do the same thing for this house, which was even more fragile. I had never mentioned the wasp dwelling to anyone, but now I decided I would go to the farm, introduce myself, and inquire about it. Perhaps I would even be permitted to handle it, or, best of all, learn how to make one myself.

I scrambled down the ladder, leaping from the third rung and landing in the frosty salad of tobacco leaves and windswept grass that collected at the foot of the barn wall. I looked down and saw that my left boot had, by no more than an inch, just missed crushing the very thing I was rushing off to seek. There, lying dry and separate on the leaves was the wasp house.

I looked up. Yes. I was standing directly beneath the spot where the sphere had hung—it was a straight fall. I picked up the wasp house, gave it a shake to see if any insects were inside, and, discovering none, took it home.

My awe of the craftsman grew as I unwrapped the layers of the nest. Such beautiful paper! It was much tougher than any I had encountered, and it held a curve (something my experimental paper airplanes never did), but it was very light, too. The secret at the center of the swirl turned out to be a neatly made fan of tiny cells, all of the same size and shape, reminding me of the heart of a sunflower that had lost its seeds to birds. The fan hung from the sphere's ceiling by a stem the thickness of a pencil lead.

The rest of the story is a little embarrassing. More impressed than ever, I decided to pay homage to the creator of this habitable sculpture. I went boldly to the farmhouse. The farmer's wife answered my knock. I showed her the nest and asked to speak with the person in the house who had made it. She blinked and frowned. I had to repeat my question twice before she understood what I believed my mission to be; then, with a gentle laugh, she dispelled my illusion about an ingenious old paper smith fond of wasps. The nest, she explained, had been made entirely by the insects themselves, and wasn't that amazing?

Well, of course it was. It still is. I needn't have been so embarrassed—the structures that animals build, and the sense of design they display, should always astound us. On my way home from the farmhouse, in my own defense I kept thinking, "But I couldn't build anything like this! Nobody could!"

The most natural thing in the world for us to do, when we are confronted with a piece of animal architecture, is to figure out if we could possibly make it or live in it. Who hasn't peered into the dark end of a mysterious hole in the woods and thought, "It must be pretty weird to live in there!" or looked up at a hawk's nest atop a huge sycamore and shuddered at the thought of waking up every morning with nothing but a few twigs preventing a hundred-foot fall. How, we wonder, do those twigs stay together, and withstand the wind so high?

It is a human tendency always to regard animals first in terms of us. Seeing the defensive courage of a mother bear whose cubs are threatened, or the cooperative determination of a string of ants dismantling a stray chunk of cake, we naturally use our own behavior as reference for our empathy. We put ourselves in the same situation and express the animal's action in feelings—and words—that apply to the way people do things.

Sometimes this is useful. But sometimes it is misleading. Attributing human-like intentions to an animal can keep us from looking at the animal's sense of itself in its surroundings—its immediate and future needs, its physical and mental capabilities, its genetic instincts. Most animals, for example, use there five senses in ways that human beings cannot possibly understand or express. How can a forty-two-year-old nearsighted biologist have any real idea what a two-week-old barn owl sees in the dark? How can a sixteen-year-old who lives in the Arizona desert identify with the muscular jumps improvised by a waterfall-leaping salmon in Alaska? There's nothing wrong with trying to empathize with an animal, but we shouldn't forget that ultimately animals live animal lives.

Animal structures let us have it both ways—we can be struck with a strange wonder, and we can empathize right away, too. Seeing a vast spider web, taut and glistening between two bushes, it's easy to think, "I have no idea how that is done; the engineering is awesome." But it is just as easy to imagine climbing across the bright strands, springing from one to the next as if the web were a new Epcot attraction, the Invisible Flying Flexible Space Orb. That a clear artifact of an animal's wits and agility stands right there in front of us—that we can touch it, look at it from different angles, sometimes take it home—inspires our imagination as only a strange reality can. We needn't move into a molehill to experience a life of darkness and digging; our creative wonder takes us down there in a second, without even getting our hands dirty.

But what if we discover some of the mechanics of how the web is made? Once we see how the spider works (or the humming bird or the bee), is the engineering no longer awesome? This would be too bad: we don't want to lose our sense of wonder just because we gain understanding.

And we certainly do not lose it. In fact, seeing how an animal makes its nest or egg case or food storage vaults has the effect of increasing our amazement. The builder's energy, concentration, and athletic adroitness are qualities we can readily admire and envy. Even more startling is the recognition that the animal is working from a precise design in its head, a design that is exactly replicated time after time. This knowledge of architecture—knowing where to build, what materials to use, how to put them together—remains one of the most intriguing mysteries of animal behavior. And the more we develop that same knowledge, the more we appreciate the instincts and intelligence of the animals.

Questions for "Animal Craftsmen" by Bruce Brooks

LEVEL 1

General Understanding

- What kind of text is this? (informative/nonfiction, fiction, etc.)
- Where does the majority of the action take place?
- What does the narrator find in the barn? What does he think this strange discovery is?
- When the narrator returns for the winter, what has happened to the sphere?
- Where does the narrator eventually find the nest?

Key Details

- What makes Brooks think the nest is made by humans?
- How does Brooks initially describe the nest?
- Is the narrator afraid of the nest at first?
- What is the narrator's state of mind at the beginning of the essay?

LEVEL 2

Vocabulary

- What is a "martin hotel"? What is its significance to the main idea of the essay?
- What is the tone of the essay? How does it reveal the author's purpose?
- How does the narrator describe the nest when he examines it? How does word choice tell us about his feelings toward the structure and the animals who built it?

Structure

- What time period does this narrative span?
- What is the narrator's concern at the end of Paragraph 2?
- When does the narrator's opinion of who built the nest change? Why?
- How does the author make sense of the structure in the center of the nest?
- In Paragraph 16, Brooks uses questioning to illustrate his point—what conclusion is he trying to lead the reader to?

Author's Craft

- How does the narrator use past experiences to infer where the nest might be?
- In Paragraph 7, Brooks says, "I didn't ask myself why anyone would want to give wasps a bivouac; it seemed no more odd than attracting birds." What flaw in his logic is he pointing out? Does it change his thinking about who built the nest?
- Examine the occasional moments of dialogue in the text. How does it help to reveal the author's purpose?

- What comparison does the author use to justify his disbelief that animals built the nest?

- Brooks says, "We put ourselves in the same situation and express the animal's action in feelings—and words—that apply to the way people do things." Is this the best way to understand how animals work? Why or why not?

- How does the author use comparisons to illustrate how humans relate to animal structures?

LEVEL 3

Author's Purpose

- At first, who does the narrator assume made the sphere? Why?

- By the end of Paragraph 5, how has the sphere changed the narrator's opinion of wasps?

- When the farmer's wife reveals the builders of the nest, how does the narrator react? Why?

- According to the author, what do humans naturally do when they see something made by animals?

- What is the difference between how animals and humans use their senses? Why is this significant?

- What happens to our sense of awe when we understand how something is made?

Intertextual Connections

- Conduct research on human inventions that have been inspired by nature. Write an informative paragraph describing one such invention and how it sprung from natural origins. In a second paragraph, relate this invention to Brooks's essay and his description of how humans often interpret natural phenomena relative to their own personal experiences.

- Research the Fibonacci numbers and the Golden Ratio. How do these concepts relate to what Brooks describes in his essay?

LEVEL 4

Opinion With Evidence or Argument

- In Paragraph 16 Brooks says, "Attributing human-like intentions to an animal can keep us from looking at the animal's sense of itself in its surroundings—its immediate and future needs, its physical and mental capabilities, its genetic instincts. Most animals, for example, use their five senses in ways that human beings cannot possibly understand or express." What difference is he pointing out? Do you agree or disagree? Compose a two-minute argumentative speech in which you use your personal experience and evidence from the text to present your position and support your thinking.

REFERENCES

Adams, M. J. (1990). *Beginning to read: Thinking and learning about print*. Cambridge, MA: MIT Press.

Adler, M. J., & Van Doren, C. (1972). *How to read a book*. New York, NY: Touchstone.

Angelou, M. (1969). *I know why the caged bird sings*. New York, NY: Random House.

Baumann, J. F., Kame'enui, E. J., & Ash, G. E. (2003). Research on vocabulary instruction: Voltaire redux. In J. Flood, D. Lapp, J. R. Squire, & J. M. Jensen (Eds.), *Handbook of research on teaching the English language arts* (2nd ed., pp. 752–785). Mahwah, NJ: Erlbaum.

Beck, I. L., McKeown, M. G., Hamilton, R. L., & Kucan, L. (1997). *Questioning the author: An approach for enhancing student engagement with text*. Newark, NJ: International Reading Association.

Berkun, S. (2010). *Confessions of a public speaker*. Sebastopol, CA: O'Reilly Media.

Billings, L., & Fitzgerald, J. (2002). Dialogic discussion and the paideia seminar. *American Educational Research Journal, 39*(4), 907–941.

Biography. (n.d.) The Official Website of Will Rogers. Retrieved April 26, 2014, from http://www.cmgww.com/historic/rogers/about/biography.html

Boyles, N. (2013). Closing in on close reading. *Educational Leadership, 70*(4), 36–41.

Bransford, J. D., Brown, A. L., & Cocking, R. R. (Eds.). (2000). *How people learn: Brain, mind, experience, and school*. Committee on Developments in the Science of Learning and Committee on Learning Research and Educational Practice. Washington, DC: National Academy Press.

Britton, J. (1983). Writing and the story of the world. In B. Kroll & E. Wells (Eds.), *Explorations in the development of writing theory, research, and practice* (pp. 3–30). New York, NY: Wiley.

Brooks, G. (1960). *The bean eaters*. New York, NY: Harper & Row.

Brown, S., & Kappes, L. (2012). *Implementing the Common Core State Standards: A primer on "close reading of text."* Washington, DC: The Aspen Institute.

Callender, A. A., & McDaniel, M. A. (2007). The benefits of embedded question adjuncts for low and high structure builders. *Journal of Educational Psychology, 99*(2), 339–348.

Carson, R. L. (1962). *Silent spring*. New York, NY: Mariner.

Castek, J., & Beach, R. (2013). Using apps to support disciplinary literacy and science learning. *Journal of Adolescent & Adult Literacy, 56*(7), 554–564.

Chi, M. T. H., & Bassock, M. (1989). Learning from examples via self-explanation. In L. Resnick (Ed.), *Knowing, learning and instruction: Essays in honour of Robert Glaser* (pp. 251–282). Hillsdale, NJ: Erlbaum.

Cisneros, S. (1991). *Woman hollering creek*. New York, NY: Vintage.

Collins, S. (2010). *The hunger games*. New York, NY: Scholastic.

Colon, J. (2001). *Kipling and I*. In I. Stavans (Ed.), *Wáchale!: Poetry and prose about growing up Latino in America* (pp. 37–41). Chicago, IL: Cricket Books.

Common Core State Standards Initiative (CCSSI). (2010a). *Common Core State Standards for English language arts & literacy in history/social studies, science, and technical subjects*. Retrieved from http://www.corestandards.org/ELA-Literacy

Common Core State Standards Initiative (CCSSI). (2010b). *Common Core State Standards for mathematical practice*. Retrieved from http://www.corestandards.org/math

Covey, S. R. (2004). *The seven habits of highly effective people*. New York, NY: Simon & Schuster.

Cromley, J., Perez, T., Fitzhugh, S., Newcombe, N., Wills, T., & Tanaka, J. (2013). Improving students' diagram comprehension with classroom instruction. *Journal of Experimental Education, 81*(4), 511–537.

Daniels, H., & Harvey, S. (2009). *Comprehension and collaboration: Inquiry circles in action*. Portsmouth, NH: Heinemann.

Darwin, C. (1859/2003). *Origin of the species by means of natural selection* (150th anniversary ed). New York, NY: Signet Classics.

Denenberg, D., & Roscoe, L. (2001). *50 American heroes every kid should meet*. Brookfield, CT: Millbrook Press.

Douglass, F. (1845/1995). *The narrative life of Frederick Douglass. An American slave. Written by himself*. New York, NY: Dover Thrift Editions.

Duarte, N. (2008). *Slide:ology: The art and science of creating great presentations*. Sebastopol, CA: O'Reilly Media.

Edwards, R. E. (2008). *Competitive debate: The official guide*. New York, NY: Penguin.

Eeds, M., & Wells, D. (1989). Grand conversations: An exploration of meaning construction in literature study groups. *Research in the Teaching of English, 23*(1), 4–29.

Eisner, E. W. (1991). *The enlightened eye: Qualitative inquiry and the enhancement of educational practice*. New York, NY: Macmillan.

Fisher, D., & Frey, N. (2008). *Word wise and content rich, grades 7–12: Five essential steps to teaching academic vocabulary*. Portsmouth, NH: Heinemann.

Fisher, D., & Frey, N. (2012). Close reading in elementary schools. *The Reading Teacher, 66*, 179–188.

Fisher, D., & Frey, N. (2014a). *Better learning through structured teaching: A framework for the gradual release of responsibility* (2nd ed.). Alexandria, VA: ASCD.

Fisher, D., & Frey, N. (2014b). *Close reading and writing from sources*. Newark, DE: International Reading Association.

Frey, N., Fisher, D., & Gonzalez, A. (2010). *Literacy 2.0: Reading and writing in 21st century classrooms*. Bloomington, IN: Solution Tree.

Gallagher, K. (2011). *Write like this: Teaching real-world writing to modeling and mentor texts*. Portland, ME: Stenhouse.

Gault, T. (2013, October 29). *10 most common rookie mistakes in public speaking*. Retrieved from http://speakfearlessly.net/10-most-common-rookie-mistakes-in-public-speaking/

Gazzaniga, M. S., Ivry, R. B., & Mangun, G. R. (2009). *Cognitive neuroscience: The biology of the mind* (3rd ed.). New York, NY: W. W. Norton.

Gernsbacher, M. (1991). Cognitive processes and mechanisms in language comprehension: The structure building framework. *Psychology of Learning & Motivation, 27*, 217–263.

Hamilton, V. (1993). *The people could fly: American Black folktales*. New York, NY: Knopf.

Hansen, J. (2001). *When writers read* (2nd ed.). Portsmouth, NH: Heinemann.

Hesse, K. (1997). *Out of the dust*. New York, NY: Scholastic.

Hillary, E. (2000). *View from the summit: The remarkable memoir from the first person to conquer Everest*. New York, NY: Gallery.

Jiménez, F. (1999). *The circuit*. New York, NY: Houghton Mifflin.

Kurland, D. J. (1995). *I know what it says . . . what does it mean? Critical skills for critical reading*. Belmont, CA: Wadsworth.

Lally, P., van Jaarsveld, C. H. M., Potts, H. W. W., & Wardle, J. (2010). How are habits formed: Modeling habit formation in the real world. *European Journal of Social Psychology, 40*(6), 998–1009.

Lovejoy, A. O. (1936). *The great chain of being: A study of the history of an idea*. Cambridge, MA: Harvard University Press.

Malthus, T. R. (1798). *An essay on the principle of population*. Retrieved from https://www.marxists.org/reference/subject/economics/malthus/ch09.htm

Marzano, R., Pickering, D., & Heflebower, T. (2011). *The highly engaged classroom*. Bloomington, IN: Marzano Research Laboratory.

Mason, J. M., Stahl, S. A., Au, K. H., & Herman, P. A. (2003). Reading: Children's developing knowledge of words. In J. Flood, D. Lapp, J. R. Squire, & J. M. Jensen (Eds.), *Handbook of research on teaching the English language arts* (2nd ed., pp. 914–930). Mahwah, NJ: Erlbaum.

McLaughlin, M., & DeVoogd, G. (2004). *Critical literacy: Enhancing students' reading comprehension*. New York, NY: Scholastic.

Meany, J., & Shuster, K. (2005). *Speak out! Debate and public speaking in the middle grades*. New York, NY: International Debate Education Association.

Mezuk, B., Bondarenko, I., Smith, S., & Tucker, E. (2011). The influence of a policy debate program on high school achievement in a large urban public school system. *Educational Research and Reviews, 6*(9), 622–635.

Nagel, R. (Ed.). (2007). *U-X-L encyclopedia of science*. Farmington Hills, MI: Gale Cengage Learning.

Newkirk, T. (2012). *The art of slow reading*. Portsmouth, NH: Heinemann.

NGSS Lead States. (2013). *Next Generation Science Standards: For states, by states*. Washington, DC: The National Academies Press.

Nichols, W. D., Rupley, W. H., & Rasinski, T. (2009). Fluency in learning to read for meaning: Going beyond repeated readings. *Literacy Research and Instruction, 48*(1), 1–13.

Norgay, T., & Ullman, J. R. (May 9, 1955). Tenzing: The tiger of Everest. *Sports Illustrated, (2)*19, 37–49. Retrieved from http://sportsillustrated.cnn.com/vault/edb/reader.html?magID=SI&issueDate=19550509&mode=reader_vault

Northwest Regional Education Laboratory. (1998). *Speech and presentation rubric*. Portland, OR: Author.

Nystrand, M. (2006). Research on the role of classroom discourse as it affects reading comprehension. *Research in the Teaching of English, 40*(4), 392–412.

Nystrand, M., & Gamoran, A. (1991). Instructional discourse, student engagement, and literature achievement. *Research in the Teaching of English, 25*(3), 261–290.

Paschen, E., & Mosby, R. P. (2001). *Poetry speaks: Hear great poets read their work from Tennyson to Plath*. Naperville, IL: Sourcebooks Media Fusion.

Peverly, S. T., & Wood, R. (2001). The effects of adjunct questions and feedback on improving the reading comprehension skills of learning-disabled adolescents. *Contemporary Educational Psychology, 26*(1), 25–43.

Pfaffinger, K. (2006). Research paper baby steps. *English Journal, 95*(4), 75–77.

Reynolds, G. (2011). *Presentation Zen: Simple ideas on presentation design and delivery* (2nd ed.). New York, NY: New Riders.

Reznitskaya, A. (2012). Dialogic teaching: Rethinking language use during literature discussions. *The Reading Teacher, 65*(7), 446–456.

Rilke, R. M. (1929/1993). *Letters to a young poet.* M. D. Herter-Norton (trans). New York, NY: W. W. Norton.

Rosenman, S. (Ed.) (1938). Inaugural address, March 4, 1933. In *The public papers of Franklin D. Roosevelt, volume two: The year of crisis, 1933* (pp. 11–16). New York, NY: Random House. Retrieved from http://historymatters.gmu.edu/d/5057

Roberts, T., & Billings, L. (2012). *Teaching critical thinking: Using seminars for 21st century literacy.* Larchmont, NY: Eye on Education.

Salinger, J. D. (1951). *The catcher in the rye.* New York, NY: Little, Brown.

Sperry, L., Neitzel, J., & Engelhardt-Wells, K. (2010). Peer-mediated instruction and intervention strategies for students with autism spectrum disorders. *Preventing School Failure, 54,* 256–264.

Spiegelman, A. (1986). *Maus I: A survivor's tale.* New York, NY: Pantheon.

Therrien, W. J. (2004). Fluency and comprehension gains as a result of repeated reading: A meta-analysis. *Remedial & Special Education, 25*(4), 252–261.

Toulmin, S. E. (1954). *The uses of argument.* Cambridge, UK: Cambridge University Press.

Trueman, T. (2000). *Stuck in neutral.* New York, NY: HarperCollins Publishers.

Wallechinsky, I., Wallace, D., & Wallace, A. (1977). *The book of lists.* New York, NY: William Morrow.

Webb, N. L. (2002). *Alignment study in language arts, mathematics, science, and social studies of state standards and assessments for four states.* Washington, DC: Council of Chief State School Officers.

White, T. G., Graves, M. F., & Slater, W. H. (1990). Growth of reading vocabulary in diverse elementary schools: Decoding and word meaning. *Journal of Educational Psychology, 82,* 281–290.

Wilde, O. (1891/1992). *The picture of Dorian Grey.* New York, NY: Modern Library.

Wilder, T. (1938/2003). *Our town: A play in three acts.* New York, NY: HarperCollins.

Wilkerson, I. A. G., & Son, E. H. (2011). A dialogic turn in research on learning and teaching to comprehend. In M. L. Kamil, P. D. Pearson, E. B. Moje, & P. P. Afflerbach (Eds.), *Handbook of Reading Research* (vol. IV, pp. 359–387). New York, NY: Routledge.

Wineburg, S., Martin, D., & Monte-Sano, C. (2011). *Reading like a historian: Teaching literacy in middle and high school history classrooms.* New York, NY: Teachers College Press.

Zusak, M. (2005). *The book thief.* Sydney, NSW, Australia: Picador.

Zywica, J., & Gomez, K. (2008). Annotating to support learning in the content areas: Teaching and learning science. *Journal of Adolescent & Adult Literacy, 52*(2), 155–165.

INDEX

ABOUT THE AUTHORS

Douglas Fisher, PhD, is professor of educational leadership at San Diego State University and a teacher-leader at Health Sciences High & Middle College. He is the recipient of an IRA Celebrate Literacy Award, the NCTE's Farmer Award for Excellence in Writing, and a Christa McAuliffe Award for Excellence in Teacher Education. A former board member for the Literacy Research Association and a current board member for the International Reading Association, Doug is also a credentialed English teacher and administrator in California. Doug can be reached at dfisher@mail.sdsu.edu.

Nancy Frey, PhD, is professor of educational leadership at San Diego State University and a teacher-leader at Health Sciences High & Middle College. A credentialed special educator, reading specialist, and administrator in California, Nancy is also the recipient of both the 2008 Early Career Achievement Award from the Literacy Research Association and a Christa McAuliffe award for Excellence in Teacher Education from the American Association of State Colleges and Universities. Nancy can be reached at nfrey@mail.sdsu.edu.

Nancy and Doug collaborate often. *Text Complexity* (IRA, 2012) and *Rigorous Reading* (Corwin Literacy, 2013), among their many best-selling texts, focus on how students can achieve a deeper understanding of complex texts with the right kind of instruction.

ABOUT THE CONTRIBUTORS

 **Heather Anderson** is an English and higher-level Spanish teacher at Health Sciences High & Middle College. Heather earned her MA in Curriculum and Instruction from San Diego State University, is BCLAD-certified, has extensive experience in staff development, and spent part of her career as an elementary math specialist. Heather has shared her passion for education while presenting at conferences and consulting at individual school sites emphasizing the use of Gradual Release of Responsibility, differentiated instruction, close reading, and collaborative grouping.

 **Marisol Thayre** is an English teacher at Health Sciences High & Middle College. She is interested in how students use different types of media to develop their own expertise as writers, and she has recently begun to share her knowledge with other teachers across the country as a presenter on topics that include close reading and the Gradual Release of Responsibility. Marisol earned her MA in English and Composition from Cal Poly San Luis Obispo and is BCLAD- and Leading Edge–certified.

BECAUSE ALL TEACHERS ARE LEADERS

Also Available

Jim Burke
On what the 6–8 and 9–12 standards really say, really mean, and how to put them into practice

Harvey "Smokey" Daniels & Nancy Steineke
On the social-academic skills central to college, career, and life readiness

Michael Smith, Deborah Appleman & Jeffrey Wilhelm
On where the authors of the standards go wrong about instruction—and how to get it right

Harvey "Smokey" Daniels & Elaine Daniels
On that single method for transforming students from passive spectators into active learners

Lapp, Wolsey, Wood & Johnson
On using graphic organizers to make the complex comprehensible

ReLeah Lent & Barry Gilmore
On practical strategies for coaxing our most resistant learners into engagement and achievement

N14787